THE UNITED STATES AND CUBA

A great power and a weaker, rival neighbor can eventually achieve normal relations. Prior to 1959, Cuba and the United States did not enjoy normal relations and during the Cold War, Cuba's alliance with the Soviet Union rendered any chance of U.S.–Cuba normality even more elusive. What the United States and Cuba now face is the task of relating to each other as normally as possible, a task made all the more difficult by the shadow of the Cold War. After 1989, regime change returned to the heart of U.S.–Cuba policy, a major obstacle for Washington–Havana dialogue. In turn, Cuban leaders have generally shirked their share of the responsibility in easing the fifty-year enmity with the United States.

This book systematically covers the background of U.S.–Cuban relations after the Cold War and the tensions persisting into the twenty-first century. The authors explore the future of this strained relationship under Obama's presidency and in a post-Castro Cuba.

Marifeli Pérez-Stable is professor of sociology at Florida International University and non-resident senior fellow at the Inter-American Dialogue. She writes a regular column on Latin America in the *Miami Herald* and her opinion pieces have appeared in a broad range of U.S., Spanish and Latin American outlets. She is the author of *The Cuban Revolution: Origins, Course, and Legacy* (2nd edn.) and the editor of *Looking Forward: Comparative Perspectives on Cuba's Transition*. In 2001–2003, she chaired the task force on Memory, Truth, and Justice which issued the report, *Cuban National Reconciliation*.

Other Titles in the Contemporary Inter-American Relations
Series edited by Jorge I. Domínguez and Rafael Fernández
de Castro

The United States and Mexico
Between partnership and conflict
Jorge I. Domínguez and Rafael Fernández de Castro

The United States and Chile
Coming in from the cold
David R. Mares and Francisco Rojas Aravena

The United States and Venezuela
Rethinking a relationship
Janet Kelly and Carlos A. Romero

The United States and Argentina
Changing relations in a changing world
Deborah Norden and Roberto Russell

The United States and Peru
Cooperation at a cost
Cynthia McClintock and Fabian Vallas

The United States and Brazil
A long road of unmet expectations
Mônica Hirst, with an essay by Andrew Hurrell

The United States and the Caribbean
The transformation of hegemony and sovereignty in the post Cold War era
Anthony P. Maingot and Wilfredo Lozano

The United States and Central America
Geopolitical realities and regional fragility
Mark B. Rosenberg and Luis G. Solís

The United States and Mexico, Second Edition
Between partnership and conflict
Jorge I. Domínguez and Rafael Fernández de Castro

The United States and Cuba
Intimate enemies
Marifeli Pérez-Stable, with an essay by Ana Covarrubias

THE UNITED STATES AND CUBA

Intimate Enemies

Marifeli Pérez-Stable

WITH AN ESSAY BY ANA COVARRUBIAS
AN INTER-AMERICAN DIALOGUE BOOK

Routledge
Taylor & Francis Group

NEW YORK AND LONDON

First published 2011
by Routledge
711 Third Avenue, New York, NY 10017

Simultaneously published in the UK
by Routledge
2 Park Square, Milton Park, Abingdon, Oxon OX14 4RN

Routledge is an imprint of the Taylor & Francis Group, an informa business

© 2011 Taylor & Francis

The right of Marifeli Pérez-Stable to be identified as author of this work
has been asserted by her in accordance with sections 77 and 78 of the
Copyright, Designs and Patents Act 1988.

Typeset in Bembo by Wearset Ltd, Boldon, Tyne and Wear

Library of Congress Cataloging-in-Publication Data
Pérez-Stable, Marifeli, 1949-
The United States and Cuba : intimate enemies / Marifeli Pérez-Stable ;
with an essay by Ana Covarrubias.
    p. cm. – (An inter-american dialogue book)
1. United States–Foreign relations–Cuba. 2. Cuba–Foreign relations–
United States. 3. United States–Foreign relations–1989- I. Covarrubias
Velasco, Ana II. Title.
E183.8.C9P4657 2011
327.7307291–dc22   2010030552

ISBN13: 978-0-415-80450-9 (hbk)
ISBN13: 978-0-415-80451-6 (pbk)
ISBN13: 978-0-203-87448-6 (ebk)

To María Cristina Herrera Fernández (1934–2010)

CONTENTS

Preface   xi
Abbreviations and Acronyms   xiv

1   **The United States and Cuba Have Never Had Normal
    Relations**   1
    The "Ever-Faithful Isle" 2
    The Missile Crisis 4
    An Uncommon Expectation of Equality 7
    A Cold War Might-Have-Been 10
    Cuban Miami Flexes Its Muscles 17
    What Wasn't and Might Yet Be 23

2   **"Next Christmas in Havana"**   24
    The End of the Cold War and the Bilateral Relationship 25
    The International Arena 41
    A Momentous Fork in the Road 49

3   **"Half Drunk and Throwing Bottles at Each Other"**   56
    Cuba's Return to Normalcy 57
    The Clinton Administration II 65
    Cuban Miami on the Eve of the New Century 75

4   **"We Need to De-Americanize the Problem of Cuba"**   84
    A Harder-Line Policy in Slow Motion 85
    The Regime Sails on 93
    Cuban Miami in the New Century 97
    After Fidel (Sort of) 103
    Cuba in the International Arena 107

5   **"The Policy We've Had in Place for 50 Years Hasn't
    Worked"**   112
    In the Age of Obama 114
    A Softer-Line Policy in Slow Motion 119
    U.S. Policy and Human Rights in Cuba 122
    The International Community 127
    Cuba's Crossroads 135
    What's Next? 140

    Mexico and Cuba: The End of a Convenient Partnership   147
    ANA COVARRUBIAS
    *Revolutionary Cuba and Mexico (and the United States) Become
      Convenient Partners 148*
    Mexico, Cuba and the United States in the post-Cold War World 152
    Democracy and Human Rights in the Bilateral Relationship 157
    The Second PAN Government: A "Normal" Relationship? 161
    The Future: Relations Between a Caribbean Island and Mexico 163

    Notes   165
    Index   204

PREFACE

The United States and Cuba: Intimate Enemies is a renewed attempt to understand the relationship between the two neighbors.[1] My goal was to put aside the familiar arguments and create a book that would be useful for policymakers in Washington and Havana. Four central ideas guided my writing.

The United States and Cuba is the ninth of a ten-book series published by Routledge and edited by Jorge I. Domínguez and Rafael Fernández de Castro on the United States and Latin America after the Cold War. Sounds straightforward enough but not necessarily regarding Cuba. Was the Cold War over for the island as well? I concluded it was. No doubt the revolution's siding with the former Soviet Union elevated tensions between the two countries to unprecedented levels, but the Cold War did not fully account for the troubled relationship after 1959. That's the first idea.

Relations between a great power and its weaker neighbor are rarely easy. In the nineteenth century, Cuba lay at the doorstep of a rising United States while still a Spanish colony. The United States looked on the island as a crucial, geopolitical piece in the greater Caribbean Basin. Cubans dissatisfied with Madrid viewed Washington with admiration for its democracy, even as they mistrusted its imperiousness. Before the revolution, the United States and Cuba never had normal relations in the sense that the two never consolidated a mutually beneficial and respectful relationship. That task is still pending and that is the second main idea in this book.

Though tempted to structure the book primarily around the bilateral relationship, I did not. The international community—whether the United Nations, the European Union or countries such as Spain and Canada—was and is an actor on its own right. Because of the Cuban Democracy and Helms-Burton acts, Havana has at times played an outsized role in the relationship between the United States and its allies, occupying a place where it clearly does not belong. At the same time, the Cuban government has excelled at advancing its interests through an activist foreign policy that has allowed Cuba to achieve an unusual importance in world affairs well beyond any objective measure of what the island actually represents.

Miami's Cuban-American community is a second complement to the bilateral relationship. If allied with the United States against the revolution, the exiles have always had their own agenda. More often than not Cuban Americans have been perceived as doing the U.S. bidding and/or as the caricatures that Havana rendered of them—*gusanos* (worms) and the Miami mafia come to mind. I have woven the strands of Cuban Miami into the narrative of this book. Without Cuban Americans and the international community, any review of the U.S.–Cuba relationship loses depth. The third idea then was to include actors beyond the two main parties who, if not on a par, at least played important supporting roles.

Ultimately, it is up to the American and Cuban governments to commit themselves to what inevitably will be a slow, incremental, sometimes regressive process of overcoming the well of mistrust accumulated over more than five decades—indeed from Havana's perspective, over more than a century—so that in the end, the two countries can establish normal relations for the first time ever. Conditioning the process to impossible demands—the United States that Cuba move toward a democratic transition, Havana that Washington lift the embargo wholesale—only extends the stalemated status quo. Even though the Obama administration has taken baby steps in that direction, both capitals sorely need to make a concerted effort at *realpolitik*.

The United States and Cuba is an Inter-American Dialogue book with good reason. Peter Hakim, then the Dialogue's president, agreed to make this project part of my portfolio during the time I was vice president for democratic governance. While at the Dialogue, three assistants—Christian Gómez, Landen Romei and Jaclyn Shull-González—and a battalion of interns—Fabián Borges-Herrero, Anahi Cortada, Nathan T. Doyel, Tanwina Hossien, Maïté Hostetter, Matthew Dugan Kane, Greta Levy, César Antonio López, Roberto Mallén and Emily Phan-Gruber—worked tirelessly on my never-ending requests. I thank you all.

Jorge I. Domínguez read the manuscript and provided me with on-the-mark commentary. I almost always revised the text accordingly. At Routledge, I am grateful to Michael Kerns and Mary Altman for their patience as I finished the manuscript. My friend and copy editor—who wishes to remain anonymous—did an outstanding job.

Family and friends were always there even if I wasn't when this book absorbed me most. Mercedes Arce, Luis Arias, María Ignacia Díaz Moya de Collazo (1933–2010), Rosendo Collazo, Manela and Tony Diez, Lino Fernández, Emilita Luzárraga García de Fernández (1938–2008), Javier Miyares, Alina

Pérez-Stable, Carlos Pérez-Stable and Mercedes Almánzar, Eliseo Pérez-Stable and Claudia Husni, Yaul and Alejo Pérez-Stable, Yolanda Prieto and Annabelle Rodríguez are all markers in my life.

And then there is María Cristina Herrera. Early on María Cristina forged a strong Cuban and Catholic identity in her native Santiago. During the 1950s, Cuban Catholicism blossomed, and so did she within it. At first the revolution offered rich opportunities to meld her patriotism and her faith. In 1959, she joined a church-sponsored literacy drive. Not long thereafter, María Cristina and many other Cubans of goodwill rejected the revolution's Communist turn and went into exile.

Hers is a story not unlike that of other Cuban exiles arriving in the United States in the early 1960s: hard times at first, then success and recognition. In 1970, she joined the faculty of Miami Dade Community College—now Miami Dade College—where she taught until she retired in 2003. Her crowning professional achievement is the Institute of Cuban Studies (ICS), *el Instituto*. Founded in 1969, the ICS has brought together three generations of Cubans—most in the diaspora but also on the island—in a commitment to scholarship, dialogue and pluralism.

Dialogue and pluralism brought on María Cristina the wrath of the militant right in Cuban Miami. On May 26, 1988, a bomb exploded at her home that aimed to derail an ICS symposium on U.S.–Cuba relations. Though the Miami hotel where the event was to take place canceled the booking, the University of Miami opened its doors to *el Instituto* and its 400-strong, mostly Cuban-American audience. Later that year the Miami chapter of the American Civil Liberties Union honored her with an Act of Courage Award.

Official Cuba has also found María Cristina nettlesome. She is against the U.S. embargo while insisting on a democratic Cuba. Though Cuban authorities have kept her from traveling to the island since 1992, she has continued to mend bridges with Cubans from all walks of life there and, of course, with the Cuban Catholic Church at all levels, now more vibrant than at any time in the past five decades. For her, national reconciliation is an ethical imperative.

For a life well lived and for all that lies ahead, María Cristina, this book is for you.

Marifeli Pérez-Stable
Miami
June 2010

ABBREVIATIONS AND ACRONYMS

ACP	Africa, Caribbean, Pacific
AIPAC	American Israel Public Affairs Committee
ALBA	Bolivarian Alternative for the Americas
ARENA	Nationalist Republic Alliance (El Salvador)
CANF	Cuban American National Foundation
CC	Central Committee
CCD	Cuban Committee for Democracy
CCPDH	Cuban Committee for Human Rights
CDA	Cuban Democracy Act
CEA	Center for the Study of the Americas
CFC	Center for a Free Cuba
CIA	Central Intelligence Agency
CLC	Cuban Liberty Council
CP	Common Position
CSG	Cuban Study Group
CTC	Central Organization of Cuban Trade Unions
CUCs	Cuban convertible pesos
DAI	Development Alternatives Incorporated
DEA	Drug Enforcement Administration
EC	European Community
EEC	European Economic Commission
EIDHR	European Instrument for Democracy and Human Rights
EU	European Union
ExCom	Executive Committee
FAA	Federal Aviation Administration
FACE	Facts about Cuban Exiles

FDR	Franklin Delano Roosevelt
FIU	Florida International University
FMC	Federation of Cuban Women
FMLN	Farabundo Martí National Liberation Front (El Salvador)
FTAA	Free Trade Area of the Americas
GAD	Group to Support Democracy
GAO	Government Accountability Office
GATT	General Agreements on Tariffs and Trade
HRC	UN Human Rights Council
HRW	Human Rights Watch
IAJC	Inter-American Juridical Committee
ICAO	International Civil Aviation Organization
ICCPR	International Covenant on Civil and Political Rights
ICESCR	International Covenant on Economic, Social and Cultural Rights
ICS	Institute of Cuban Studies
IMF	International Monetary Fund
INS	Immigration and Naturalization Service
MEP	Member of the European Parliament
NAFTA	North American Free Trade Agreement
NAM	Nonaligned Movement
NARAS	National Academy of Recording Arts and Sciences
NATO	North Atlantic Treaty Organization
NCAM	New Cuban+American Majority PAC
NGO	Non-governmental organization
NORAD	North American Aerospace Defense Command
OAS	Organization of American States
OFAC	Office of Foreign Assets Control
OLAS	Organization of Latin American Solidarity
PAC	Political Action Committee
PAN	National Action Party
PCC	Cuban Communist Party
PP	Popular Party (Spain)
PRD	Party of the Democratic Revolution
PRI	Institutional Revolutionary Party (Mexico)
PSOE	Spanish Socialist Workers' Party
TSRA	Trade Sanctions Reform and Export Enhancements Act
UN	United Nations
UNCHR	UN Commission on Human Rights
UNHCR	UN High Commissioner for Refugees
UPR	UN Universal Periodic Review
USAID	United States Agency for International Development
U.S.S.R.	Union of Soviet Socialist Republics
WTO	World Trade Organization

1

THE UNITED STATES AND CUBA HAVE NEVER HAD NORMAL RELATIONS

The Cold War, it is often said, has not ended for the United States and Cuba. Yet a key source of tension between the United States and Cuba—the dynamics between a great power and its weaker neighbor—antedates the U.S.–U.S.S.R. conflict. Pursuing what it saw as its Manifest Destiny during the nineteenth and early twentieth centuries, the United States never considered the rightful interests of neighbors like Cuba.[1] Indeed, "what was good for the United States was good for Cuba" could have been the motto stamped on the U.S. calling card. For its part, Cuba viewed the United States with ambivalence: admiration for U.S. democracy and progress, mistrust of U.S. presumptuousness. The island, moreover, had an uncommon expectation of equality that Washington rarely considered. As a result, the United States and Cuba have never had normal ties.

In the years before Fidel Castro came to power in 1959, the two countries had failed to establish a stable, mutually beneficial relationship as Mexico and the United States had done after 1940. When the revolution aligned Cuba with the former Soviet Union, U.S.–Cuba relations grievously deteriorated. More than two decades after the fall of Communism in Europe, Washington and Havana are still far from resolving their long-standing predicament: How can the great power learn to take into account Cuban sensibilities as its weaker neighbor turns geographic proximity to the United States into an asset? Because the Cold War so estranged the two countries, normalizing relations years after it ended has not been easy for either party. Nor will it be. Without doubt, Cold War legacies burden the prospect of ending a fifty-year enmity that has served neither country well. But they do precisely because, as the superpowers faced off against each other, Cuba upended Washington's expectations of loyalty. A brief period of détente in the 1970s opened a door to a U.S.–Cuba rapprochement that ultimately closed. Had it not, a book about Cuba and the United States after the Cold War would not have been subtitled *Intimate Enemies*.

Cuban domestic affairs have always been at the crux of the U.S.–Cuba relationship. In the nineteenth century, the United States feared that political instability on the island could create opportunities for European powers other than Spain to gain influence over Cuba. Until the 1890s, the United States, in effect, preferred that Cuba remain a Spanish colony. As the United States rose over the Caribbean Basin early in the twentieth century, political stability in Cuba remained imperative to safeguard U.S. investments, national security and access to the Panama Canal. Immediately after World War II, nothing signaled the fact that Cuba would bring the Cold War ninety miles from U.S. shores. That, when it did, the United States sought to undermine the revolution was to be expected. Washington failed as a result of its own mistakes but also because of the character of the revolution. In the early years, a decisive majority of the Cuban people lent the revolutionary government inordinate strength. The confrontational nature of the U.S.–Cuba nexus became one of the pillars in the relationship that Fidel Castro and the revolution forged with ordinary citizens. The call for a *patria digna*, a homeland of dignity, in short, a *Cuba para los cubanos*, elicited in response impregnable loyalty from the Cuban people. Millions then established such a strong emotional bond with the revolution that *la revolución* became a quasi-mystical symbol whose pull is still felt in some sectors of Cuban society. By the 1970s, the United States and socialist Cuba appeared ready to make peace. Given the Cold War, U.S. recognition offered to imprint the government in Havana with a mark of permanence. As it had in the past, however, Washington brought to the table a set of expectations commensurate with its status as a great power. At the same time, the prospect of normalization did not lead Cuba to curtail the activist foreign policy that had so enhanced its international standing. The great power–weaker neighbor conundrum remained intact.

The arc of U.S.–Cuba relations after the Cold War does not, therefore, start in the late 1980s. The two countries carry exceptionally heavy historical baggage that the superpower conflict gravely compounded.

The "Ever-Faithful Isle"[2]

"Why should the Americans have the right to put missiles at our doorstep and we not have a comparable right?" asked Nikita Khrushchev in the spring of 1962 as the U.S. Jupiter missiles in Turkey were about to become operational.[3] A few months later, the Soviet premier answered his own question by emplacing nuclear missiles with offensive capabilities in Cuba. Rumors had swirled for weeks before U.S. intelligence confirmed, on October 16, that the missiles were on the island. The Cuban Missile Crisis had begun. For thirteen days, President John F. Kennedy and his advisors—the Executive Committee (ExComm) convened to deal with the situation—deliberated on how the United States should respond.

All options were on the table: a comprehensive blockade, an air strike on the missile sites, sweeping strikes against military bases and a full-scale invasion. At the same time, Kennedy worried that the U.S. "fixation on the subject of Cuba" might give European allies pause at whatever course he decided to follow.[4] Europeans, after all, lived with Soviet medium-range ballistic missiles at their doorstep and thought that, in the president's words, "We're slightly demented on this subject."[5] On October 22, Kennedy announced his decision: a naval blockade on incoming ships bearing military cargo and a demand for the immediate removal of all missiles from the island. He chose a moderate course that, nevertheless, signaled his unequivocal refusal to accept the Soviet missiles in Cuba while giving himself and Khrushchev time to ponder their next moves.[6]

"But Cuba's so small compared to the world," General David M. Shoup said to Kennedy during the ExComm deliberations.[7] Cuba is, of course, small. Yet the island had loomed large in the U.S. purview since the early nineteenth century. In 1823, Secretary of State John Quincy Adams wrote the classic statement on how the United States viewed Cuba:

> There are laws of political as well as of physical gravitation; and if an apple severed by the tempest from its native tree cannot choose but fall to the ground, Cuba, forcibly disjoined from its own unnatural connection with Spain and incapable of self-support, can gravitate only towards the North American Union, which by the same law of nature cannot cast her off from its bosom.[8]

Until the Missile Crisis, U.S. interest in Cuba spanned the three decisive fronts in the making of U.S. foreign policy: national security, domestic politics and economic development.[9] Whether as a bulwark against European expansionism, a defense outpost for the Panama Canal or an "ever-faithful" ally in the budding East–West conflict after World War II, Cuba lay at the heart of U.S. national security. Domestic politics also shaped U.S.–Cuba relations. Before 1860, slaveholders favored the annexation of the island to maintain the equilibrium within the Union. Turn-of-the century progressives looked at a possible annexation of Cuba through the lenses of a United States engaged in modern, "good" imperialism. New Dealers showcased their Cuba policy as evidence of their good neighborliness to counter domestic criticism of U.S. interventions in Central America and the Caribbean. When a revolutionary wave swept Cuban society in 1933, Franklin Delano Roosevelt (FDR) dispatched, not the Marines, but Sumner Welles—assistant secretary of state and an architect of the Good Neighbor Policy—to mediate the crisis. On the economic front, beet growers never lost sight of quotas and tariffs on Cuban sugar entering the U.S. market.

Between the late nineteenth century and 1959, the United States and Cuba were important trading partners.[10] In 1953, the island ranked sixth in the world as a destination of U.S. exports.[11] In 1958, per capita U.S. investments in Cuba ($143) far surpassed that in the rest of Latin America ($39).[12]

Kennedy was right to worry about the "fixation" that might dampen European enthusiasm for the U.S. response to the crisis in Cuba. His ExComm military and some of his civilian advisors adamantly (if fruitlessly) insisted that the missiles altered the strategic balance between the superpowers and recommended immediate military action. The president and most of his civilian advisors worried that any military strike might put the world over the brink of nuclear Armageddon. Kennedy himself thought that the Soviet Union's gutsy missile placement implied a trade of Cuba for West Berlin, an idea the president and his advisors were unwilling to consider.[13] In 1962, the United States was much more interested in preserving a free West Berlin than in promoting change towards a free Cuba. Still, the United States had grown accustomed to the "ties of singular intimacy"—William McKinley's memorable phrase in his State of the Union message after the Spanish-American War—that had long marked the U.S.-Cuba relationship.[14] In 1945, no one in the United States could have predicted that the most dangerous confrontation of the Cold War would happen over Cuba. So yes, there were reasons aplenty for the emotional undercurrents that intermittently charged the ExComm's discussions. Fortunately, cooler heads prevailed.

The Missile Crisis

Cuba was an actor in the October Crisis, as Havana calls the Cuban Missile Crisis. Without Cuban acquiescence, the Soviet Union could never have placed the missiles in Sagua La Grande, in central Cuba, and in Guanajay and San Cristóbal, west of Havana. Fidel Castro consented to the Soviet request in a show of "solidarity with the socialist camp" and, especially, in the hope of deterring the full-throttled U.S. invasion that both Havana and Moscow then considered likely.[15] What else were the Cubans and the Soviets to make of the two major military exercises held in April and May of 1962? The first executed an amphibious assault on Vieques, an island off the coast of Puerto Rico; the second summoned more than 40,000 troops, 79 ships and over 300 aircraft for a maneuver on the southeastern coast of the United States.[16] From Havana's vantage point, Operation Mongoose—Kennedy's covert plan (1961–1962) aimed at sparking a revolt against Castro, which could well have been considered state-sponsored terrorism—inevitably pointed to another invasion (Mongoose would be a factor in the Soviet decision to station the missiles on the island). In April 1961, the botched invasion attempt at the Bay of Pigs had actually bolstered the revolutionary government. So much so that, in August 1961 at a meeting in Punta del Este, Uruguay, that set up the Alliance for

Progress, Ernesto Ché Guevara told Kennedy emissary Richard Goodwin: "Thank you for Playa Girón [Bay of Pigs]. Before the invasion, the revolution was shaky. Now, it is stronger than ever."[17] Bay of Pigs also created a nightmare for the United States: To Khrushchev, Kennedy looked weak, an impression that was not altered by the first meeting between the two leaders in Vienna two months later. Only in the crucible of the thirteen days in October 1962 would the Soviet premier realize the determination that the U.S. president, chastened by his mistakes, was capable of mustering.

Cuba, however, had no say in the resolution of the Missile Crisis. On October 28, Castro learned from Radio Moscow that Khrushchev had accepted Kennedy's proposal: that, subject to on-site verification, the United States would pledge not to invade Cuba if the Soviet Union removed the missiles. Khrushchev had not told Castro of his decision, which made Cuba look like a pawn. Nothing ever maddened Castro more than being treated as a subordinate. And yet, the Comandante had had a "say": Alarmed by his bellicosity in their letter exchange, Khrushchev ended the crisis. Naturally, Castro never agreed to an on-the-ground inspection. He also thought Khrushchev weak for not insisting on a public, *quid pro quo* removal of the Jupiter missiles from Turkey, instead of the discreet dismantlement that took place in April 1963. Decades later, Castro would learn that his instincts had been right regarding the Soviet Union's decision not to go public with their 1962 missile agreement. In 1989, Theodore Sorensen, a former Kennedy aide, noted that such a disclosure would have made it harder for the United States to force the removal of the missiles; the world might have simply accepted the Soviet–Cuban agreement as the counterpart of the U.S.–Turkey accord on the Jupiters.[18] Had Khrushchev accepted Castro's advice in this instance, Soviet missiles in Cuba might not have taken the world to the brink of nuclear war.

Neither was Cuba an integral part of the eventual historiography on the Missile Crisis. In the late 1980s, Brown University launched an oral history project on the crisis that brought together historical actors and scholars to examine newly declassified documents and explore new interpretations.[19] Only U.S. participants attended the first conference in 1987 at Hawks Cay, Florida. In 1989, project organizers planned a second meeting in Moscow with American and Soviet participants. Upon learning that Cubans would also be in attendance, James G. Blight, the project coordinator, candidly expressed his amazement.

> Before the 1989 conference, the Soviets told us, "Oh, by the way, we've invited thirteen Cubans." At the time, I did not know the Cubans had anything to do with the Cuban missile crisis. At most, Cuba had been the parking lot for the missiles.[20]

After Moscow, a conference in Cuba became inevitable.

In January 1992, American and Russian participants met in Havana with their Cuban counterparts. A couple of days before the meeting, the Kennedy–Khrushchev letters exchanged during the Missile Crisis were declassified, and they made it clear that Kennedy had not issued an outright pledge not to invade Cuba. Only if Havana had agreed to an on-site verification would such a pledge have been operational. Until that point, Castro may not have realized the stark conditionality of the U.S. pledge on his acceptance of an inspection system.[21] Had Khrushchev perhaps hinted at a firmer U.S. commitment than was actually the case?[22] In Havana's view, the Missile Crisis had had one saving grace: the pledge that shielded Cuba from U.S. aggression. And no matter what the status of the pledge was immediately after the crisis, Castro also knew that in 1970 the United States had issued an understanding of nonaggression that removed the on-site verification issue from the table. In answering a Soviet request to clarify the status of the 1962 terms, Richard Nixon made U.S. restraint on the use of force against Cuba conditional on the Soviet Union's keeping offensive weaponry out of the island.[23]

After the release of the letters and infuriated once again by the October Crisis that had so humiliated him, Fidel Castro decided to attend the conference. As a result, Robert S. McNamara, Kennedy's defense secretary, was able to ask him directly if he would have recommended the use of nuclear weapons in the event of a U.S. invasion. Only Castro could have given the following answer:

> Now, we started from the assumption that if there was an invasion of Cuba, nuclear war would erupt. We were certain of that. We would be forced to pay the price that we would disappear. Would I have been ready to use nuclear weapons? Yes, I would have agreed to the use of nuclear weapons. I would have agreed, in the event of the invasion, with the use of tactical nuclear weapons. If Mr. McNamara or Mr. Kennedy had been in our place and had their country been invaded or their country was going to be occupied, I believe they would have used nuclear weapons.[24]

Castro's mind-set—his willingness to defend Cuban national sovereignty even at the risk of a nuclear catastrophe—shocked American participants. Even more distressing was the Russian disclosure that Moscow had not only emplaced medium-range nuclear missiles capable of taking out major U.S. cities, but had also supplied Soviet troops on the island with tactical nuclear weapons to be used at their discretion in the event of a U.S. invasion. In one case, the commander of a Soviet submarine heading towards the Caribbean—having lost communication with Moscow and exhausted from the cat-and-mouse game with the U.S. Navy—ordered the nuclear torpedo on board to be made combat ready.[25]

An Uncommon Expectation of Equality

Great powers have rarely tempered their actions out of respect for their weaker neighbors. Take, for example, the United States and Mexico. In the nineteenth century, the doctrine of Manifest Destiny propelled U.S. expansion into California, Texas and the southwest. The Mexican–American War (1846–1848)—largely forgotten in the United States but painfully remembered south of the border—sealed Mexico's loss of half of its territory and suffused Mexican culture with a mistrust of its powerful neighbor that lingers still. All the same, after 1940, Mexico and the United States slowly crafted a mutually beneficial relationship. As in Cuba in 1933, FDR's restraint in Mexico after Standard Oil was nationalized in 1938 gave heft to the Good Neighbor Policy: By not intervening, Washington let the nationalization stand and, thus, handed Mexican nationalism a landmark victory. As the Institutional Revolutionary Party (PRI) stabilized Mexican politics and put the economy on a path of sustained growth until the 1970s, the United States paid more heed to Mexican sensibilities. While Mexican presidents maintained cordial relations with Havana, Washington never badgered Mexico. Instead, U.S. and Mexican intelligence services discreetly cooperated on matters of mutual interest regarding the island. Havana, in turn, never meddled in Mexican internal affairs as it did in many other Latin American countries by supporting guerrillas. As the economic crisis deepened in Mexico in the 1980s, the PRI cast aside the state-centered policies that no longer promoted growth and adopted a market-friendly course. Closer ties with the United States and a cautious political liberalization ensued.[26] In 1992, Mexico joined Canada and the United States in the North American Free Trade Agreement (NAFTA).[27] NAFTA also abetted the forces within Mexico that had slowly been pushing towards democratization since the late 1970s.[28]

In contrast, Cuba and the United States never found a stable path toward a mutually advantageous relationship. Even more so than in the U.S.–Mexican case, glaring disparities marked U.S.–Cuba relations. Cuba, moreover, had an uncommon expectation of equality vis-à-vis great powers. During the nineteenth century, for example, Cubans proposed three alternatives to Spanish colonialism based on parity: joining the United States as a state, gaining autonomy as a province of Spain and establishing an independent republic. After the Civil War, U.S. interest in annexing Cuba waned. Spain never seriously heeded the autonomists' demands that Cuba be given the same rights as peninsular provinces. When independence finally arrived in 1902, the new Cuban republic was saddled with the Platt amendment, an addendum to the Cuban Constitution of 1901 that enabled U.S. intervention if order and property were threatened on the island. Even those who had advocated statehood decried the amendment for placing Cuba in the subservient position of a protectorate. Until the Roosevelt administration abrogated it in 1934, the Platt amendment curtailed Cuban sovereignty.[29] Like the Mexican–American War, the amendment left barely a trace in the U.S. imagination. Cuba, on the other hand, has an ele-phantine memory that bristles still.

Twenty-five years passed between the amendment's demise and the triumph of the revolution. The United States and Cuba, nonetheless, did not make much progress in normalizing relations. In 1940, a new Cuban Constitution came into effect. It was a socially progressive document that tended to social welfare as well as to the institutional architecture of democracy, and one that had broad support from the Cuban citizenry. The Constitution of 1940, more-over, reflected a broadly based pact among all factions in the contested upheav-als of the 1930s; it marked the only time Cuban political elites successfully crafted a democratic governing consensus while keeping the United States at bay. During these years, Fulgencio Batista Zaldívar was Cuba's dominant polit-ical figure, emerging from power broker in the 1930s to constitutional presid-ent from 1940 to 1944.[30] In 1944, Ramón Grau San Martín won the presidency (1944–1948) and Carlos Prío Socarrás succeeded him. Both men belonged to the Auténtico Party, which embodied the revolutionary ideals of the 1930s and, consequently, awakened great hopes in the citizenry that Cuba would, at last, find good governance. The Grau and Prío administrations enacted socioeconomic reforms that benefited ordinary Cubans. At the same time, the Auténticos let corruption run rampant, deeply disillusioning the Cuban electorate.[31] A moral outrage at the unfulfilled promises of the young republic grew in the polity. Batista's coup stoked that outrage further and the revolution exploited it: The revolutionaries promised a Cuba rid of the *poli-tiquería* of the past and of the machinations that had led to broken promises. Regarding the United States, the Auténtico administrations began laying the foundations for a different relationship. The party platform—nationalism, social justice, democracy and anti-Communism—was embraced by a majority of Cubans and complemented the U.S. agenda of the early Cold War. Prío, moreover, assumed the presidency with a commitment to economic diversifi-cation and modernization: It was patently clear that sugar—historically at the foundation of the Cuban economy—alone no longer sufficed. His government created the National Bank of Cuba and other state institutions to enhance eco-nomic development, and instructed the foreign ministry to make national eco-nomic interests its priority. It was the closest Cuba ever came to turning geographic nearness to the United States into an asset. Unfortunately, the opportunities created by the abrogation of the Platt and the return of demo-cracy in 1940 came to naught.

On March 10, 1952, Batista's coup against Prío preempted the presidential election set for June, thus trampling on the Constitution of 1940. While not a promoter of the coup, Washington welcomed Batista's reentry into Cuban politics and generally backed his regime throughout the 1950s.[32] Under the Cold War's pernicious logic, friendly dictators were preferable to nationalist or unruly democracies that might open a flank to Communism. Still, without the Platt amendment, Washington had long ceased to interfere directly in Cuban affairs. Though Cuba lived in the shadow of U.S. hegemony, the United States no longer imposed the same strictures on Cuban sovereignty.[33] All the same, pre-1959 U.S.–Cuba relations, especially the U.S. support of Batista in the 1950s, fueled anti-U.S. sentiments among *Fidelistas* and Cubans in general.

After January 1, 1959, Washington faced a government in Havana with an unremitting will for independence, and it did not know how to respond, except imperiously. All that the United States had ever feared in Cuba—threats to national security and U.S. investments—materialized at the height of the Cold War, a mighty conflict with consequences that far surpassed the geopolitical concerns of old. In the spring of 1959, the Eisenhower administration was already planning to replicate in Cuba the success it had in Guatemala when it toppled Jacobo Arbenz.[34] Unlike Guatemala, however, Cuba was undergoing an enormously popular nationalist revolution. Fidel Castro, moreover, was a relentless visionary without qualms about the means used to pursue his ends—a truly sovereign and just Cuba. Arbenz had been a reformer with mundane political skills. Forged in the struggle against Batista, Castro's Rebel Army never divided as Guatemala's military did when a faction joined the U.S.-backed coup against Arbenz. In 1959–1960, millions of Cubans felt that Cuba was truly theirs for the first time and Castro's call for a *patria digna*, a homeland of dignity, sounded the deepest chords of nationalist defiance. Early on, the newspaper *Revolución* captured the national mood: "Cuba is not a simple geographical reference."[35]

Badly managed and never fully supported by the Kennedy administration, the principal actors in the Bay of Pigs invasion—the brigade of Cuban exiles who landed and the U.S. officials who backed them—also revealed a tragic disconnection from the popular sentiments on the island.[36] Democracy and anti-Communism motivated the Cuban invaders; rolling back Communism ninety miles from Key West propelled the Eisenhower and Kennedy administrations. Neither the exiles nor the U.S. government grasped the depths of the searing cry, *Cuba sí! Yanquis no!* often heard in response to Castro's open-air speeches to the Cuban people. Two days after landing on April 17, 1961, the *brigadistas* were routed, a victory for the Cuban Army that inspired the revolutionary leaders to be even more audacious. The spirit of the Platt amendment had finally expired: Cuba had defied the United States, and it had prevailed. Cuban nationalism achieved a great victory but, unlike Mexico's in 1938, it was at the cost of an enmity that has lasted half a century. Across the Florida Straits, the Cuban exile community began to lay down roots, even if most still cherished the dream of returning to a democratic Cuba. Over the ensuing decades, Cuban Americans would learn to flex their political muscle in favor of the U.S. embargo, and have significant influence in shaping U.S. policy toward Cuba after the end of the Cold War.

A Cold War Might-Have-Been

Normalization of relations between Cuba and the United States could well have happened during the Cold War. After the Missile Crisis, Kennedy reflected on ways other than military and covert actions to advance the U.S. national interest.[37] Castro, it seems, also sought alternatives to better advance Cuba's national interest. In the fall of 1963, Cuba's UN ambassador, Carlos Lechuga, approached U.S. Ambassador William H. Attwood about opening talks to normalize relations.[38] On a parallel track, Kennedy sent Castro a message with French journalist Jean Daniel, the gist of which was, "Everything is possible with a Cuban nationalist state, even one that is communist. Nothing is possible with a Cuban state that is a vassal of the Soviet Union."[39] On November 22, 1963, Daniel was having lunch with the Comandante when news of Kennedy's assassination in Dallas came through. Three times Castro uttered, "This is bad news."[40] Attwood and Lechuga continued their contacts after Dallas. Soon thereafter, however, Lyndon Johnson "put the talks on ice": In an electoral year, he was not about to appear "soft on anything, especially Cuba."[1]

In the year before his death, Kennedy's views on the Third World had been in flux. The Missile Crisis had impressed upon him the urgency of "a strategy for peace" that would limit the nuclear arms race.[42] He tended to see neutrality in the Third World as an opportunity for the United States, not as the threat that John Foster Dulles had perceived it to be in the 1950s.[43] During his presidency, the White House gained its own voice in Africa, where it had previously been a sort of "junior partner of France and England", and became "less suspicious of genuine nonalignment."[44] Kennedy's message delivered by Daniel suggested that the United States might normalize relations with "an independent communist state" in Cuba. Kennedy had told Daniel:

> In part owing to my country's policies during the Batista regime, I believe that we created the Castro movement out of whole cloth and without realizing it. I can assure you that I have understood the Cubans. I approved the proclamation which Fidel Castro made in the Sierra Maestra, when he justifiably called for justice. In the matter of the Batista regime, I am in agreement with the first Cuban revolutionaries. That is perfectly clear. But it is also clear that the problem has ceased to be a Cuban one. I am the President of the United States and not a sociologist; I am the President of a free nation which has certain responsibilities in the Free World. I know that Castro betrayed the promises made in the Sierra Maestra, and that he has agreed to be a Soviet agent in Latin America. The world was on the verge of nuclear war in 1962. The Russians understood this very well; but so far as Fidel Castro is concerned, I don't know whether he realizes this, or even if he cares about it.[45]

At exactly the same time, however, the Central Intelligence Agency (CIA) was plotting to assassinate Castro, a sign that Washington still held out hope of reversing the revolution. Then, as Vietnam consumed the Johnson administration, interest in the island waned. Cuba would never again be front and center in U.S. foreign policy.

The Missile Crisis temporarily soured Soviet–Cuban relations, but Castro and Khrushchev mended relations quickly. In January 1963, Khrushchev wrote Castro a 7,000-word letter inviting him to visit and "see, on a sunny day, the ground covered with snow and the forests silvery with frost." The Soviet leader impressed upon him the importance of developing the Cuban economy, "the revolutionary example" that "the monopolists and the imperialists most fear."[46] In late April 1963, Castro traveled to the Soviet Union and stayed for a month, longer perhaps than his hosts had wished. All the same, the visit dispelled the tensions of the previous October. Fidel and Nikita engaged in marathon sessions on the Missile Crisis itself, how best to govern a socialist society, the Soviet model of economic development and their shared mistrust of the United States. In January 1964, Castro returned to Moscow and secured additional trade agreements. From then on, Cuba–U.S.S.R. relations settled on a pattern whereby Moscow supplied Havana military equipment *pro bono*, covered Cuba's yawning trade deficits and extended development credits on generous terms.[47] Though not always tension-free, the relationship proved to be remarkably stable until the Communist superpower disintegrated. By 1970, Havana's radicalism— which scorned Soviet orthodoxy on socialist economics while promoting revolution in Latin America and Africa—had wrought disaster. At home, the economy had collapsed; abroad, guerrillas had failed miserably in replicating the Cuban experience.

Cuba did a volte-face and launched a process of institutionalization that accepted the basic tenets of Soviet socialism.[48] With more orderly governance and economic management, Cuban society acquired a profile more akin to state socialism.[49] In that sense, the revolution receded from the daily lives of Cubans, even if *la revolución* remained central to the collective political imagination. Cuba's closer ties with Moscow also brought stronger economic backing.[50] Even then, however, Havana never quite fit the mold of a Soviet satellite. The revolution's national origins and Fidel Castro's leadership afforded Cuba an independence vis-à-vis Moscow that geography always denied Eastern Europe. During the 1970s, Cuba reaped significant benefits from abandoning radicalism at home and abroad. For the first time since the revolution, the economy sustained modest growth with commensurate improvements in living standards. By mid-decade, Argentina, Barbados, Colombia, Guyana, Jamaica, Trinidad and Tobago and Venezuela had normalized relations with Havana. In 1975, the Organization of American States (OAS) ended multilateral trade sanctions that had been levied in 1964. The two OAS meetings served as bookends on Cuba: the first commanded isolation to undermine the revolution; the second accepted socialist Cuba as a fixture in the Western Hemisphere. The United States voted with the majority to lift the multilateral sanctions. Without its prior support, the resolution would never have come to the OAS floor. Indeed, U.S. détente with the Soviet Union had achieved a climate of stability that favored a rapprochement between Washington and Havana. In the 1970s the United States went back to the type of approach that Kennedy had begun testing after the Missile Crisis: that U.S. national interests might best be promoted by easing tensions with Cuba to counterbalance Moscow there. From June 1974 to February 1976, the United States and Cuba held a discreet dialogue initiated by the administration of Gerald R. Ford.[51] Both countries dropped preconditions to hold bilateral talks: Washington would not insist that Cuba sever all military ties to the Soviet Union; Havana held back demands that the United States lift the embargo. After communicating through special channels for six months, U.S. and Cuban emissaries held a series of meetings in New York and Washington "to explore the possibilities for a more normal relationship between our two countries." Drawing lessons from détente, the United States underscored the usefulness of dealing with specific issues of mutual interest and benefit. Both sides made gestures of goodwill. Washington's most important signals were the OAS vote and the Ford administration's subsequent modifications of the embargo: licensing U.S. foreign subsidiaries to do business with Havana, abolishing foreign-aid penalties on countries that traded with Cuba and allowing foreign ships involved in commerce with the island to refuel in U.S. ports. Cuba, in turn, released a U.S. citizen with CIA ties captured in 1965 and returned the $2 million ransom paid by Southern Airways after the 1972 hijacking of one of its planes. In March 1975, the State Department issued a review of U.S. Cuba policy that concluded: "If there is benefit to us in an end to the state of 'perpetual antagonism' it lies in getting Cuba off the domestic and inter-American agendas, in extracting the symbolism from an intrinsically trivial issue."[52]

At the outset of the secret talks, Kissinger instructed U.S. emissaries to mind their tone: "It is better to deal straight with Castro. Behave chivalrously; do it like a big guy, not like a shyster."[53]

Superpower détente likewise reinforced the American idea that Castro might respond favorably to U.S. overtures. Might Cuba find a niche between the superpowers as India or the old Yugoslavia had? Had normalization happened, U.S. recognition would have bestowed the ultimate mark of permanence to the post-revolutionary government in Cuba. Yet, Havana's moves in foreign affairs towards the end of 1975 undermined the twenty-month dialogue. In September, Cuba introduced a resolution at the United Nations calling for Puerto Rican independence. Coming right after the OAS resolution on multilateral sanctions and the Ford administration's easing of the embargo, the timing peeved Washington. In November 1975, Castro sent 36,000 troops to support the Movement for the Liberation of Angola (MPLA) against two CIA-backed

Angolan groups and the South African Army that had invaded Angola in October.[54] From the U.S. perspective, Cuban actions in Angola torpedoed the talks. "There was absolutely no possibility that we would tolerate the Cubans' moving into a new theater, becoming a strategic base in the Cold War and still improve relations," Kissinger said.[55]

Cuba had a different understanding of why the talks failed. Ramón Sánchez-Parodi, a Cuban participant in the talks, explained: "The first excuse was Puerto Rico. Later it was Angola. But the main reason, we have always believed, was the fear that if the secret talks were revealed during the election campaign, Ford would have been severely damaged."[56]

All the same, Havana surely realized that sending troops to Angola would not advance the ongoing quiet diplomacy. From a Cuban perspective, other factors had come into play. In 1975, the United States suffered defeat in Vietnam. Angolan events presented Cuba with a unique opportunity: support of the MPLA against the U.S.-backed groups and South Africa, knowing that neither Congress nor domestic public opinion would countenance a U.S. intervention so soon after Vietnam. On December 19, 1975, Congress passed the Clark amendment, which ended all CIA-backed operations in Angola. In addition, with South Africa's entry into the Angolan civil war, Africa's support for Cuba's military deployment was assured. In a masterstroke, Havana gained an international stature well beyond what it or any other minor power had a right to expect. Would Cuba sacrifice that standing for the sake of rapprochement with the United States? In 1976, Castro did not mince words:

> It is not that Cuba rejects the ideal of improving relations with the United States—we are in favor of peace, of the policy of détente, of coexistence between states with different social systems. What we do not accept are humiliating conditions—the absurd price which the United States apparently would have us pay for an improvement of relations.[57]

Without the Ford administration's quiet diplomacy, Jimmy Carter's efforts to bridge differences with Cuba may not have made progress. In spite of Cuban involvement in Angola, the new administration set out to better relations. Two months after his inauguration, Carter lifted the ban on travel to Cuba.[58] For the first time in two decades, American tourists, artists, businessmen, professors and students visited the island. In September 1977, Interests Sections opened in Washington and Havana, a step that might have led the way to establishing embassies, much as the 1973 liaison offices did for the full restoration of U.S.–China relations in 1979. But Havana again valued its activist foreign policy more than the advancing rapprochement with Washington. In February 1978, Cuba sent 15,000 troops to help Ethiopia roll back Somalia's occupation of the Ogaden desert; as in Angola, Cuba succeeded.[59] In May, Angola-based Katanga rebels attacked Shaba province in Zaire with the intent of establishing an independent state, although in Zaire, the record mostly belies U.S. suspicions of Havana's complicity.[60] Nonetheless, any Cuban activity in Africa, real or perceived, happened with Angola and the Cold War as backdrop.

In 1977, Carter placed "the strands that connect our actions overseas with our essential character as a nation" at the core of U.S. foreign policy. The United States, he argued, should free itself from an "inordinate fear of communism which once led us to embrace any dictator who joined us in that fear" and address "the new global questions of justice, equity and human rights."[61] Still, the actual conduct of foreign policy inevitably fell short of the president's noble goals. Zbigniew Brzezinski, the national security advisor, never lost sight of the rivalry with the Soviet Union. Secretary of State Cyrus Vance, in contrast, saw conflict resolution at the heart of U.S. diplomacy and made it his charge "to slog it out," to find solutions piecemeal.[62] After Cuba sent troops to Angola, the Ford administration had ended its dialogue with Havana, a great power's response to Cuba's incursion into "a new theater" in the Cold War. In spite of Cuba's presence in Angola, Carter quickly resumed the dialogue. However, Southern Africa—with its late independence struggles in Portugal's colonies, racist regimes in South Africa and Rhodesia (now Zimbabwe) and the Cuban military mission in Angola—was fraught with instabilities that infused autochthonous regional processes with unavoidable Cold War meanings. Washington balked at what it saw as Havana's brash gamesmanship in superpower politics. Cuba, in turn, was loath to pass up the opportunity that Africa offered: a way to reaffirm the old expectation of equality that the revolution ceaselessly fanned.

Under Carter, U.S. policy toward Cuba rode an obstacle-ridden path. In no small measure, the administration wanted to square the circle: normalizing relations while forcing Havana to disengage from Africa. Cuba, in turn, was unwilling to sacrifice the international stature it had achieved with its activist foreign policy. While détente had facilitated an opening between Washington and Havana, Cold War imperatives hindered progress. Meanwhile, Carter faced a tough reelection that was made even more difficult by the Mariel exodus of 1980, when tens of thousands of Cubans streamed unimpeded into the United States, reinforcing the perception of inefficacy that besieged the administration. Eventually, talks between the two governments ended the exodus, and Washington and Havana moved forward on the normalization agenda, which was to be concluded in Carter's second term. That, of course, never happened.

Ronald Reagan took U.S. foreign policy in other directions. The Sandinista revolution in Nicaragua, Marxist Maurice Bishop's leadership in the tiny Caribbean island of Grenada and an escalating civil war in El Salvador focused Reagan's attention on Cuba as the "source" of the region's troubles.[63] The idea of approaching the Third World on its own terms—never fully articulated as policy under Kennedy or Carter—was discarded by Reagan. Instead, the administration quickly established a distinction between "authoritarian" and "totalitarian" regimes, the latter being antithetical to U.S. interests while the former were useful against the Soviet Union.[64] In short, Reagan's view—"The Soviet Union underlies all the unrest that is going on in the world"—harked back to the 1950s.[65] Nevertheless, the doors between Washington and Havana remained ajar. In November 1981, Secretary of State Alexander Haig and Cuban Vice-President Carlos Rafael Rodríguez met secretly in Mexico City; in March 1982, retired General Vernon Walters, ambassador-at-large in Reagan's first term, met with Castro and Rodríguez in Havana.[66] Even after the U.S. invasion of Grenada in 1983, Washington and Havana crafted an immigration agreement—Cuba accepted the return of 2,746 Mariel refugees, the United States allotted up to 20,000 preference visas a year for eligible Cuban citizens. However, that pact proved short-lived.[67] In May 1985, Havana suspended it after the launch of Radio Martí, the U.S. broadcasts to Cuba modeled after those of Radio Free Europe.[68]

In the two years after the broadcasts began and the migration agreement was abrogated, U.S.–Cuba relations markedly deteriorated. Havana curtailed the charter flights that delivered supplies for the U.S. Interests Section, and for a time, the two governments recalled the respective heads of their diplomatic missions. The Reagan administration froze the entry of Cubans, either from the island or from third countries where they might have migrated. During this period, almost no one from Cuba entered the United States legally. Meanwhile, economic conditions in Cuba took another downward turn, which placed pressures on Havana to reactivate the migration escape valve. In a May 1987 interview with *L'Humanité*, the French Communist Party newspaper, Castro mentioned in passing that those who "prefer a capitalist society to our socialist society" would not be kept from leaving.[69] While a meeting between U.S. and Cuban officials a year earlier had come to naught, this time the door opened by Castro led to the restitution of the immigration agreement. Much as Havana tried to put it on the table, however, the Reagan administration did not budge on Radio Martí, which continues broadcasting today. In May 1987, Kenneth N. Skoug, director of the State Department's Office of Cuban Affairs, told a University of Minnesota audience:

> There is a smaller agenda with Cuba which we share as neighbors. The United States has been ready to deal with these issues because it has believed there are better prospects for success than on those issues where Cuba's sense of revolutionary mission is so prominent. In the past 5 years, on U.S. initiative, we have sought solutions to migration and refugee issues and to radio broadcasting interference.
>
> Resumption of the migration agreement remains the key to any improvement in our bilateral relationship. While we cannot realistically expect any change on the major world issues, which stem from the fundamental approach of the Cuban leader, there is no good reason why an

agreement which has been criticized by neither side cannot be put back into force. If that happened, other issues on the small agenda could also be considered.[70]

Thus, Reagan's chief specialist on Cuban matters proposed a problem-solving agenda of mutual interest with immigration as the first item. In November 1987, the 1984 agreement was restored, keeping intact its original intent: the return to Cuba of the Mariel excludables and the issuance of up to 20,000 immigration visas a year by the United States.[71] In fact, even when tensions had been at their peak in the early 1960s, the two governments negotiated on immigration. In October 1965, Fidel Castro announced the opening of the Port of Camarioca to Cubans wishing to leave the island and authorized Cuban exiles to come by boat to pick up their relatives. After a month, Havana and Washington ended the boatlift. In December 1965, the United States established the Freedom Flights which brought more than a quarter of a million Cubans to the United States.[72] In 1973, Havana ended the airlift, claiming that the pool of disaffected Cubans had run dry. Other issues such as air piracy also underscored interests in common. Throughout the 1960s, hijacked planes often landed at Havana's José Martí International Airport. By the early 1970s, Castro expressed interest in an anti-hijacking agreement, in no small part because his government had lost 264 planes and boats between 1960 and 1970. In 1973, Cuba and the United States under Richard M. Nixon signed an anti-hijacking agreement. After the 1976 bombing of Cubana Flight 455, which killed seventy-three people, Havana abrogated it, accusing the United States of complicity in exile terrorism. Castro, nonetheless, expressed a disposition to honor the agreement's provisions.[73] Thus, the long-standing enmity did not prevent the two governments from talking on concrete issues of mutual benefit. Only under the Ford and Carter administrations, however, was the "smaller agenda" launched with the prospect of normalizing relations as the final outcome.

Most significant, however, were the four-party talks to end the Angolan civil war, establish Namibian independence and withdraw Cuban troops from Southern Africa. There was nothing small about that agenda and, yet, Washington and Havana succeeded. In 1988, the United States, Cuba, Angola and South Africa met a dozen times over five months before announcing the accords on Angola and Namibia.[74] In May 1991, the last Cuban soldiers returned home from Angola. If in the mid-1970s Kissinger had decried Cuba's entrance into a new front in the Cold War, the Reagan administration had no choice but to negotiate with Havana to bring peace to Southern Africa. The weak neighbor sat shoulder to shoulder with the great power. Its activist foreign policy had borne a substantial fruit: The United States had recognized Cuba as a player in Southern Africa, one that was an integral part of the discussions to end the region's wars. In 1975, Castro had seized the opportunities that South Africa's invasion of Angola created; a less intrepid leader may never have dared. All the same, Angola had been costly. Relative to population, Cuba had deployed more troops to Africa every year between 1975 and 1989 than the United States had in Vietnam in the war's peak year, 1968.[75] In a decade and a half, 2,016 Cubans lost their lives in Angola; the Ministry of the Revolutionary Armed Forces has never released the numbers of the seriously injured.[76] In 1975 and 1976, a majority of Cubans probably relished "the satisfaction of the great victory" in Angola.[77] By 1988–1989, however, the taste of victory had likely been lost.

Cuban Miami Flexes Its Muscles

Soon after 1959, the revolution closed all avenues for peaceful dissension in the island. As a result, Cubans from all walks of life who rejected the radical path set by Castro took up arms against him. That is what Cubans had historically done against governments they deemed unjust. Between 1960 and 1966, homegrown guerrillas—particularly in the Escambray Mountains in central Cuba—posed a serious threat to the government. The Revolutionary Armed Forces mobilized some 100,000 militias to combat the rebels, who may have totaled 8,000 at their peak in 1961.[78] The internal resistance neither received significant U.S. support, nor was it controlled by Washington. By decade's end, however, the prospect of a military victory against the revolution had virtually disappeared. Domestic opponents had been defeated or silenced, and thousands vanquished by death, imprisonment or exile. During the 1960s, both before and after the Bay of Pigs invasion, some exiles carried out—with CIA support or on their own—covert actions against the Castro government. For the most part, Cuban exiles rejected the nascent U.S.–Cuba rapprochement under the Ford and Carter administrations.

In the early 1960s, two national projects had emerged. The revolution put a premium on social justice and national sovereignty while dispensing with democracy and civil liberties. The opposition repudiated the alignment with the Soviet Union, the conflation of patriotism with unconditional loyalty to the Comandante and the revolution, and the idea that only by eliminating private property could social justice be achieved. At the same time, the opposition—most of whose members had also fought Batista's dictatorship—saw the need for a profound socioeconomic transformation and a moderate nationalism. Alberto Müller—a student leader against Batista and then against Castro—expressed this position:

> We wanted economic growth governed by the idea that it was necessary to place the economy at the service of the people. And this would not happen without an economic plan respectful of private property but controlling it; without regulating foreign investment so that it really became useful for our country; without a land reform; without a sound industrialization policy. We wanted social development: agrarian transformations,

improvements in standards of living, expansion of public education and the eradication of all types of discrimination.[79]

Defending Cuban sovereignty against the United States earned the revolution plaudits worldwide; decrying Havana's Communist turn and its alliance with the Soviet Union branded the opposition as Washington's adjuncts almost everywhere. The patriotism of the exiles was questioned while Castro's was not, even as Cuba became utterly dependent on the Soviet Union. In addition, most international activists at the time were left-of-center; as a result, the revolutionary government's human-rights violations rarely elicited the world's condemnation.[80] Jaime Castillo, a renowned Chilean human-rights lawyer, divided activists into two groups: Those who are blind in their left eye and those who are blind in their right eye. In any case, international law provides an ethical and legal framework that disallows the justifications used by the Cuban government, the violent opposition and the U.S. government for their respective actions in pursuit of their ends during the 1960s.[81] In essence, ends, however worthy they might be, require means that respect human rights. Eyes wide open—not politically colored lenses—are the first line of defense against violations.

Cuban exiles carry an open wound regarding their struggle against Castro. The opposition's objectives—indeed, the very legitimacy of a Cuba other than Castro's—disappeared in the fabric of the Cold War. In 1996, Enrique Baloyra (1942–1997), a democracy activist and scholar, well expressed the exasperation of the revolution's opponents:

> Part of the frustration that we feel after all these years is that history has been written by the victors. We can put something important on the record, the force of all those young people, idealistic people who because of number one, religious convictions, and number two, because they were evicted from the revolutionary coalition, decided to take up arms against the government.
>
> I don't think that there was a hell of a big chance in April of 1961 for us to be ready to overthrow the government. I am sorry, but I cannot blame the Americans for failure there. It was not your responsibility to liberate Cuba. It was ours. I *can* blame you for getting into a fight and then trying to take over and then diverting the fight and not allowing for the maturation of the indigenous resistance. Your fault was to get into the fight, to set it up in a way that would accomplish *your* objectives with *our* means, not *our* means with *our* objectives.[82]

While the United States and the Soviet Union played out opposing interests over Cuba, the roots of the conflict were essentially Cuban.

Well into the 1970s and 1980s, some exiles persisted in the use of violence, such as attacks against Cuban diplomatic and commercial missions as well as

Cuban ships in open sea and the assassination or kidnapping of Cuban diplomats. The most violent of the actions was the 1976 bombing of Cubana Airline Flight 455.[83] From the perspective of these exiles, their actions constituted a declaration of war "along all the world's paths" to answer Havana's "internationalism" in Angola, Ethiopia and, a bit later, Central America. Under international agreements and norms, however, these activities cannot be considered anything but terrorism.[84] Other exiles, however, welcomed the overtures by the Ford and Carter administrations, and many were targeted by terrorists for their advocacy of a change in U.S. policy. Assassinations were carried out in Miami, New Jersey and Puerto Rico. Travel agencies that chartered flights to Cuba, as well as the businesses or homes of some pro-rapprochement exiles, were bombed.[85] At the same time that the two governments were talking, Havana opened a second track of discussions with Cuban Miami. Between August 1977 and October 1978, banker Bernardo Benes met with Cuban officials—in Panama, Mexico and Havana—and with Fidel Castro himself to discuss the release of political prisoners. In Miami, Benes was ostracized and pilloried for his efforts.[86]

In November and December 1978, Havana convened two sessions of public meetings between exiles and Cuban officials that became known as *el diálogo*. In August of that year, as part of the talks with the Carter administration, Cuba had agreed to release political prisoners and to allow Cuban exiles to visit their families on the island. Thinking that both issues, but especially the prisoner release, complemented Carter's human-rights policy, Havana suggested that the administration make a public announcement. Though the State Department embraced the idea, the White House did not. Baffled by the U.S. reluctance, Havana asked if the administration would object to announcing the prisoner release and family visits as a concession to what it now called *la comunidad*, a neutral term that displaced the derogatory *gusanos* (worms). The administration quickly gave the go-ahead. The *diálogo*, therefore, was born out of Carter's refusal to acknowledge the fruits of his diplomatic efforts. The administration feared sending the wrong signal to countries that supported U.S. efforts against the Cuban presence in Africa and, thus, recoiled from acknowledging negotiations with Havana on the prisoner release.[87] All the same, Havana's initial overture to Cuban Miami had preceded the administration's decision not to take credit for the prisoner release. Cuba understood that an easing of tensions with Washington also required mending some fences with the exile community. (After the Bay of Pigs, the revolutionary government had also met with exiles, albeit in private, to discuss the fate of the invaders after their defeat. Some exiles, however, deplored the meeting: In their eyes, negotiations—even to free their compatriots—would further bolster Castro and delay their return to Cuba. In a deal reached with the Kennedy administration, the men were exchanged for $53 million in food and prescription drugs.[88])

In 1978, a majority of exiles considered the Havana-sponsored dialogue a travesty and saw the nearly 300 mostly U.S.-based Cubans who participated in it as traitors. (Three decades later, *diálogo*—the word dialogue itself—remains taboo among militant exiles. Then, as it is now, the core issue was how best to deal with Havana: through diplomacy or through confrontation.) At the time, a group of 138 political prisoners signed a letter denouncing the *diálogo* as a "farce," arguing that those "who have divided and maintain divided members of the Cuban family lack the moral standing to convene a dialogue."[89] Be that as it may, after the *diálogo*, Cuba freed 3,600 political prisoners and the United States admitted thousands of ex-prisoners and their families.[90] In 1979, 100,000 Cuban Americans traveled to the island to visit their families. While benefiting the Cuban government financially, the visits also triggered political challenges. So many *mariposas*—the popular term for the former *gusanos* returning as butter-flies—all over the island set the 1980 Mariel exodus in motion: Two decades after the triumph of the revolution, about 125,000 of its children fled the island in a chaotic boatlift from the port of Mariel. When the boatlift was finally stopped, hundreds of thousands more were left waiting to leave. The discussions with the United States and the increased contact among Cubans across the Florida Straits had served the Cuban government with one of its most trying political situations ever.

At the same time, Mariel also challenged Cuban Miami. Almost immediately, Castro's labels for the Marielitos—"antisocials, homosexuals, drug addicts and gamblers"—were appropriated by many in the exile community, Miami's Anglo establishment and the local and national media. Subsequent analysis of the immigration data showed that, at most, 10 percent of the new arrivals could be considered hardened criminals, mental patients or others deemed excludable by U.S. immigration authorities.[91] But, at the time, Cuban Miami reacted with alarm to how easily its golden story of success was being tarnished. Neither could exiles understand why the local establishment and the *Miami Herald* had suddenly turned against them, though they, too, breathed a sigh of relief when, after six months, the boatlift finally came to an end.

When in November 1980, a referendum on banning the use of public funds for education and cultural activities in languages other than English passed over-whelmingly, the exile community took the vote as rebuke.[92] After 1980, as a reaction to the helplessness experienced during the Mariel exodus and the anti-bilingual movement, Cuban Miami learned to parlay its economic power into the political arena. The rate of naturalization among Cuban exiles increased. The Cuban American National Foundation (CANF) and Facts about Cuban Exiles (FACE) developed into the community's premier organizations.[93]

A group of exile businessmen had begun organizing CANF sometime before the Mariel boatlift. Rankled by Carter's outreach toward Havana, the group modeled itself after the American Israel Public Affairs Committee (AIPAC), which had so successfully lobbied for a pro-Israel U.S. policy. At the same time, at the national level, conservative Democrats and hardline Republicans, alien-ated by the Carter administration's foreign policy, formed the nucleus of a movement that espoused a "new conservatism." Upon his election, Reagan, a long-time proponent of standing up to the Soviet Union, drew most of his foreign policy advisors from the ranks of these neo-cons. CANF, though born of Cuban Miami's frustrations, no doubt benefited from Reagan's—and the neo-cons—ascendance.[94] Founded in 1981, the foundation aimed to make sure that U.S.–Cuba policy would never again stray far from hardline policies. Its board members made annual contributions of at least $10,000 each, with some donating as much as $50,000 to CANF; trustees gave a yearly minimum of $5,000.[95] On May 20, 1983, CANF sponsored a visit by Reagan to Miami to celebrate Cuban independence. His anti-Communist rhetoric and, more important, his policies delighted exiles. The president noted:

> We will not permit the Soviets and their henchmen in Havana to deprive others of their freedom. The Soviet Union with all its military might, with its massive subsidy of the Cuban economy, can't make the system produce anything but repression and terror. You know, they say there are only two places where communism works: in Heaven, where they don't need it, and in Hell, where they've already got it. What's happening in Cuba is a failure of Fidel Castro and of communism. Some day Cuba itself will be free.[96]

Jorge Mas Canosa (1939–1997) led the Foundation to extraordinary success. When Radio Martí's launch upended the newly minted immigration accord, CANF was doubly pleased. The radio station was its signal achievement, while the agreement's cancellation suited its opposition to any and all U.S.–Cuba talks. CANF's directors, trustees and political action committee pressed their advantage unabashedly: Between 1981 and 1997, their contributions to Democrats and Republicans who advocated a tough stance toward Havana totaled more than $3.2 million.[97] The Foundation also cooperated with the Reagan administration in Nicaragua and Angola. CANF lobbied Congress on behalf of aiding the Contras and repealing the 1976 ban on U.S. aid to Angolan rebels fighting the Havana-backed government in Luanda. Mas Canosa worked closely with then-House Foreign Affairs Committee Chairman Dante B. Fascell, a Florida Democrat, to end the ban in 1985.[98] At the end of the 1980s, CANF engineered Project Exodus, a program that brought to the United States about 10,000 Cuban exiles who had been stranded for years in third countries such as Panama, Costa Rica, Peru and Spain.[99] Most of Cuban Miami embraced CANF with unbridled enthusiasm. Thanks to Mas Canosa and the Foundation, the exile community chalked up political victories and regained trust that Washington could, after all, advance exile interests.

Still, the year 1987 closed with other changes for Cuban Miami. An amendment pegged to the federal appropriations bill codified the renewed U.S.–Cuba migration accord as well as the right of Cubans in third countries to enter the

United States. Even if Havana again abrogated the accord, the 20,000 annual visas would not be suspended nor would Cubans ever again be stranded in third countries. It was, perhaps, the first time that Congress encroached on the president's prerogative on policy regarding Cuba; Reagan signed it into law. While CANF applauded the renewed migration agreement and its codification, other sectors in the exile community did not. Most in Cuban Miami looked askance at any talks between Washington and Havana, and opposed the return to the island of Mariel refugees that the Immigration and Naturalization Service (INS) had deemed excludable. CANF understood political horse trading and, more important, the U.S. interest in preventing another uncontrolled exodus. Also, the agreement had allowed Mas Canosa to launch Project Exodus, CANF's most ambitious and successful program ever.[100] On a more ominous note, terrorism returned to Miami in 1988 and 1989. Travel agencies that chartered flights to Cuba, exiles who promoted dialogue and even Little Havana's Cuban Museum of Arts and Culture, which exhibited works by artists living in Cuba, became bombing targets. In 1988, Miami led the United States for acts of terrorism.[101]

Since the nineteenth century, Cubans had been fleeing political turbulence at home by going into exile in the United States. Geographic proximity made the great power a natural destination of refuge. But the need for a safe haven alone did not lead Cubans north. From the United States, exiles plotted their return to Cuba. In the 1850s and again in the 1880s, filibuster expeditions were often organized from the United States to try to spark uprisings against Spain; none succeeded. By the 1890s, Cuban émigrés in the United States—José Martí most prominently among them—organized what in the twentieth century would become known as a national liberation movement, an alliance that cut across class and race to achieve independence.[102] The émigré community played the pivotal role in launching the War of 1895. Once the war started, émigrés lobbied Congress and the White House to extend belligerent status to the insurgents. That never happened.[103] As the loss of life mounted with no end in sight, the émigré lobby called for U.S. military intervention.[104] In keeping with its long-standing interest in Cuba, the United States complied.

During the 1950s, exiles in the United States backed the anti-Batista struggle. In late 1953, Carlos Prío—Cuba's last freely elected president—was even arrested in Miami for violating U.S. neutrality laws.[105] Though based in Mexico (1955–1956), Fidel Castro traveled to the United States to rally support and raise funds for his cause. In the 1890s, the cause of Cuban émigrés dovetailed with those of U.S. political, media and public-opinion sectors that favored war against Spain.[106] In the early 1960s, the initiatives of the Cuban exiles also coincided with U.S. interests. In contrast with the 1890s, however, two differences stand out. First, the War of 1895 was seen as the "good fight" by the United States and many other countries; fairly or not, the struggle against Castro and the revolutionary government was generally not. Second, in the late nineteenth century, Cubans (with the aid of the United States) were able to achieve independence for Cuba, albeit mediated by the Platt amendment until 1934. Since 1959, neither Cuban exile activists nor ten U.S. presidents have been able to overturn the regime installed by the revolution nor normalize relations between the two governments.

What Wasn't and Might Yet Be

In the early twentieth century, some Cubans had counseled "good government" as the best antidote against U.S. intervention. In 1919, the public intellectual Fernando Ortiz wrote:

> We need to strengthen our nationalist sentiments without yielding to quixotic illusions or anachronistic xenophobia. We can best guarantee our independence via good, honest and just government, one based on our people's hopes and cordial, intimate reciprocity with the United States.[107]

Diplomat and journalist Manuel Márquez Sterling put it succinctly: "A civic government is, after all, the definitive expression of consolidated independence."[108] Cubans, as a nation, have never heeded these wise words. Yet to achieve normalization of relations with Washington, Cuba's current or future leaders will need to come to terms with the realities that being a weaker neighbor of a great power dictates. Such realism would surely help the Cuban people establish a relationship with the United States that is more beneficial than the hit-and-miss relations it had before 1959 or the entrenched confrontation that has existed since then.

By the same token, the United States will be called upon to respect Cuban sovereignty in ways for which the historical record offers no precedent. In the end, the best way to serve U.S. national interests may well be for Washington to look on from afar as Cubans—and to a lesser extent, Cuban Americans—determine the island's future. More than two decades after the end of the Cold War, Barack Obama has begun to reconsider a policy that for fifty years has not brought Cuba any closer to democracy and freedom.

2

"NEXT CHRISTMAS IN HAVANA"

When the dominoes fell in Eastern Europe in 1989 and Mikhail Gorbachev's Soviet Union tottered, the United States again envisioned the downfall of Fidel Castro. The Cuban American National Foundation lobbied Congress and the White House intensely to step up pressure on Havana. The time had finally arrived for a post-Castro Cuba. CANF and many in Congress favored the enactment of legislation that would tighten the embargo. President George H.W. Bush, however, balked at yielding to Congress any of the powers that the Constitution grants the executive to conduct foreign policy. Still, after candidate William J. Clinton supported the Cuban Democracy Act (CDA), the White House did as well. In October 1992, Bush signed the CDA into law. CANF's donations to political candidates across the partisan aisle and the fact that Cuban Americans lived mostly in Florida and New Jersey, two states rich in Electoral College votes, were also important factors in the CDA's passage. Though *realpolitik* was guiding U.S. relations with China and Vietnam, Washington followed a different approach with the island: Once again, it began to pursue regime change in Havana. The key source of tensions in the U.S.–Cuba relationship—the dynamics between a great power and its weaker neighbor—lived on after the Cold War.

Geography again dealt Cuba a difficult hand. Beginning in the late 1970s, military dictatorships fell and civil wars ended in Latin America. In Nicaragua, for example, the Sandinistas lost the election of 1990 to Doña Violeta Barrios de Chamorro. In Chile, Don Patricio Aylwin led the center-left *Concertación* to the first of four electoral victories between 1989 and 2009. While the Christian Democratic Party was its largest member, the coalition also included the Socialist Party and two smaller ones that had supported Salvador Allende's Popular Unity government (1970–1973). In El Salvador, ARENA—the conservative

Nationalist Republican Alliance—had emerged as the dominant political force in 1989. After the 1992 peace accords, however, the Farabundo Martí National Liberation Front (FMLN) became a legal political party and the country's second political force. In short, Cuba's friends were now competing in free and fair elections. By the early 1990s and for the first time ever, all the governments in Latin America, except for Cuba, were democracies. Great expectations abounded, including that a transition in Cuba would promptly follow suit. No doubt Cuba was the odd country out in the Western Hemisphere.

With Soviet and European Communism in the dustbin, U.S. allies in Europe and the Western Hemisphere advocated engagement with Havana. If in 1962 Kennedy had worried that the U.S. fixation with Cuba would hamper European understanding of its actions during the Missile Crisis, thirty years later the world was more mystified than ever at the U.S. position. Be that as it may, neither the isolation that Washington practiced nor the openness that U.S. allies preferred brought about significant change in Cuba. Had the United States, Europe, Canada and Latin America joined forces on either confrontation or engagement, the outcome might have been different. But Cuba did not elicit the international outrage that apartheid South Africa or Augusto Pinochet's Chile had. Common ground was possible only on engagement, which the United States resisted. By the time President Clinton signed the Cuban Liberty and Democratic Solidarity Act (also known as the Helms-Burton Act) into law, Havana had served the United States and the international community with the fait accompli of its survival.

The End of the Cold War and the Bilateral Relationship

The United States

The Bush Administration

After the fall of the Berlin Wall, Bush might have walked down the road of *realpolitik*. The fruitful cooperation between the United States and Cuba that had led to the resolution of the conflicts in southern Africa did not, however, segue into a bilateral dialogue. Nor did the fact that Washington's long-standing conditions for normalization had been unexpectedly met, since concern over the Soviet–Cuban nexus had become moot. The wave of democratization that swept away military dictatorships in Latin America had left precious few revolutionary movements for Havana to support. Furthermore, Cuba was already committed to ending its fifteen-year military presence in Angola. But the Bush administration moved the goal post by making the normalization of relations conditional on Havana's making progress toward democracy and a market economy.[1] The United States was not about to bless a Caudillo-led Communist dictatorship in its backyard. Besides, the Soviet subsidies that had long sustained the Cuban economy had ended with the collapse of the Soviet Union. How could Castro survive without them? In the early 1990s, a stricter embargo made some sense.

The Bush White House reinforced the embargo by requiring all ships that carried cargo to and from Cuba to obtain a license if they were also stopping at U.S. ports in the same trip. The result was that the entry of goods into Cuba through third countries was reduced and currency flows were restricted.[2] In part, the decision had to do with internal U.S. politics. The administration hoped to derail legislation that incorporated similar restrictions but that would have encroached on the executive branch's constitutional prerogatives in matters of foreign policy.[3] At the same time, the president himself assured Moscow that the United States would not initiate an attack against the island, and subsequently high-ranking administration officials reiterated the no-aggression intentions.[4] Washington, nonetheless, launched Television Martí, an action Havana considered an ideological aggression. CANF members were pleased: Bush had fueled the hopes of Cuban Miami, expressing full confidence that the "new world order" would "sweep away our hemisphere's last dictator, Fidel Castro."[5] He also encouraged exiles to negotiate Cuba's future with the Cuban government, saying that he would be "extraordinarily interested" to hear if Castro said "something constructive, more democracy, more freedom, more openness."[6] Still, U.S. and Cuban officials intermittently discussed topics of common interest such as immigration and narcotraffic control.[7] An immigration accord was in place and another would be signed in 1995. Washington, however, held Havana at bay on an anti-narcotics agreement.

In Congress, Representative Robert S. Torricelli (D–NJ) introduced the bill that eventually became the Cuban Democracy Act. Florida legislators founded the bipartisan Cuban Freedom Caucus, which garnered the support of liberal Democrats like senators Paul Simon (IL), Carl Levin (MI) and Clairborne Pell (RI).[8] The Immigration and Naturalization Service braced itself for the migration crisis expected after Castro's fall.[9] Elliot Abrams, a former Reagan assistant secretary of state who had been a leading advocate for aid to the Nicaraguan Contras, urged Bush "to move in for the kill."[10] Former UN Ambassador Jeanne Kirkpatrick joined the more than 500 people who entered a "Predict the Fall of Fidel" contest, sponsored by a conservative think-tank.[11] Milton Friedman drew up an economic plan for Cuba's next president to consider.[12] In South Florida, local authorities prepared for the many challenges Castro's fall would bring: increased travel, rapidly expanding trade and a possible refugee crisis. They drew up security plans for post-Fidel festivities.[13] In Miami, the Cuban Municipalities in Exile pledged to help rebuild Cuba "the day after Fidel falls." Lawyers were bombarded with requests for advice on relocating businesses and claiming confiscated properties. Stickers reading *La próxima Nochebuena en La Habana* appeared in car bumpers all over Miami, reviving the next-Christmas-in-Havana dream that had lain dormant since the 1960s.[14]

Not everyone was deluded. Some Bush administration officials privately recognized that Castro's government, though in dire straits, was unlikely to collapse. A mounting economic crisis, the Sandinista electoral defeat in Nicaragua and political shockwaves from Eastern Europe all assailed the Cuban government. Castro, however, faced no immediate threats to his power.[15] Two well-positioned reports—by the Rand National Defense Research Institute (1992) and the Strategic Studies Institute at the U.S. Army War College (1993)—forecast the regime's survival in the short-to-medium term. Rand's noted:

> Castro is not inclined to cave in and accommodate to the "new world order." Even as he presents a moderate, pragmatic face to attract foreign investment, he may facilitate drug trafficking through Cuba. He may well present the United States with other types of challenges and crises over the short term (one to two years) and medium term (three to five years). Cuba today is a moving target. At present, prudence dictates that the operative policy assumption should be that Castro may remain in power over the short and perhaps medium term.[16]

The War College report struck a similar tone in terms of the regime's staying power:

> While Castro must leave sooner or later, reports of his impending demise have been much exaggerated. A *golpe de estado* is possible, but not probable. Nor is it likely, under current circumstances, that the Cuban masses would rise up and overthrow the dictatorship. And although Castro could become the casualty of assassination, suicide or natural death, this is not the kind of thing that is readily subject to prediction. Nor would it necessarily lead to the collapse of the regime. For a variety of reasons, Castro's "final hour" seems likely to last for several years, perhaps longer.[17]

All the same, Bush and Secretary of State James A. Baker III preferred to do nothing. Why should the United States do anything but harden the embargo through executive measures if Cuba no longer posed a threat? Against his better judgment, the president signed the Cuban Democracy Act in October 1992. The act prohibited U.S. subsidiaries abroad from trading with Cuba, something that had been legal since 1975, and made any improvement of relations conditional on Havana's commitment to holding free elections and respecting civil liberties. After candidate Clinton's endorsement of the Torricelli bill, Bush set aside his own misgivings about the legislation. The lure of Cuban-American votes in Florida and New Jersey persuaded both Clinton and Bush of the bill's merits. The CDA actually had two tracks. Track I was predicated on the assumption that Havana could not survive economic sanctions without the

Soviet Union to buffer their impact. Track II soft-pedaled Track I with people-to-people contacts. It allowed for exchanges of all kinds—cultural, academic, media, scientific and family travel—that might prompt some openings in Cuba to which Washington could respond in "carefully calibrated ways."[18] Though not wanting in logic, the act was flawed by determinism and wishful thinking. Orthodox Marxism and embargo supporters aside, economic crises alone have never determined societal change anywhere. Castro always excelled in politics, and nowhere did the CDA acknowledge the intangible resources still at his disposal. Havana, in fact, was already resisting the full-force winds of democracy that had swept away other dictatorships in Latin America.

The Clinton Administration I

George Bush and Bill Clinton were mirror images of each other: Bush, a patrician New Englander, the last World War II veteran to serve as president, a public servant with an exceptional understanding of foreign affairs; Clinton, a Southerner of humble roots, the first baby-boomer to hold the office, a masterful politician with a laser-beam understanding of ordinary Americans. Had the Republican been reelected, the White House would have likely exercised a steadier international leadership than Clinton did at first. Then again, even such an archetypal foreign-policy president as Bush might have had trouble finding his footing in a new era that no longer had the lodestar of anti-Communism. A new, robust internationalism might have taken its place, but it ran counter to the inward-looking currents of U.S. public opinion at the time.[19] In 1994, the passage of the North American Free Trade Agreement (NAFTA) and the first Summit of the Americas in Miami marked one of the high points of internationalism during the 1990s, offering a compelling vision for the Western Hemisphere that Bush had laid out and Clinton realized (though not entirely, as the Free Trade Area of the Americas (FTAA) eventually fell by the wayside).[20]

In 1992, the faltering U.S. economy and the third-party candidacy of Ross Perot cost Bush the election; adherence to the now-famous motto, "It's the economy, stupid!" won it for Clinton, albeit with an underwhelming mandate of 43 percent. Domestic issues being his forte, the new president embraced them with gusto. Cuba was also a domestic matter, a fact that a young Governor Clinton learned the hard way in 1980 when rioting Mariel Cuban inmates at Fort Chaffee, Arkansas, helped frustrate his reelection bid. The Democratic president would thus not take any chances on Cuban issues. The Cuban Democracy Act had laid out a foundation that the new administration accepted fully. The CDA handed the White House a ready-made template that had both some logic at the time and the blessing of voter-rich South Florida.

Still, hardliners were fearful that Clinton might soften the embargo, while those favoring a more proactive policy were frustrated over the lack of initiatives towards Cuba. When two Washington, DC, think-tank analysts—Peter

Hakim of the Inter-American Dialogue and Joseph Tulchin of the Woodrow Wilson Center—testified in January 1993 before Congress that a "fresh and more activist approach" was in order rather than continuing "a policy of passively waiting for the Cuban authorities to take the first steps," Torricelli, Ileana Ros-Lehtinen (R-FL), Lincoln Díaz-Balart (R-FL) and Robert Menéndez (D-NJ) blasted their testimonies and implicitly cautioned the White House against taking their advice.[21] Three months later, the subcommittee on Western Hemispheric Affairs in the House of Representatives passed a unanimous resolution that called for an international embargo on Cuba, perhaps issued more as a signal to the White House than in anticipation that the world would band together against Havana.[22] At his confirmation hearings, Secretary of State-designate Warren Christopher said, "It is hard to envisage normal relations with Cuba with Castro still in place," and reiterated his backing of the Cuban Democracy Act which, in any case, was the law of the land. As Carter's deputy secretary of state, Christopher had been a leading proponent of normalizing U.S.–Cuba relations.[23] In May 1993, Vice-President Albert A. Gore Jr. told the *Miami Herald*'s editorial board:

> Castro's chickens are coming home to roost. His policies have been an utter failure and always have been. Let us not forget that our principal policy for hastening the departure of Castro is to convince the people of Cuba that his leadership is an abject failure. And our policy is to stay the course. There are tremendous opportunities in Cuba if they just get rid of this dictator.[24]

In the 1990s, most bills to end or soften the embargo and ease or lift the travel ban were introduced by Democrats in Congress.[25]

Unsurprisingly, migration presented the Clinton administration with its first Cuban crisis. Under the 1984 migration agreement, the Reagan administration had alloted 20,000 annual preferential visas to eligible Cuban citizens. Between 1988 and 1993, an average of 12,342 Cubans a year were legally admitted to the United States.[26] As long as the Cuban Adjustment Act (1966) remained in effect and the U.S. government did not grant the full 20,000 immigrant visas a year, Havana argued, illegal migration would continue. In fact, with the economy plunging, the number of Cubans risking passage of the Florida Straits had spiked dramatically, from 467 in 1990 to 2,203 (1991), 2,557 (1992) and 3,656 (1993).[27] In 1984, Havana had agreed to the return of Mariel Cubans who had never been legally admitted to the United States. By November 1992, only 1,013 of the 2,746 detainees that the INS deemed excludable had been deported.[28] In October 1993, officials representing forty federal agencies met at the State Department to review contingency plans, including blocking off the Florida coast, in case of a mass exodus from Cuba. One attendee suggested that the political weight of Cuban Miami kept fresh ideas at bay: "People have been intimidated by the political pressure from taking out a clean sheet of paper and saying: What are our options?"[29] The summer of 1994 tested the Clinton administration.

The *balsero* (rafter) crisis started with a rush of hijackings in Havana and the Port of Mariel. In mid-July 1994, forty-one people, including twenty children, drowned when transportation ministry boats pursued and sunk a tugboat that had been commandeered in Havana Harbor.[30] In late July and early August, four other hijackings resulted in the deaths of at least two policemen and one Navy officer.[31] On August 5, thousands gathered on the *Malecón*, Havana's waterfront: The city had been bustling with rumors of ships sailing from Florida to carry back all who wanted to leave. Though galvanized by the prospect of leaving the island, the demonstrators also shouted anti-government slogans such as "Freedom! Freedom!" and "Down with Fidel!" After several hours, regime supporters and plainclothes police dispersed the protesters, and the demonstrations, which became known as the *Maleconazo*, ended. Special forces from the interior ministry had stood by in plain view, ready to take action had it become necessary. Official sources reported thirty-five people injured and 700 detained. In a televised address, Castro labeled the demonstrators part of "the fifth column of American imperialism" and warned Washington that his government would lift restrictions on Cubans leaving by sea if the United States did not change policies that encouraged illegal migration.[32]

In response, the White House declared in no uncertain terms that a Mariel-like sealift, that is, one in which Havana encouraged Cuban Americans to sail south and pick up their relatives, would be stopped even if it meant mobilizing the U.S. Navy to blockade the island. Cuban Miami cooperated with the federal government and exercised prudence in the matter. Castro, however, upped the ante: He ordered the Cuban Coast Guard to let those attempting to leave illegally pass without incident. Almost immediately, Cubans set out toward the United States in *balsas*, makeshift rafts often made with inner tubes and Styrofoam. Clinton then ordered the U.S. Coast Guard to intercept the *balseros* and take them to Guantánamo Naval Base. Between August and September 1994, the Coast Guard intercepted 32,362 Cuban citizens.[33] At the same time, the Clinton administration banned family remittances, family visits and all academic travel in an effort to turn the economic screws on the regime further. In September, the United States and Cuba reached a new migration accord. Like Reagan, Clinton agreed to 20,000 immigrant visas a year. Havana had floated numbers as high as 100,000 but ultimately agreed to the U.S. figure while making a commitment to do everything possible to stop illegal departures and accept the Mariel Cubans still in U.S. prisons. Like Reagan, Clinton also refused to discuss the embargo as Cuba wanted and stuck exclusively to a migration-related agenda.[34]

Not until May 1995 would the issue of the Cubans in Guantánamo be settled. The Clinton administration and the Cuban government agreed that most of the rafters still at the U.S. naval base would receive passage to the U.S. mainland. Thenceforth all Cuban rafters intercepted by the U.S. Coast Guard would be returned to Cuba, except those who met international standards for political asylum. Cuban authorities also consented to treat the returnees fairly and allow U.S. diplomatic personnel at the Interests Section to check up on them. In effect, Clinton brought the right of Cubans to seek political asylum in the United States in line with the Refugee Act of 1980, which bestowed the status of refugee only to those individuals "with a well-founded fear of persecution" due to race, religion, nationality, membership of a particular social group or political opinion.[35] The administration, in effect, revised the Cuban Adjustment Act, which allowed Cubans automatic political asylum without any questions asked, a privilege that unintentionally encouraged illegal migration. Thus, the 1995 agreement attained a normalcy of sorts on the issue of migration, even if the so-called wet-foot dry-foot litmus test—those found at sea, even within U.S. waters, would almost certainly be returned, those setting foot on U.S. soil would not—had the unintended consequence of ramping up human trafficking.[36] Jointly known as the Migration Accords, the 1994 and 1995 agreements set up a schedule for bilateral talks on migration every six months.

Predictably, critics abounded. Senator Jesse Helms (R–NC), chairman of the Foreign Relations Committee, reproved:

> The administration's announcement that the United States will hereafter cooperate with Castro's brutal security apparatus to capture Cubans fleeing Castro's repression and turn them over to his thugs in Havana is seen by many as the first of these "calibrated steps" that may bring the two countries closer.

Representative Dan Burton (R–NC) said: "The president has made a grave mistake. These are people who are fleeing a barbaric Communist regime." Representative Porter Goss (R–FL), however, expressed support:

> We must take steps to regularize Cuban immigration, to bring order to what has been a chaotic situation for far too long. If this agreement works, it should have the net effect of drastically reducing the danger of another Mariel overwhelming Florida's shores and resources.

Florida's Democratic governor, Lawton Chiles, noted: "It's a lose-lose situation. But I think it's one of those tough decisions that a president has to make. I think he made the right decision." Actually, it was a win-win situation for the governor, who won reelection in November, an outcome that might have been different without the agreement. General John Sheehan, commander of the U.S. Atlantic Command, stated: "I would like to applaud the effort to regularize this process." Senator Bob Graham (D–FL) declared: "This agreement makes it clear that the United States is in control of our borders and that we will not allow Fidel Castro to use immigration as a foreign policy weapon." A *Miami Herald* poll tallied over 65 percent of non-Cuban Americans interviewed and 45 percent of Cuban Americans agreeing with the statement: "The United States was right to admit Cuban refugees in the past, but the time has come to sharply limit Cuban immigration." Notwithstanding, Cuban Miami erupted in protest. Over several days, hundreds of demonstrators blocked traffic in major highways, marched in downtown Miami and staged other nonviolent actions. CANF Chairman Jorge Mas Canosa complained that he had not been consulted on the decision and issued a strong rebuke: "To destroy in secret negotiations with Cuba the institution of political asylum is totally unacceptable." In Havana, National Assembly President Ricardo Alarcón acknowledged: "It is a fair accord that is in the interests of both the United States and Cuba. Both sides are winners."[37]

Nearly three years after taking office, Clinton issued his first foreign-policy initiative on Cuba: a package of measures under CDA tutelage. Among these were eased regulations for travel and academic exchanges; licenses to open media bureaus in Cuba; authorization to Western Union to open offices on the island; permission to U.S. non-governmental organizations (NGOs) to send faxes, computers, copiers and financial assistance to Cuban NGOs; a $500,000 grant to Freedom House for the promotion of democracy; and diligent enforcement of the U.S. Neutrality Act. The latter served notice to exiles that their transgression of Cuban airspace and territorial waters would no longer be tolerated.[38] Concurrently, the administration bolstered the Office of Foreign Assets Control (OFAC), the Treasury Department's agency charged with enforcing the embargo. Clinton's carrot-and-stick approach revealed the jagged terrain of making Cuba policy. The administration sought to facilitate U.S.–Cuba contacts without provoking excessive criticism from the hardline ranks; hence, OFAC's improved capacity to enforce sanctions and the grant to Freedom House. At the same time, Washington wanted Havana to respond favorably in order to advance a bilateral agenda on immigration, narcotraffic and the environment; hence, mentions of the U.S. Neutrality Act and the facilitation of remittances.

In any event, neither the Cuban government nor the hardline embargo forces welcomed the measures. In Havana, Alarcón decried: "What do they expect from us? To say, 'Oh, thank you. Welcome. Do whatever you want in this country.' If they're interested in the Cuban people, please lift the damn embargo once and for all." In Washington, Senator Phil Gramm (R-TX) also blasted the measures: "The president is putting out a welcome mat to Castro instead of tightening the noose around his aging neck." Representative Menéndez (D-NJ) was dismayed:

> It is wrong to go ahead and give one-sidedly without seeing some reforms within Cuba, without seeing economic reforms, which would improve

the living conditions of Cubans and their families. The Republicans are playing politics with this. They certainly know the sentiments of the Cuban-American community.

In Miami, thousands of Cuban Americans welcomed the measures that eased restrictions on travel and remittances by calling travel agencies and Western Union.[39] Thousands more protested Clinton's measures and hailed the Helms-Burton bill that was then making its way through Congress.[40] Graham (D-FL) summed up the president's predicament:

> There are some who resist any opening, whether it's to the government or the Cuban people, out of fear that it will rebound to Castro's benefit economically or in political prestige. Then there are others who want more visitations and contacts and would have liked the president to go further. He has struck a good balance.[41]

Helms (R-NC) and Burton (R-IN) had introduced their bill in February 1995, shortly after the Republicans won control of Congress. Neither was interested in striking a balance on the subject of Cuba. Slowly, Helms-Burton made its way through the House of Representatives and the Senate. Inevitably, the presidential campaign of 1996 tinged the debate; Senate majority leader and presidential candidate Robert Dole (R-KS) and the president competed on being "tough on Castro" and bidding for Cuban-American votes.[42] In September, the House voted 294–130 in favor of the bill; the White House threatened a veto, even though the vote margin allowed for an override.[43] If the CDA (about 3,200 words) curtailed the president's foreign-policy prerogatives, Helms-Burton (more than 17,500) amounted to a full-bore assault. From issuing general guidelines on how to conduct policy towards Cuba, Congress now served the White House with a detailed roadmap. In late October, the Republican-controlled Senate passed a toothless version without Title III, the section that would grant U.S. citizens holding certified claims—including Cuban Americans who were citizens of Cuba at the time their properties were confiscated—the right to sue foreign corporations and nationals for "trafficking" in their expropriated properties. The House and Senate conference on the Helms-Burton bill, officially called the Cuban Liberty and Democratic Solidarity (LIBERTAD) Act, was set to take place in February 1996.[44]

Cuba

After 1989, Havana certainly had reason to worry. Not since the early 1960s had survival been so much in question. Thirty years of revolution had taken their toll on the citizenry. In the late 1980s, the Cuban government did not command the popular enthusiasm of yore, nor did ordinary Cubans harbor much hope for the future. By the mid-1980s, the economy had skidded into recession; in the early 1990s, it contracted by at least 35 percent, and already austere living standards plummeted further.[45] The withering away of Communism in Eastern Europe and, especially, the Soviet Union made the Cuban economy quake. At the 1991 Cuban Communist Party Congress, Castro detailed the shortfalls in Soviet deliveries of oil, raw materials and food products to explain the economic plight.[46] The Comandante gave not the slightest hint of awareness that the long list undermined his claims to have upheld Cuban independence—in general, not just from the United States—nor that it constituted an indictment of his economic policies. A year earlier Havana had declared a *período especial*, a special period of austerity in the face of turbulent international changes.

Unlike China and Vietnam, Cuba eschewed comprehensive reforms in no small part because it was aware of the changes that economic reforms had brought to the Communist Party in each of those countries. Chinese and Vietnamese Communists had staked their power on far-reaching economic reforms and improving living standards. In the process, they largely left behind ideology and mass mobilizations. How could they have kept these alive when alternatives to state employment were sprouting everywhere, state enterprises were subjected to budgetary discipline, and fiscal reforms allowed regions and local communities to retain more of their revenues?[47] Citizens going about their business had better things to do than wave flags, shout slogans and march. Admiring though he was of the Chinese and Vietnamese for retaining power, Castro could not fathom a similar transformation in Cuba. Like Joseph Stalin and Mao Zedong in their time, he thrived on keeping politics at the center. Since 1959, Cuban politics rested on the tripod of mobilizational authoritarianism: Castro's leadership, mass mobilizations and the defense of *la patria* (the homeland).[48] Politics in Cuba was rooted in the praetorian imperatives of maintaining unity against *los imperialistas yankis* and needed the United States as an essential adversary. With Castro at the helm, the Cuban Communist Party (PCC) never quite acquired the bureaucratic, institutional routines of the Soviet Union and Eastern Europe, let alone those of reform-driven China and Vietnam. Castro, in short, could never entreat Cubans as Deng Xiaoping had the Chinese: "To get rich is glorious!"

Still, Cuban elites had to address the economic crisis. Some liberalization of foreign trade and foreign investment took place. There was a new emphasis on tourism, which quickly challenged the primacy of sugar. In 1993, the government made the U.S. dollar legal tender. Self-employment in various occupations was legalized; agricultural cooperatives were granted more autonomy. Agricultural, industrial and artisan markets soon bustled with sellers and buyers. The Constitution was amended to include multiple forms of property.[49] When faced with adversity, Castro always returned to what he considered the essence of socialism: central control of the economy, a calling on the Cuban people to sacrifice and a relentless affirmation of national sovereignty vis-à-vis the United States. Modest economic reforms aside, he resisted domestic and international appeals to let markets loose to improve productivity and living standards, to allow unrestricted self-employment and to legalize small- and medium-sized enterprises. Regime reformers had proposed these measures both to bring back the economy and ease tensions with the Clinton administration.[50] Yet, in mid-1995, Castro stated: "If there has to be more opening, we will do it, though I do not see an immediate need for that."[51] Stabilizing the economy, albeit at low levels, proved to be enough for the regime, which prized political and economic control over improving the lives of ordinary Cubans.

Political reform was another matter altogether. Though half-hearted, the economic reforms prodded Cuba a bit from central planning and allowed for some non-state property rights. There was, however, no stepping back at all from the Communist Party's monopoly on power: Plural forms of political expression remained anathema. For an instant, it seemed that a change of some import might come about in the Popular Power assemblies. Since 1976, Cuba held direct elections at the local level. In 1991, the party authorized direct elections of National Assembly deputies. A few months later, Carlos Aldana, then-PCC ideological secretary, suggested that the National Assembly could be pluralist "in ideas, opinions and points of view."[52] The suggestion was stillborn. Elections remained uncompetitive, and the ban on campaigning stayed in place. Castro, moreover, warned: "We can never make the mistake of accepting multiple parties. We have the majority and the sacred obligation to maintain it."[53] Notwithstanding, the 1992 local elections shocked the regime: In Havana, up to one-third of voters cast invalid ballots—blank or defaced—in effect, anti-government votes; though at lower rates, citizens in the rest of the country also cast invalid ballots.[54] When Cubans elected national deputies in February 1993, the regime summoned mobilizational authoritarianism full-force: an omnipresent Comandante, masses all over the island and incessant patriotic appeals. Expectations of change duly deflated, Castro applauded "an Olympic victory."[55]

"We are the only ones and there is no alternative," Castro had asserted before the 1991 Party Congress.[56] Unlike its Eastern European counterparts, the Cuban government stood on its own politically. The Red Army had neither brought the Cuban revolution to power nor propped it up to keep it in place. Under Castro, even in the midst of an economic disaster, Cuban elites manifested an unflinching will to stay in power against the odds that the United States in particular was betting on. "We will crack heads open," said a general in an apt if unusually frank public expression of the leadership's mentality.[57] In the early 1990s, Havana unveiled a national-security blueprint intended to dissuade Washington from military action; it consisted of a defense and national security law, a decree to suspend civilian institutions in case of a national emergency and the creation of a National Defense Council. A national emergency, however, could just as likely emerge from chaos in the streets or divisions within the elites; the blueprint also served notice to citizens and closet reformers to toe the line.[58] Castro was determined to avoid what he considered the blunders of Eastern Europe, the former Soviet Union and Nicaragua: allowing reformers to fester within the Communist Party, launching political and economic reforms simultaneously and calling an unwinnable election. The bloody events in Beijing's Tiananmen Square in 1989 offered up their own crucial lesson. Hundreds of thousands of Cubans acting on their own initiative and making demands on the government would never fill *la Plaza de la Revolución*, Havana's central square. The *Maleconazo* had also served the regime with its homegrown wake-up call.

Nevertheless, a new peaceful opposition had already emerged. In 1976, the Cuban Committee for Human Rights (CCPDH) was founded by Ricardo Bofill, Elizardo Sánchez Santa Cruz, Marta Frayde and others.[59] Influenced by the Helsinki Accords and the fledgling human-rights movements in the Soviet bloc, the CCPDH stood on a platform of nonviolence and human rights. Like the historical opposition, these human-rights activists had also supported the revolution but had stayed within its ranks longer. Many had been members or fellow travelers of the old Communist Party and broke ranks over the Fidelista heterodoxy on socialism and support for guerrillas in Latin America and Africa. Unlike the historical opposition, these dissidents brandished only their beliefs, but the regime still persecuted them, and so they truly became prisoners of conscience. In the mid-1980s, these activists began to attract international attention to the violations of human rights in Cuba, at first from jail, then from outside prison and, eventually for some, from exile. In the late 1980s, human-rights activists submitted reports on Cuba's violations to the UN Commission on Human Rights (UNCHR).[60] These authoritative reports—and those rendered by Of Human Rights, an exile organization—helped build the case in favor of putting the Castro government on the UNCHR docket.[61]

After the tidal-wave year of 1989, Washington and Cuban Miami banked on the regime's quick demise. Castro's Cuba, however, refused to oblige and survived largely on its own terms, that is, by implementing modest economic reforms and holding firm in the political realm. The limited economic openings, moreover, served useful political purposes by rewarding those whose loyalties were battle-tested. Top elites and their families began to prosper in tourism and other areas that welcomed foreign investment. More comprehensive reforms would have involved many more ordinary Cubans who might not have been so closely contained. All the same, Cuban society was changing. The Cuban people no longer professed the will, energy and passion that had once bolstered the revolution. As a result, Havana's defiance of the United States stood on a weaker platform than in the past. The regime's continued dependence on Fidel Castro's leadership also belied its cocky claim of being forever secure. The Comandante, after all, was mortal. In addition, the economic reforms, modest as they were, somewhat lessened the state's centrality in people's livelihood, sowed corruption and created a two-tiered society. With U.S. dollars, Cubans could purchase goods and services that made their lives considerably easier, even comfortable. Most citizens, however, lived with pesos and endured a more austere drudgery than ever. Stability partly hinged on a fragmented civil society crisscrossed by support, yes, but also by fear and apathy. As long as ordinary Cubans concentrated their energies on their daily needs, their actions would not tip the regime's delicate balance. Would Havana have survived on the same terms had tensions with the United States lessened? While the answer lies in the realm of speculative history, the actual outcome suggests more interaction than coincidence. Confrontation with the United States was similarly a factor in regime stability.

Cuban Miami

In South Florida, the Cuban American National Foundation was riding high in the early 1990s. Though mostly Republican, its members lobbied and courted both political parties. After a meeting with CANF's leader Mas Canosa in Tampa, Clinton lunched with a group of influential Cuban Americans at Versailles Restaurant in the heart of Little Havana. The candidate netted $275,000 for his campaign chest at a time when it was running low.[62] CANF's influence inside the Beltway helped to sideline a realist Cuba policy. Just as important, however, was the euphoria that the events in Eastern Europe in 1989 unleashed in Washington and the certainty that the regime in Cuba could not but be next.

After 1989, some in Cuban Miami revived their dreams of armed struggle. A year earlier, the anti-Castro militant Orlando Bosch had returned to the United States from Venezuela. There, he had twice been tried and acquitted for the 1976 bombing of Cubana Airlines Flight 455 but had remained imprisoned for eleven years until all legal procedures against him were exhausted. Upon arrival, U.S. marshals arrested him for parole violations related to a 1968 conviction for attacking a Polish freighter docked in Miami's Biscayne Bay. A pediatrician before the revolution, Bosch became a terrorist in the fight against Castro. Like other militant exiles, he had a history with the CIA. For many in Miami, his reappearance after so many years seemed fortuitous, a good omen for a free Cuba.[63] In early 1990, Alpha 66—a long-standing exile group advocating insurrection in Cuba—recruited thirty to fifty men to train in the Everglades and get them ready to support an eventual armed uprising on the island. Former CIA Cuban operatives founded the Association of Veterans of Special Missions "to get close to the Cuban coast to announce its willingness to cooperate with anyone longing for liberty."[64] In late 1991, three exiles from Comandos L—a paramilitary group bent on overthrowing Castro by the force of arms—infiltrated Cuba, where they were caught in the act of preparing explosives. The men were tried, found guilty and sentenced to death by firing squad. Only one was executed; the other two had their sentences commuted to thirty years in prison.[65] In October 1992, Comandos L strafed the Spanish-Cuban Hotel Meliá in Varadero Beach causing little damage and no casualties; this time the exile raiders returned safely to their undisclosed base.[66] In July 1990, Orlando Bosch was released after protracted legal actions; thousands of Cubans had signed a petition calling for his freedom and hundreds of Cuban-owned businesses held a three-hour strike. "The community believes the struggle against Castro is a war, and in a war that kind of activity is not frowned upon," said Alfredo Durán, who had been chairman of the Florida Democratic Party during the Carter administration.[67] Bush never pardoned Bosch. His administration initially sought to deport him, but since only Cuba would have him, Bosch was released.

In the meantime, hardline sectors started to pull the levers of power to pursue their ends. In 1985, Xavier Suárez was elected mayor of Miami, the first Cuban American to occupy the post. When Claude Pepper—a liberal, anti-Communist Democrat who served Florida in the Senate (1936–1951) and South Florida's 18th District in the House of Representatives (1963–1989)—passed away, Republican Ileana Ros-Lehtinen won the special election to succeed him. Campaigning for her, President Bush declared: "I am certain in my heart I will be the first American president to step foot on the soil of a free and independent Cuba."[68] Dexter Lehtinen, Ros-Lehtinen's husband, served as U.S. Attorney for the Southern District of Florida (1988–1992). In 1993, fellow Republican Lincoln Díaz-Balart joined Ros-Lehtinen in the House of Representatives. Rare before 1980, victory for Cuban candidates in local elections— the Florida State Legislature, county and city commissions and local mayoralties—slowly became commonplace.

Political power can be used or abused. Corruption often follows an ethnic community's political successes, and Cuban Americans were no exception.[69] In addition, Cuban Miami often worked the system to harass Cuban Americans who held moderate views on Cuba. Given the centrality of anti-Castro intransigence to the exile identity, it was not surprising.[70] In the 1970s, after all, dissident exiles had been targets of terrorism. With access to the halls of power, the community resorted to political shenanigans, an improvement of sorts. For the most part, the fact that the ends-justify-the-means mentality mirrored the Cuban regime's went unrecognized. The difference, of course, lay in the contexts in which these mentalities operated. In Cuba, no institutional checks curbed Castro's power, no public accountability kept the PCC in check. In the United States, the U.S. Constitution protected civil liberties, even if Cuban Miami often tried to constrain them when citizens expressed opinions on Cuba outside the hardline mainstream. In 1992, Human Rights Watch (HRW) issued a report, *Dangerous Dialogue*, that documented systematic intimidation against some exiles for their views and activities.[71] Freedom of expression, HRW concluded, was under attack in Miami. The following incidents depict well the ambience of the late 1980s and early 1990s.

- For showing works of artists still in Cuba, the Cuban Museum of Arts and Culture suffered politically motivated investigations, threats to cut off funds and an eviction notice from the city-owned property it had long leased from the City of Miami. In 1991, a federal judge blocked the eviction as improper government conduct. None of the allegations against the Cuban Museum was ever proven.
- Artists who had ever performed in Cuba or who did not subscribe to hard-line wisdom were banned or harassed in Miami. In 1989, for example, the Kiwanis Club of Little Havana barred singers Denise de Kalafe, a Brazilian, and Andy Montañez, a Puerto Rican, from participating in the annual festival, Calle Ocho; the festival had received $15,000 from the Miami City Commission. In 1986, Dolores Prida saw her comedy *Coser y cantar* (Sew and Sing) dropped from the Hispanic Theater Festival; the playwright favored the normalization of relations with Havana.
- In 1988, terrorists sought to derail a forum sponsored by the Institute of Cuban Studies (ICS) by exploding a bomb at the home of its director, María Cristina Herrera. When the hotel where the event was to take place cancelled, the University of Miami offered to host it and more than 400 people attended. In 1989, the Florida State Legislature considered a CANF-backed bill to set up a Cuban studies institute at Florida International University (FIU). FIU, however, would retain little or no control over the institute, as the bill called for CANF to nominate six of its nine trustees. The institute would also have been exempt from Florida's Sunshine Laws that guarantee public access to the records of public institutions. FIU faculty unequivocally opposed an institute born under the proposed conditions and the university administration backed them. While the funds were never approved, the legislature allocated a million dollars for CANF to support scholarly research on Cuba. Guided by academic protocol and the legal requisite of transparency, FIU inaugurated the Cuban Research Institute in 1991.[72]
- In 1992, the *Miami Herald* published an editorial opposing the Torricelli bill, which CANF strongly backed. For that editorial and for what it considered "unfair coverage of Cuban Americans," the foundation embarked on a three-month campaign against the Herald. CANF leased billboards and placed ads on Dade County buses saying, "I don't believe in the *Miami Herald*." *Herald* vending machines were vandalized, the newspaper's offices received bomb threats and publisher David Lawrence's life was threatened. Mas Canosa eventually called for "calm and reason."[73]
- U.S. Treasury agents confiscated 220 paintings from the home and office of Ramón Cernuda—a major collector of Cuban art who at the time was the Miami representative of Elizardo Sánchez and other dissidents in Cuba who were calling for dialogue—on alleged violations of the U.S. embargo. Cernuda sued for their return and won. The judge in the case said: "I find

it somewhat unusual that the U.S. attorney has announced that he's not going to prosecute less than five kilograms of cocaine and then expends his resources going after paintings." Subsequently, the Florida Department of Labor and the Internal Revenue Service investigated Cernuda and his business; no infractions were found. All told Cernuda's legal costs for retrieving his artwork and clearing the other investigative hurdles totaled $150,000.

In 1994, a second HRW report found that intimidation still threatened freedom of expression in Miami, though law enforcement agencies were doing better in protecting individuals under attack.[74]

Even so, some in Cuban Miami drew lessons from the experience of peaceful resistance in Eastern Europe. Inspired by a similar action carried out by Polish émigrés off the Baltic Coast in 1982, a group of exiles sent 1,500 helium-filled balloons bearing freedom messages in Havana's direction. Unfavorable winds, however, spread most of the messages around the Florida Keys. A month later, 200 helium-filled balloons, larger in size than the first batch, carried messages of solidarity, packets of coffee and disposable razor blades. About thirty blew back to Key West; whether the rest reached Cuba was never determined.[75] Some 200 Cuban Americans organized a Cuban Freedom Flotilla and sailed to a point twenty-three miles off the coast of Havana "to send a message of solidarity" to the Cuban people.[76] Still others focused on the successful negotiations that led to the collapse of Eastern European regimes one after the other. The Democratic Platform—*la Plataforma Democrática*, which brought together Christian Democrats, Social Democrats and European-style liberals—sought to be an interlocutor in a prospective dialogue with Havana and the dissidents. *Cambio Cubano* (Cuban Change)—founded by Eloy Gutiérrez Menoyo, a participant in the anti-Batista struggle and later imprisoned under Castro—emphasized that only Cubans, on the island and in exile, should take part in solving Cuba's problems. Founded by Cuban Americans in business, academia and the professions, the Cuban Committee for Democracy (CCD) hoped to promote changes in U.S. policy toward Cuba. By embracing dialogue with Havana, *la Plataforma*, *Cambio Cubano* and the CCD strayed farthest from the traditional exile demand of Castro's unconditional ouster.

Exile intransigence extended across the Florida Straits to dissidents in Cuba who called for an inclusive dialogue. When Gustavo Arcos (1926–2006) and other dissidents called on the opposition, the exile community and the Cuban government to join a national dialogue, Cuban Miami lashed out. Arguing that dissidents should have checked with exile leaders before making any sort of proposal, Mas Canosa added: "That small space, that small umbrella that protects them from the fiercest repression, is due to exile militancy."[77] Apparently, CANF's chairman was unaware of the dogged efforts that courageous dissidents in Cuba had made well before this discord. Armando Valladares, a former political prisoner, deemed Arcos a "traitor" and the initiative, naturally enough, "treason." Traditional exiles believed the dialogue strategy would only help Castro remain in power. Writer Carlos Alberto Montaner struck a different note: "We are not trying to prolong the regime but to end it without bloodshed. There is no reason why it cannot work, except for the intransigence of some people in Cuba and Miami." Ricardo Bofill, who served time in Cuban jails for his beliefs, lost his Miami job as a radio and television commentator for supporting the Arcos initiative.[78] While opposed to any dialogue with the regime, a former Cuban prime minister, Manuel Antonio de Varona (1908–1992), noted: "The first person who will govern a free Cuba is there now."[79] At the time, de Varona was one of the few traditional exiles who recognized that Cubans on the island were the principal architects of Cuba's future. "Whether they like it or not, exile leaders will have to accept that the center of gravity of change in Cuba is not in Miami but in Havana," Cernuda said.[80] Over the course of the 1990s, Cuban Miami would come to accept that the center of gravity had, indeed, shifted.

The International Arena

In the Cold War's aftermath, Washington and Havana sought to rally support in a world that partly agreed with each. International public opinion decried the U.S. embargo, but also chided Cuba for its human-rights violations and meager economic reforms. The United States and its allies differed on whether confrontation or engagement would best promote a transition in Cuba. Even after it was clear that the regime in Havana would not go away quickly, Washington did not relent on the embargo nor did Canada, the European Union and Latin America abandon engagement. The David–Goliath syndrome favored Cuba internationally, as did the lingering aura of what the Cuban revolution had once been. At the same time, the United States and hardline Cuban exiles underscored the parallels between Castro's Cuba and Pinochet's Chile or apartheid South Africa, the latter two justifiably having earned the world's repudiation while Cuba elicited no more than ambivalence. Without Havana's moving decisively on economic transformation or, at the opposite end, a Tiananmen Square-style massacre in Cuba, the United States and the rest of the world were likely to remain in a stalemate on how best to deal with the government in Havana. The stalemate favored official Cuba: The world widely rebuked the embargo while less intensely censuring the regime's record on human rights.

The United Nations

At the peak of its U.S.-imposed isolation in the 1960s, Cuba established a bridge to the non-Communist world through the United Nations. Even as Latin American countries banished it from their UN caucus, Havana found allies in the Nonaligned Movement (NAM). When two Latin American seats on the

United Nations Development Program's council became vacant in 1969, the Latin American caucus nominated Mexico and Argentina. The General Assembly elected Mexico but not Argentina; Cuba ran as an independent and won despite hemispheric opposition.[81] In 1979, after Cuba hosted the Nonaligned summit in Havana and Castro addressed the General Assembly as NAM's president, Cuba sought a seat on the Security Council. Colombia and Cuba battled through 154 ballots, Cuba leading each round but falling short of the stipulated two-thirds majority. After the Soviet invasion of Afghanistan in December, support for Cuba faltered, and Havana withdrew in favor of Mexico.[82] Ten years later, in the twilight of the Cold War, the General Assembly elected Cuba to a two-year term (1990–1991) on the Security Council.[83] It was quite a feat for a Caribbean island deprived of its long-standing allies and nearing economic collapse.

When Saddam Hussein occupied Kuwait in 1990, Havana found a welcome spotlight in the first major crisis after the end of the Cold War. Ricardo Alarcón—Cuba's UN ambassador (1966–1978 and 1990–1992)—presided over the Security Council during the Persian Gulf crisis. In December, U.S. Secretary of State James Baker and Cuban Foreign Minister Isidoro Malmierca met privately in New York to discuss the ultimatum the United Nations would soon give Iraq. Though it had voted to condemn the invasion of Kuwait, Cuba issued one of two dissenting votes—Yemen's was the other—against the resolution that authorized military action if Iraq did not withdraw its troops by January 15, 1991. In November, Havana had tried in vain to persuade Hussein to pull out under the aegis of the four NAM members of the Security Council—Cuba, Yemen, Malaysia and Colombia.[84] By the time Baker and Malmierca met, war was all but inevitable. Still, Cuba's effort to give Iraq a face-saving cover to withdraw from Kuwait and thus avert the UN-backed war was noteworthy. Like the 1988 southern Africa talks in 1988, Havana played a constructive role even if, in 1990, the odds of success proved too long.

Human rights and the U.S. embargo drove the U.S.–Cuba feud at the United Nations. In 1986, Armando Valladares, jailed for twenty-two years, published his memoir, which garnered international renown.[85] Subsequently, the Reagan administration named him U.S. ambassador to the UN Commission on Human Rights. His presence there and the reports submitted by dissidents on the island and the exile-based organization Of Human Rights, built momentum for bringing Cuba before the commission. In part due to heightened UNCHR interest in Cuba and the reformist winds blowing in the Soviet Union and Eastern Europe, Havana took the unprecedented step of inviting outside observers, including the UNCHR Cuba working group. Even more unusual, the government allowed these observers to visit some prisons.[86] Between 1988 and 1991, the commission considered resolutions on UN monitoring of human rights in Cuba. In 1990, a U.S.-initiated resolution expressed "concerns" that witnesses who had met with commission representatives during a visit to the island had been harassed, notwithstanding Havana's earlier pledge to the contrary. Cuban UN Ambassador Raúl Roa railed against the non-NATO (North Atlantic Treaty Organization) countries that sided with the United States: "They are countries that have been led like oxen, pulled around by their nose rings to vote against Cuba," he said.[87] In February 1991, Secretary General Javier Pérez de Cuéllar submitted a report on conditions on the island that, though short on substance and criticism, still prompted the UNCHR to call for a UN special representative to monitor human rights in Cuba.[88] Carlos Menem's Argentina was the only Latin American country to side with the United States. In June 1991, Pérez de Cuéllar named Colombian diplomat Rafael Rivas Posada to assume the charge. Alarcón dismissed the new post as part of Washington's "aggressive policy toward Cuba," adding: "There is no justification for it."[89] That fall, Havana tried to place the U.S. embargo on the General Assembly agenda; Washington opposed the effort, on the grounds of "interference in internal affairs."[90] Cuba withdrew the motion in light of insufficient support, Mexico, Colombia and Venezuela being particularly lukewarm.[91]

The UN Commission on Human Rights first censured Cuba in 1992. Rivas Posada tendered a report noting an alarming increase in political persecution. He had been denied entry to the island, so he sent Havana inquiries on 128 individuals whose human rights had allegedly been violated. Rivas Posada never received a response. Though no longer subject to the decades-long sentences common in the 1960s, political prisoners continued to endure poor living conditions, physical violence and questionable psychiatric treatment. Rivas Posada drew his findings from interviews with Amnesty International, Americas Watch and Cuban exiles. In contrast to previous years, Cuba stood alone in the debate. Havana questioned the UNCHR's stature to review its record, which did not sit well with the membership. The resolution passed with a record number of Latin American votes (Argentina, Chile, Costa Rica and Uruguay), all Western democracies, plus the former Cuban allies of Russia, Bulgaria, Czechoslovakia and Hungary. The Russian delegation, moreover, held a party in honor of three Cuban exiles who traveled to Geneva for the debate.[92] In the fall, however, the General Assembly passed a nonbinding resolution against the U.S. embargo. Now foreign minister, Alarcón declared it Cuba's "greatest diplomatic victory in a long time." That victory came with the unintended help of the Cuban Democracy Act, which was enacted that year. It tipped UN opinion in Cuba's favor when the anti-embargo resolution came to a vote; a year earlier, the same motion had died of indifference. Carl-Johan Groth, later special UN rapporteur for human rights in Cuba, called U.S. policy "totally counterproductive" and "the surest way of prolonging an untenable internal situation" on the island. Two weeks later, the General Assembly passed a U.S.-sponsored resolution critical of the Cuban government's record on human rights.[93]

The U.S.–Cuba *pas de deux* at the United Nations continued throughout the decade. The Commission on Human Rights in Geneva reproached Cuba, and the General Assembly in New York denounced the embargo. Between 1992 and 2000, Cuba's resolution against the embargo went from 59 to 167 votes in favor. Except for 1998, the UNCHR passed resolutions condemning Havana for human-rights violations each of those years. In 1998, the resolution failed as the commission recognized the religious freedoms conceded for Pope John Paul II's January visit. In 1999, however, the UNCHR returned to its standard condemnation of Cuba. An unidentified Latin America envoy commented on the "undiplomatic" manners of Havana's UN ambassador in Geneva. "People gave Cuba a break last year and now they go around putting more dissidents in jail," he said.[94] Until 1999, Cuba garnered no Latin-American votes against the UNCHR reprimands; Latin American and the Caribbean countries either abstained or voted in favor. Then Mexico, Peru and Venezuela joined Havana in opposing the resolution; Peru and Venezuela remained on Havana's side in 2000. Between 1991 and 1998, Mexico had abstained but it supported Cuba in 1999, citing the UNCHR's unfair singling out of Havana and not condemning the U.S. embargo.[95] When Mexico reverted to abstaining in 2001, the stage was set for the spectacular rift between Mexico and Cuba that took place after Vicente Fox's election.

Iberoamerican Summits

In 1990, Portugal and the countries of Latin America welcomed Spanish Prime Minister Felipe González's initiative to open an annual forum for Iberoamerica to forge new bonds of cooperation in the emerging world order. Cuba was a special Iberoamerican concern, and Havana had a marked interest in the summits. Since the early 1960s, Havana had not participated in regular gatherings of Latin-American countries. The yearly events would provide a setting for strengthening ties with Iberoamerican nations and a platform for denouncing the U.S. embargo. Like its election to the UN Security Council, the Iberoamerican summits opened doors for Cuba at a time when its erstwhile friends were slamming them shut. In July 1991, the first summit was held in Guadalajara, Mexico. A few months after Guadalajara, Castro met presidents César Gaviria of Colombia, Carlos Salinas of Mexico and Carlos Andrés Pérez of Venezuela in Cozumel, Mexico. Initially, Cuba had banked on its cultural and historical ties with these countries to secure material assistance at its hour of need. But neither from Guadalajara nor from Cozumel did the Comandante take more than diplomatic support back to Havana. In July, Castro had unequivocally stated: "We want to integrate into Latin America," and the region seemed ready to respond—if Cuba moved in the direction of reform.[96]

At every summit, Castro confronted the consensus on democracy and markets. At the gathering in Barcelona (1992), Felipe González had Cuba in mind when he stated: "We must be clear that neither intolerance nor authoritarianism are acceptable instruments in the dawn of the new millennium."[97]

After Cozumel, González, Salinas and Gaviria continued a dialogue with Castro in the hope of prodding him down a path of reform that would lessen tensions with the United States. Gaviria later revealed that the Comandante had promised to "respect the will of the people" if the Communist Party lost the elections for the local Popular Power assemblies. At the 1994 summit in Cartagena, Colombia, Castro again met privately with González, Gaviria and Salinas, who pressed him: "You're among friends. You'd better deal with us while you can." Testily, he demanded Spain and Latin America respect "our criteria as we respect yours."[98] By 1996, when Iberoamerican leaders met in Viña del Mar, Chile, and issued the summits' most forceful declaration of democratic principles, no one was under any illusion that the Comandante would give substance to the signature he affixed to the final document.[99]

Cuban matters inevitably elicited uncommon attention around the Iberoamerican summits, which always concluded with a *de rigueur* rebuke of the U.S. embargo. After the summit in Spain (1992), Alfredo Cristiani, El Salvador's president, hosted a meeting of Central American presidents with Cuban exiles from the Democratic Platform; a delegation from *la Plataforma* also met with Spain's González.[100] A week before the summit in Bahía, Brazil (1993), the Cuban government released a document pledging not to export revolution and asking to be respected as a legitimate part of "Latin American political plurality."[101] At San Carlos de Bariloche, Argentina (1995), presidents Menem and Castro exchanged wine and cigars—a thaw in relations prompted by Cuba's agreeing to pay the $1.3 billion debt in preferences to Argentine businesses.[102] In Chile (1996), Hortensia Bussi, Salvador Allende's widow, urged Fidel to mend his ways and heed the calling of democracy.[103] At Isla Margarita, Venezuela (1997), four Cuban dissidents sent a respectful letter to Castro, exhorting him to adhere to the Viña del Mar declaration he had signed a year earlier.[104] In 1998, the Portuguese summit reproved the International Monetary Fund (IMF), World Bank and the leading industrial powers for their part in the financial crisis that had started in Asia in the summer of 1997. Castro profitably seized the opportunity to rail against the ills of capitalism.[105]

The summits highlighted the persona of Fidel Castro. Whether because his presence elicited admiration, repulsion or curiosity, his comings and goings almost always grabbed center stage. His continued defiance of the United States was a source of secret satisfaction for many participants; his unyielding stubbornness amid a world he no longer fully understood intrigued them as well. When Castro declared himself a "monarchist" after meeting King Juan Carlos at the Barcelona summit (1992), Prime Minister González urged him to hold elections within a year, designate a prime minister and become king. Unlike Carlos Andrés Pérez, Alberto Fujimori and Gaviria, who had to rush back due to domestic crises, Castro remained for an extended stay, visiting the Barcelona Olympic Games facilities, Seville's World Fair and his father's native Galicia.[106] Some leaders like Argentina's Carlos Menem (1989–1999) and Spain's José

María Aznar (1996–2004) relished their intermittent public sparring with the Comandante over democracy and human rights. In Cartagena (1994), Fidel's *guayabera* grabbed the headlines—it was the first time he had been seen in public out of his olive-green fatigues.[107] In Oporto, Portugal (1998), Nobel laureate José Saramago held a "private party" of 5,000 supporters in his honor.[108]

Constructive Engagement by U.S. Allies

Only after the end of the Cold War did Cuba truly become a contentious issue between the United States and its allies. There were, of course, moments of tension before 1990, particularly around the Missile Crisis but, for the most part, the bipolar world closely aligned the capitals of Europe and the Western Hemisphere with Washington. Mexico, the only country in Latin America that defied the 1964 OAS motion to break relations with Havana, cooperated with U.S. intelligence on Cuba-related matters. In spite of an unsalvageable ideological chasm, trade between Castro's Cuba and Francisco Franco's Spain had flourished.[109] The generalissimo himself explained why after a 1961 spat on Cuban television between the Comandante and the Spanish ambassador: "In the future, we don't attack or criticize Fidel Castro. He's a communist leader. I'm a Catholic one. But we are both strong *gallegos*. We will do business with him."[110] After the Spanish transition, Prime Minister Adolfo Suárez became the first Western head of government to visit Cuba. His government implemented a policy toward Latin America, based on the idea of community, that started with Cuba. Canada—a veteran practitioner of diplomacy that also never broke relations with Havana—trod carefully so as not to cross the United States beyond certain limits. Trade with Cuba continued after 1959 but Ottawa abided by the U.S. ban on strategic materials, did not transship goods of U.S. origins and even reputedly allowed an official at the Canadian embassy in Havana to work with the Central Intelligence Agency.[111]

Under the Cold War umbrella, these differences—at best, irritants—never weakened the Western alliance against Communism. The post-1990 world, however, was not so clearly bisected and thus the disagreements over Cuba were magnified. For Mexico and other Latin American countries, the U.S. insistence on respect for human rights and an eventual democratic transition were not the source of tensions with the United States. On the UN Commission on Human Rights, Mexico mostly abstained; others in Latin America either abstained or voted to condemn Cuba. All European members cast votes to censure Cuba and keep Havana's record under the UNCHR's watch. No, the bone of contention was the U.S. effort to extend the embargo through the Cuban Democracy Act of 1992 and, especially, the Cuban Liberty and Democratic Solidarity (LIBERTAD) Act of 1996. In the 1960s, the embargo prohibited U.S. subsidiaries abroad from trading with Cuba; it also barred the sale to Havana of any item that included U.S.-origin components and the re-export of

U.S. products from third countries. In 1975, however, the Ford administration lifted the restrictions on U.S. subsidiaries. Since the late 1940s, the General Agreements on Tariffs and Trade (GATT) had helped to create a multilateral system of expanding free trade that, in 1994, resulted in the World Trade Organization (WTO). Thus, in the 1990s, the CDA's and especially Helms-Burton's pretensions of extraterritoriality made Cuba an exception in a free-trade consensus that bound the United States and its allies more strongly than ever.

As world trade boomed, Washington insisted on the embargo, Helms-Burton in particular calling for its internationalization. To be sure, there were a few instances in which the international community had agreed on embargoes. After Saddam Hussein invaded Kuwait in 1990, the United Nations put in place an embargo to pressure Iraq's withdrawal that, unlike the U.S. Cuba embargo (until 2000), exempted medical supplies, food and other goods of humanitarian need. After the Gulf war, further sanctions were added to prod Iraq to come clean on weapons of mass destruction. But with the Cold War over, U.S. allies simply did not see Cuba rising to a comparable threat—one that merited a UN-backed embargo against Havana. Meanwhile, U.S. subsidiary trade with the island had developed at a moderate pace between 1975 and 1988. As the world turned in 1989 and Cuba's network of trade partners frayed beyond recognition, U.S.–Cuba trade jumped from $246 million (FY 1988) to $705 million (1990) and $718 million (1991). It then declined to $499 (1992) before the CDA came into effect and banned all subsidiary trade. Falling sugar purchases by U.S. subsidiaries largely accounted for the decline; U.S. exports to Cuba from third countries had actually risen by $24 million in 1992.[112] Canada, Great Britain, the European Economic Commission (EEC), Mexico and Japan roundly condemned the CDA, with Canada and Britain threatening U.S. subsidiaries with fines and their executives with jail terms if they obeyed the U.S. law. Japan's ambassador in Havana noted that the CDA "constitutes the extraterritorial application of U.S. domestic legislation which is not permitted in international law."[113]

Canada and Spain—middle powers in the post-Cold War world—offer contrasting examples of engagement with Cuba. In 1993, Jean Chrétien's election as Canada's prime minister initiated a new era in relations with Havana. His predecessor, Brian Mulroney (1984–1993), had struck a close relationship with the Reagan White House and Ottawa's policy toward the island became one of "studied neglect."[114] Mulroney, moreover, saw relations with Latin America in general as an extension of Canada's ever-increasing ties with the United States, although Joe Clark, Mulroney's secretary of state for external affairs, pushed to move Canadian policy toward more active involvement with Havana. Chrétien, in contrast, placed Canadian–Latin American relations in a multilateral context. During his administration, Canada expanded trade, one-way tourism, NGO ties with Cuban counterparts, financial support for Canadian investors in the island

and contacts among high-ranking officials. Ottawa also reinstated Cuba's eligibility to receive official development assistance and advocated its readmission to the OAS. For a while, Ottawa became Cuba's most important trading partner. "Canadian values must be represented by Canadian foreign policy, but it is in Canada's interest not to be taken for a more important or bigger nation that we are," Foreign Affairs Minister André Ouellet observed in an apt expression of how ordinary Canadians see their country. Chrétien's Cuba policy distanced Canada from Washington, which pleased public opinion precisely because Mulroney's overall closeness to Reagan had struck most as being un-Canadian. The U.S. embargo, moreover, did not meet Canada's traditional conditions on economic sanctions: that the international community take a common position, that Canadian public opinion agree with imposing them and that there be a reasonable chance of success.[115] They were, no doubt, sensible standards that made all the more sense, and not just to Canadians, after the demise of Soviet-style Communism. In short, Chrétien put relations with Cuba on a normal course of trade and diplomacy, which made Canada a "constant partner" for the island in the uncertain 1990s.[116]

Like U.S.–Cuban relations, those between Madrid and Havana carried the weight of history and intimacy. In mid-July 1990, for example, Spain recalled its ambassador and postponed a meeting on bilateral trade amid a churlish exchange over Cuban asylum seekers. In a week, four men had made their way into the Spanish embassy; one of them had been shot at, but not hurt by Cuban police as he jumped over the fence. When the Spanish foreign minister condemned the incident, Havana blasted him as an "anguished colonial overseer," seeped in "historic amnesia, paternalism and scandalous ignorance." In response, Madrid accused Havana of behavior "alien to the minimum standards of international coexistence," and froze its aid.[117] The EEC suspended a review of development projects.[118] After having fired the verbal fusillade, Castro lamented: "The way I feel is like a hurt relative."[119] As had similar crises during the same period with Italy, Switzerland, Belgium and Czechoslovakia, the stand-off with Spanish ended when the asylum seekers turned themselves over to Cuban authorities.[120] Afterwards, Felipe González did his part to improve relations through increased trade, investments and economic cooperation. Castro, however, made no moves to embrace broad reforms that would open the economy, and so there was not a great deal of progress in their economic relations.[121] In 1996, the Popular Party defeated the Socialists and José María Aznar became prime minister. A new era of recrimination would begin. Unlike the ties between Canada and Cuba, Spanish policy toward Cuba was also a domestic matter.

At first glance, Castro's response to the asylum seekers in 1990 may have seemed self-defeating in light of Cuba's desperate economic straits and lack of allies. Yet Havana's long-standing policy had been to deny safe passage out of the country to those who made their way into Western embassies. These intermittent crises, in Castro's view, were nothing more than planned "provocations" to recreate the type of chaos that reigned in the months preceding the 1980 Mariel exodus. In the summer of 1990, Castro acted to prevent what he saw as a potential threat, made all the more dangerous precisely because he stood so alone. Understanding that U.S. allies also believed that his government's days were numbered, the Comandante had to be constantly on the alert. Europe, Canada and Latin America all argued that diplomacy, trade, investments and exchanges of all kinds—in short, having a foothold in Cuba—would make it easier for the island to make the expected democratic transition. Both the U.S. embargo and constructive engagement were tools to pressure Havana for change: Washington turned the screws tighter; U.S. allies stepping up the interface. Neither policy brought a happy ending, in no small part because Castro held firm, listening to no other counsel than his own, while Cuban elites closed ranks and subsumed whatever internal differences existed among them.

A Momentous Fork in the Road

Since the late 1980s, the U.S. corporate world had expressed interest in exploring opportunities in Cuba in the hope of gaining a foothold on the island with Castro still in power. When the Clinton administration lifted the embargo against Vietnam, editorials across the nation, the conservative Wall Street Journal included, had asked why Cuba should not be next. The Cuban government, in turn, had encouraged U.S. corporate interest by opening a U.S. department in the ministry of foreign investments. In 1994–1995, nearly 300 U.S. executives visited Cuba, including representatives of one-third of the Fortune 500 companies. Executives from the largest U.S. pharmaceutical firm, Merck & Company, Inc., visited biotechnology facilities on the island. While U.S. law prohibited formal agreements between U.S. companies and the Cuban government, letters of intent were allowed; by the end of 1994, more than sixty had been signed. At about the same time, a U.S. consortium announced a proposal to raise a $2 billion Cuba investment fund.[122]

Faced with the prospect of Helms-Burton, American executives called their senators and representatives with concerns about losing investment and trade opportunities. The U.S. Chamber of Commerce complained that Helms-Burton "harms American companies and does nothing to Castro." After months of research, the U.S.–Cuba Trade and Economic Council found not a single major American company in favor of the bill.[123] In New York City for the United Nations' fiftieth anniversary, Castro dined with forty-seven CEOs from General Motors, Hyatt Corporation, J.C. Penny, K-Mart, Travelers Insurance, Harley-Davidson and Charles Schwab, among others. He met with Dwayne Andreas, chairman of Archer Daniels Midland Company and was feted by Mortimer Zuckerman at his Fifth Avenue apartment.[124] In the meantime, Helms was telling a CANF-organized rally in Miami:

All loopholes in the embargo must be closed. You can dress [Castro] up in a suit, make him take a bath and have him sip tea with French intellectuals, but it does not alter the fact that Castro is an evil, cruel, brutal, murdering thug.[125]

By issuing measures that strengthened enforcement of the embargo in October 1995, the White House hoped to deflect the bill's support in Congress. By month's end, it had succeeded: The Senate deleted the controversial Title III, which gave U.S. certified claimants, including Cuban Americans, the right to sue foreign entities in U.S. courts. Still, Helms-Burton undercut the president's constitutional prerogatives in the conduct of foreign policy by itemizing the conditions that a transitional Cuban government would have to meet before the normalization of relations. Among these were the legalization of all political activity; dissolution of the interior ministry's state security machinery; organization of free and fair elections that did not result in a victory by either Castro brother; establishment of an independent judiciary; and respect of the basic freedoms as per the UN Universal Declaration of Human Rights. However desirable, these conditions left the White House with little wiggle room, something that was especially needed in a case as intractable as Cuba's. Gone were the CDA's "calibrated ways," the give-and-take indispensable for a realist foreign policy.

The CDA already framed U.S.–Cuban relations in terms unacceptable to the Cuban government. How could it be otherwise when the United States claimed the right to promote change in the island's political system? If passed in full, Helms-Burton would be even more presumptuous and intrusive. More emphatically than with the CDA, Havana invoked the memory of the Platt amendment. And yet, given U.S. political realities, the best possible scenario was to keep the CDA as the sole guide of U.S. policy—that is, if Havana were truly interested in coexisting with Washington with fewer tensions. Demanding, as the Cuban government did, the unconditional lifting of the embargo was tantamount to saying that Cuba wanted no change at all in U.S.–Cuban relations. In the early 1990s, Cuban elites might have convincingly embraced economic reforms or enacted a token political opening; such domestic loosening might have set off a new dynamic in U.S. Cuba policy. But, under Castro's incontestable leadership, the regime could not engage in "calibrated ways" of any sort with the United States. By mid-decade, a hamstrung political system lacked the flexibility needed to improve relations with Washington. The Cuban government, moreover, was beset by a latent weakness: The revolution no longer commanded the genuine support of the majority. More open, tolerant politics and greater economic opportunities to earn a living surely found broad support with the citizenry. But if granted, those concessions would challenge the Fidelista model of governance. All the more reason why Cuban elites had little room to maneuver domestically and, thus, could not enter into a dialogue with the Clinton administration as they had with those of Ford and Carter.

By the end of 1995, it looked as if Helms-Burton would be diluted, if not outright defeated were it to include its most offensive titles. That scenario spurred the Clinton administration to define Cuba policy around the CDA's Track II of responding in "calibrated ways" to changes in Cuba. This would not be risk-free, as conservative Republicans, CANF and many Cuban Americans had come to see it as appeasement. Havana, in turn, would have to settle for a bilateral agenda that did not immediately address the embargo. Yet for both sides, the weakening of the Helms-Burton bill, or its defeat, would mean at least a slackening of tensions. The Clinton White House clearly favored crafting a policy across the center, and it seemed that the new year would bring modest progress in U.S.–Cuba relations. In January 1996, two bipartisan groups of Congressional staffers traveled to Cuba; a third group of visitors to the island, led by Representative Joe Moakley (D-MA), consisted of religious leaders, businesspeople and academics.[126] Also in January, Representative Bill Richardson (D-NM) spent four days in Havana talking to Cuban officials, including the Comandante, from whom he requested the release of fifteen political prisoners. A month later, Richardson returned to take three of the prisoners to the United States.[127] Sectors within the Cuban leadership almost certainly wanted to improve relations with the United States as well, although Castro did not, aware as he was that a more centered U.S. policy would partly depreciate the David–Goliath syndrome that had served him so well at home and abroad. Without Helms-Burton, U.S.–Cuban relations would have required a finesse that had rarely been exercised by either side in their long history together, but at least there might have been talks. On March 12, 1996, however, Helms-Burton became the Cuban Liberty and Democratic Solidarity (LIBERTAD) Act, with Titles III and the equally troublesome Title IV, which denied visas to executives of foreign corporations that invested in American properties seized by Cuba, fully reinstated.

On February 24, 1996, Cuban Air Force MiG pilots shot down two unarmed U.S. Cessnas over international waters, killing their four Cuban-American crew members. The planes belonged to Brothers to the Rescue—an organization founded to search for and rescue rafters in the Florida Straits. José Basulto, a Bay of Pigs veteran who was Brothers' president, was piloting a third Cessna that did violate Cuban airspace but escaped the MiG assault. Since its creation in 1991, the organization had rescued 4,300 rafters. Its core mission had ended with the Migration Accords, which stanched the flow of *balseros* from the island, but Basulto—seething with anger at the Clinton administration for the wet-foot/dry-foot policy of repatriating those who did not step on U.S. soil—had another mission for the organization: political confrontation of the Cuban regime. On at least three occasions and in violation of international law, the Brothers had entered Cuban airspace. In July 1995, its pilots dropped political flyers over or near Havana; in January 1996 they returned twice to drop flyers over or near central Cuba. Basulto, who only admitted to the July overflight, called it "an act of civil disobedience," an example to the Cuban people of peaceful resistance against the regime. Even before the first known incursion into Cuban airspace, a U.S. aviation official had cautioned Basulto that such actions might lead Cuba to force him to land the plane or to shoot it down.[128]

In late July 1995, the Federal Aviation Administration (FAA) pulled Basulto's pilot license, but a court order reinstated it. Between July and October 1995, the FAA and the U.S. State Department made public statements or warned Basulto directly about Cuba's determination to defend its boundaries. Sometime that fall, U.S. officials decided not to caution Basulto further, for he became so agitated that their warnings were "more likely to provoke him than to quiet him down."[129] In the meantime, the Cuban government registered numerous complaints with the U.S. Interests Section in Havana regarding the overflights and warned Washington of its fading patience. In early February 1996, retired Admiral Eugene Carroll traveled to Cuba with a delegation of other retired officers. In a meeting with Cuban generals, the Americans were asked what the U.S. reaction might be should the Cuban Air Force shoot down a Brothers' plane. Carroll told them the world would condemn Cuba as a "brigand"; upon his return to Washington, he promptly informed the administration of what he considered to have been a "calculated warning."

Evidence mounted in early 1996 that Havana aimed to take action against Brothers to the Rescue. Several weeks before the Cessna shootdown, U.S. intelligence had reported MiG practice strikes against slow-moving planes. On February 23, an internal FAA communication reported a warning from the State Department: "It would not be unlikely that the [Brothers would] attempt an unauthorized flight into Cuban airspace tomorrow." The administration had ordered a special alert nationwide to watch over the Florida Straits (which almost always meant being on the lookout for drug smugglers, but not this time). When the MiGs were spotted, the North American Aerospace Defense Command (NORAD) ordered two F-15 fighter jets at Homestead Air Reserve Base to get ready for action, but the go-ahead never came. Orders had been misunderstood, NORAD said. In late 1995, a U.S. official had summed up his concerns about Basulto: "One, because we have to worry about the man's safety. Two, flying over Cuba is clearly a violation of international law. And three, obviously it affects foreign policy. It risks provoking an international confrontation." Did the F-15s remain on the ground to avoid an encounter with the MiGs? In any case, the Clinton administration had contemplated a scenario where Cuba shot down a Brothers' Cessna that had crossed into Cuban airspace. That Cuba might blow up two Cessnas over international waters had not entered their purview.

On February 24, the FAA sent Havana the flight plan, as it customarily did with the Brothers' flights to avoid an accidental clash. But there was nothing accidental about the MiGs' actions that day. No sooner had Cuban radar detected the Cessnas flying south than the MiGs at San Antonio de los Baños Air Force Base received the order to start their engines. A few minutes later, the fighter jets took off. Basulto's Cessna was fifty nautical miles north of Cuba's twelve-mile limit, and the other two aircraft were even farther away. It was just before 3:00 pm; by 3:30 the two unarmed Cessnas and their crew had exploded over the Caribbean Sea, never having entered Cuban airspace. After hitting the first, the MiG pilot said: "We hit him, *cojones*. We hit him." Mission accomplished, the pilots might have thought, except that a second Cessna had just been located. "Follow it," ground control said. "Is the other authorized?" the MiG pilot asked. "Authorized to destroy." And so the second Cessna met its fate. At no point did the records later examined by the International Civil Aviation Organization (ICAO), a UN agency, show that the command at the San Antonio de los Baños base had been at all interested in determining whether the Brothers' Cessnas had entered Cuban airspace.

Might the Clinton administration have acted more forcefully to ground the Brothers? On May 16, 1996, almost three months after the MiGs shot down the Brothers' Cessnas, the FAA again revoked Basulto's license, threatening him with fines and even arrest if he persisted in flying into Cuban airspace. The timing, however, was largely coincidental. With a nod from the White House, the FAA had opened a formal investigation on Basulto in August 1995. Before it could issue an "emergency order of revocation" of his license, the FAA had to gather solid evidence of wrongdoing, including asking Cuba for proof of an alleged incursion on January 13, 1996, which Havana provided in the form of radar plots, photocopies of flight plans and transcribed aircraft communications.[130] By letting the FAA process run its course, the White House hoped to minimize the risk of another court order overturning the decision to yank Basulto's license. Though Brothers appealed the May 16 order at a cost of $100,000, this time Basulto lost his pilot's license once and for all. Needless to say, Cuban Miami decried the Clinton administration's "political vendetta." Havana, in contrast, praised the FAA move.

With the downing of the Cessnas, Cuba had wanted to send a strong signal to the United States, Cuban Miami and the world. By the mid-1990s, the international attention on its human-rights record gnawed at the regime's patience: The UN Commission on Human Rights was condemning Havana year after year and the European Union was pressuring the leadership to show progress on human rights as a condition for a cooperation agreement. Castro—never one to make concessions on principles—was absolutely determined not to yield an inch on domestic political matters. The European Union (EU) sought to establish a cooperation agreement with Cuba, the only country in Latin America and the Caribbean without one. A standard agreement included economic benefits but also required respect for democratic and human rights. In addition, the EU, having just signed a cooperation agreement with Vietnam after Hanoi accepted its democratic clause, wanted a similar disposition from Cuba. It was insisting that penal-code reform, an amnesty for political prisoners and a broadening of economic reforms be part of any cooperation agreement with Havana. Manuel Marín, an EU vice president charged with taking the first steps toward an EU–Cuba cooperation agreement, traveled to Havana in mid-February; he left empty-handed a few days before February 24. By shooting down the Cessnas, Cuba had sent Europe an unequivocal message.

That tragic Saturday was also meant to speak to Cubans on the island. Though in July 1995 Castro had declared the economic-reform process finished, at least two very different, unconnected groups of Cubans had not quite heeded him: Concilio Cubano and the Center for the Study of the Americas (CEA). On October 10, 1995, the opposition in the island launched its most daring project, Concilio Cubano, an umbrella organization of 130 groups committed to a peaceful democratic transition that included amnesty for political prisoners and the right of all Cubans to participate in forging Cuba's future. More than 200 well-known international figures, including eleven Nobel Prize laureates, supported Concilio's program. Concilio's leaders asked the government for the license to hold a meeting in Havana on February 24–27, 1996. The European Union had suggested that Havana grant Concilio's request as an expression of interest in an economic cooperation agreement. But from the outset, the regime unleashed a wave of persecution, incarcerations and beatings against the members of Concilio throughout the island that culminated in the week before February 24, when more than 150 activists were arrested. In the end, Concilio, which had planned to go ahead with a meeting even though its permission request had been denied, cancelled the gathering.[131]

The Center for the Study of the Americas, founded in 1977, had an almost twenty-year history of first-rate scholarship. Taking their cues from the Italian philosopher Antonio Gramsci, CEA members saw themselves as "organic intellectuals" who supported the "revolutionary project" with critical perspectives. Between 1977 and 1995, CEA received glowing evaluations from Communist Party higher-ups. In 1996, however, the regime was no longer interested in pursuing even modest reforms. CEA—never a favorite of the hardliners—was in the crosshairs. The party convened a commission that fired most of the CEA researchers and criticized them for their *naïveté*—being unaware that they were tools of the imperialists—and for their pedantry—thinking that they could act outside the official discourse. Politburo member José Ramón Balaguer told them: "Fidel Castro is the man we admire and love. Official discourse is the discourse of Fidel Castro." At most, the CEA researchers had overreached by tending bridges to other Cuban institutions—such as Popular Power, trade unions, the office of Vice-President Carlos Lage, the foreign ministry and the mass media—to exchange ideas on economic reforms. That was the CEA's downfall: Its interactions with other institutional actors had set in motion a lateral process of dialogue that was raising the need for political openings that the top-down PCC simply could not tolerate.[132]

After the Cold War ended, the Cuban government faced serious challenges. Near economic collapse and the consensus in the international community that Havana would be the next Communist regime to disintegrate led Castro to yield on modest economic reforms while reaffirming political control. That last decision precluded the natural give-and-take of diplomacy. Castro was a master of this art, but he had categorically refused to engage in diplomacy when concessions might compromise the regime's survival.[133] The decision to shoot down the Brothers to the Rescue planes—Fidel Castro later told *Time* magazine, "I take responsibility for what happened"—guaranteed that Clinton would sign into law the Helms-Burton Act, complete with Titles III and IV, precisely the two measures that U.S. allies fiercely opposed for their extraterritoriality.[134] A weaker Helms-Burton would not as readily have rallied the world against the United States. The Cuban government well understood the consequences of downing the Cessnas.[135]

After the shootdown, the Clinton administration retracted the looser regulations on travel and remittances adopted in October 1995, issued an indefinite suspension of all U.S.–Cuba charter flights and moved quickly to sign the Helms-Burton bill. The UN Security Council strongly condemned the Cuban Air Force attack; reminded Cuba that all states are bound by international law and asked the UN agency ICAO to fully investigate the incident. The European Parliament likewise repudiated Cuban actions against the two Cessnas, but it also deplored the passage of Helms-Burton and reaffirmed the right of Europeans to conduct normal commercial relations with the island. In July 1996, the Montreal-based ICAO concluded that the downing of the Cessnas took place over international waters, and that the MiGs had not given the Cessnas the requisite warning before firing. It also noted that civilian aircraft should only be used for civilian purposes. The report stopped short of putting full blame on Cuba for the incident; it implied that the Brothers' occasional violations of Cuban airspace were an unusual activity for civilian planes. Nonetheless, ICAO left no doubt that the two downed Cessnas never crossed Cuba's twelve-mile limit.[136] To this day, Havana refutes that finding.

In mid-1996, the United States and Cuba reached a fork in the road and chose diametrically opposed directions. Neither listened to the other, as a big power and its weaker neighbor must if they are to learn to live in peace. Both set forth unconditional demands—Washington's framed by Helms-Burton, Cuba's by an all-or-nothing stand on the embargo—and neither budged, as they had been willing to do under the Ford and Carter administrations. Fruitful talks between foes never start with a maximalist agenda. In the 1970s, Washington and Havana had kept their maximal goals in mind but had defined smaller, concrete issues as starting points for discussions. After Helms-Burton, the Clinton administration seemingly lost all flexibility in its policy toward Cuba. Cuba, in turn, flaunted its national sovereignty, no matter the costs—precisely the point in the shootdown of the Cessnas. Seeing some reason on each side, Canada, the European Union and other U.S. allies were caught in the impasse.

3

"HALF DRUNK AND THROWING BOTTLES AT EACH OTHER"

On November 5, 1996, President Bill Clinton was reelected when he defeated Bob Dole and Ross Perot. While the Electoral College outcomes were similar (379–159 in 1996 versus 370–168 in 1992), the president won reelection by a larger plurality of the popular vote (49 percent versus 43 percent). He lost three states he had carried in 1992—Montana, Colorado and Georgia—and won two that had previously eluded him—Arizona and Florida. The latter was a hard-won victory. In 1992, Clinton had campaigned intensely in Miami's Cuban neighborhoods, a first for a Democratic presidential candidate. His support of the Cuban Democracy Act had paid off; he garnered about a quarter of the Cuban-American votes and cut into the 80 percent share the Republicans had marshaled since Ronald Reagan. In 1996, Clinton won Florida with 48 percent of the vote, in no small part due to his larger share of Cuban-American supporters—about 35 percent.

While mindful of Cuban Miami, many of the decisions Clinton made in terms of Cuba policy during his second term had as much to do with a desire to reaffirm his executive authority, which Helms-Burton attempted to restrain. In asserting his presidential prerogatives in foreign policy Clinton forged a more flexible Cuba policy than the law had intended. Internationally, Clinton benefited from two Cuba-related developments. In December 1996, the European Union announced a Common Position (CP) that placed a democratic transition in Cuba and the regime's respect for human rights at the center of its policy toward Havana. Then, in January 1998, Pope John Paul II traveled to Cuba, providing the White House with the opportunity to ease travel restrictions and renew charter flights to the island and to authorize larger remittances from the United States. The Pope's message—"May Cuba open itself up to the world, and may the world open itself up to Cuba"—was a clarion call for Havana and Washington.

Fidel Castro, too, had reasons to celebrate. He had survived the end of the Cold War unscathed, at least in what mattered most, his hold on power. With smug satisfaction, he welcomed Iberoamerican dignitaries to Havana for the 1999 summit. Years earlier, when Cuba had been selected as the host country for the last summit of the decade, no one had expected Castro to be around for the actual meeting. In Havana, he reminded his guests that Cuba had rejected entreaties to change its Communist ways: "The advice rained down from everywhere, but we thought of another way and decided to struggle."[1] The Comandante had, moreover, held on to power on his own terms, ignoring calls from within the elite and the citizenry for broader market reforms and dismissing all talk of political concessions. In Giuseppe di Lampedusa's *The Leopard*, a young Italian aristocrat-turned-revolutionary says to his uncle, a Sicilian prince: "If we want things to stay as they are, things will have to change." And so it had been for Castro and his regime.

By the end of the 1990s, moreover, the tide had begun to turn against market reforms in Latin America. While still holding the democratic ideal in high regard, the region's citizens were becoming increasingly impatient with the practice of democracy. Continued inequalities and stagnant living standards were stirring popular anger. In December 1998, Venezuelans fired the first salvo by electing Hugo Chávez president. Chávez took office two months later and quickly launched an institutional transformation aimed at limiting the checks on power at the heart of liberal democracy. As the new century neared, Havana faced a more auspicious regional environment than it had earlier in the decade.

Cuba's Return to Normalcy

Ten days before the pope's arrival in January 1998, Castro remarked: "Cuba isn't changing. Cuba is reaffirming its position, ideals and objectives. It's the world that's changing."[2] Well before John Paul II made his call for openness, the Comandante had already decided to disregard any and all such suggestions. In the early 1990s, in the midst of a severe economic crisis, the leadership had entertained modest economic reforms. Some mid-level cadres even argued for deepening the reforms in order to reduce tensions with Washington and negotiate a cooperation agreement with the European Union. Cuba's decision to shoot down two Cessnas piloted by Cuban exiles and the subsequent enactment of Helms–Burton had stifled the prospects for change in U.S.–Cuban relations.

Looking Inward

The Cuban leadership had turned its attention inward. The times called for rallying around *la patria* and professing revolutionary ideology. Though Castro had long rallied and professed on his own, the role of the Cuban Communist Party now gained importance even if, when he deemed it necessary, Castro continued making decisions and informing the party afterwards. In August 1996, the PCC claimed a greater and more effective reliance on state institutions, mass organizations and individual militants than ever before.[3] Still, at the heart of Cuban politics lay the tension between Castro's charismatic leadership and the party's institutional authority. Between 1992 and 1997, PCC membership grew at the rate of 46,000 persons a year, a 70 percent increase from the 1980s rate.[4] While some in Washington and Miami still believed that a transition in Cuba was imminent, leaders in Cuba prepared for the long haul. Whether out of conviction, self-interest or a combination of both, some ordinary Cubans were seconding the leadership by joining the party.

In October 1997, the PCC summoned its Congress. Its documents and resolutions relayed the anti-market, nationalist rhetoric—nationalism being always more salient in Cuba than Marxism-Leninism—as well as a newfound bravado for having survived. As it had in the past, the Central Committee (CC) offered a glimpse into the thinking of Castro and his closest associates. The leadership reduced the membership of the Central Committee by a third, saying it wanted to have less cumbersome and expensive meetings. Yet, a look at the sectors cut from the CC suggested other reasons. Nearly half came from the ordinary citizens who had been tapped for CC membership in 1991. In effect, the party was giving up the symbolism of having *el pueblo* represented at its highest levels. Mass organizations like the Central Organization of Cuban Trade Unions (CTC) and the Federation of Cuban Women (FMC) also suffered mightily in the reduction. Suddenly, the CC was dominated by party cadres. And for the first time since 1965, the military increased its CC share slightly. The number of state administrators also increased, by 15 percent.[5] Favoring party, military and administrative cadres at the expense of other sectors conveyed a preference for control over anything else. Since 1959, Castro had shown inordinate abilities to configure and reconfigure the ruling elites. Now, in a time of crisis, he had done it again. At first, few international observers grasped the long-term import of the Cuban government's success at reconstituting itself without changing the basic contours of its power. The political system would still be largely based on Castro's leadership, mass mobilizations and a nationalistic emphasis on the homeland's defense. As a result, the government did not feel it had to respond to pressures from the United States and the European Union to make political concessions nor, for that matter, to heed the Pope's call for openness.

All the same, ordinary Cubans had changed. In 1995, a Costa Rican firm associated with the Gallup Organization conducted a public-opinion survey on the island. The results gave the regime scant comfort. Some 64 percent of respondents said they had not attended a political meeting in the last thirty days, while 20 percent had been to church. Only 21 percent described themselves as Communist or socialist, though an additional 48 percent considered themselves revolutionaries. When asked who could aid or guide citizens who disagreed with the government, a combined 46 percent answered "nobody," "don't know" or left the question blank. Given a choice between equality and freedom, 50 percent favored equality while 38 percent opted for freedom. More than 53 percent wanted to set up their own businesses. And 39 percent said that the government, not the people, was benefiting the most from foreign investment. Nearly half refused to name what they considered to be the revolution's principal failure. Eighty-eight percent said they were "very proud" to be Cuban.[6]

In the early 1990s, the PCC had acknowledged the pervasiveness of *la doble moral*—the fact that Cubans by and large were apt to say one thing in public while believing another—and called on the citizenry to speak out without *el afán de unanimidad*, the zeal of unanimity.[7] "We need to learn to disagree with those in charge. We don't say anything in meetings but we talk endlessly in hallways," Raúl Castro said, though clearly he did not mean disagreement with the Comandante, himself or the party.[8] Might not the relentless insistence on loyalty to the PCC, the revolution and comrade Fidel stymie the public expression of honest but politically incorrect points of view? Would not citizens therefore be acting reasonably in seeing official meetings as nothing more than a charade? Without autonomous institutions and civil liberties, the political system could neither overcome *la doble moral* nor break the stranglehold of unanimity. Cuban politics was absolutist, that is, it allowed no quarter for compromise on the vision of *patria* consecrated by the revolution. Ironclad unity was the *sine qua non* of national sovereignty, and the Comandante's incontestable primacy was an inviolable imperative. Though it is unlikely that Gallup's respondents disclosed the full gamut of their opinions, the survey still showed a significant gap with official discourse. The regime could have helped itself, for example, by legalizing the small-business sector, which a majority wanted, but it did not, out of political and ideological considerations. The reconstituted regime was also unable to refresh its relationship with ordinary Cubans by providing their material well-being. On the contrary, politics as usual further heightened the disconnect between the citizenry and official Cuba.

Human Rights

At the same time, Castro and his government faced a growing number of initiatives from human-rights advocates and opposition groups, even if quite small and limited in reach. No sooner had Concilio Cubano been squashed than another group gained center stage. In July 1997, the Internal Dissident Working Group—made up of Vladimiro Roca Antúnez, Martha Beatriz Roque Cabello, Félix Antonio Bonne Carcassés and René Gómez Manzano—issued a strong riposte to the guiding document for the PCC's October Congress.[9] All four had been part of official Cuba for decades and understood its convolutions well. Had PCC members and state administrators read the manifesto, *La patria es de todos* (The Homeland Belongs to All), many would likely have agreed with at least some of its content. The document hit hard against a "regime anchored in the past, that lives in the past, a rather remote past at that," one that substituted entreaties for "patriotic and revolutionary behavior" for real solutions to the nation's problems. The four dissidents were immediately arrested and held in jail for twenty months before they were tried. In February 1999, a draconian legislation against "sedition" went into effect. Providing the United States with information harmful to Cuban national interests, establishing unauthorized contacts with foreign diplomats and distributing or possessing publications "subversive" of Cuba's economy and political system could warrant imprisonment for up to twenty years.[10] In March, the four were tried retroactively under the new law, found guilty and sentenced to from three-and-a-half to five years behind bars. Not surprisingly Washington denounced the regime's actions, but Havana also earned the rebuke of the European Union, many Latin-American governments and even some of its traditional allies on the Left.[11]

The revolution had never put a premium on civil liberties and individual rights, but in the 1960s, when violations had been more flagrant, the responses from Europe and Canada had been more muted. Most countries in Latin America were then either under military rule or restrained in their criticisms by domestic constituencies, and if the Cuban revolution alarmed committed democrats and those who had long lived privileged lives, many others across the region cheered it on. Nonetheless, there was some criticism: In the early 1960s, Chile's Eduardo Frei had proclaimed a "revolution in freedom," a bold alternative to Cuba's path; and Caracas submitted proof to the Organization of American States of Castro's support of Venezuelan guerrillas, which helped to make the case for the Cuban government's exclusion and a hemispheric-wide embargo.[12] Also, between 1962 and 1983, the Inter-American Commission on Human Rights had issued seven reports on the island's human-rights record.[13] But in the early 1990s, Felipe González repeatedly pressured Castro to reform, while the European Union saw no reason why Cuba could not accept the democratic clause as Vietnam had done for the sake of a cooperation agreement. So, Castro was right: Cuba stood firm on its "position, ideals and objectives" while the world turned its attention to human rights and economic reforms. The world had, indeed, changed.

A Two-beat Engagement: The Papal Visit and the Havana Iberoamerican Summit

Cuba, in essence, had not changed in the forty-plus years since the triumph of the revolution, at least insofar as the medulla of Castro's power was concerned: his categorical authority, appeals to the masses and defense of national sovereignty. In consequence, Havana was not in a rush to engage meaningfully with the EU and Canada. Putting out occasional fires on human rights such as the yearly condemnation by the UN Commission on Human Rights was a small price to pay for having beaten the odds and survived. The Cuban government, nonetheless, could not totally ignore the international concern over its human rights violations. The papal visit in January 1998 and the Havana Iberoamerican Summit were cases in point. The Pope and the Iberoamerican dignitaries who gathered at the annual summits had long opposed the U.S. embargo, but no top-level visitor had ever pressed the regime over democracy and human-rights publicly, as they did.

Pope John Paul II's visit to Cuba marked a high point of engagement for the regime. While a papal visit had been under discussion since the 1980s, it was only after the end of the Cold War that the Cuban government agreed to host him. Cuba saw the Pope's presence on the island as a moral slap at the United States, particularly since John Paul II had recently denounced the social ills of unfettered capitalism with almost the same fervor he had mustered against Communism. In Cuba, after decades of ostracism, the Catholic Church had slowly regained a foothold in society. Since the mid-1980s, an ongoing, often difficult dialogue between the bishops and the government had opened up spaces for Catholic action. Indeed, the church displayed impressive mobilizational abilities in preparing the papal visit. Lay activists visited almost every Cuban household; dioceses throughout the island held outdoor masses; Cardinal Jaime Ortega explained the pastoral significance of the papal journey in a televised address. In 1997, after a three-decade ban, the government declared Christmas Day a holiday in honor of John Paul II.[14] Cuba was ready to receive the Holy Father.

The visit itself produced extraordinary images and let loose a multitude of sentiments. For five days, hundreds of thousands gathered for religious celebrations; millions watched or listened to masses that were broadcast live to the nation. In his homilies, John Paul II delivered a message of inclusion, freedom, reconciliation and respect for the dignity of individuals. "It is the hour to walk down the paths demanded by the times of renovation in which we live!" the Pope declared in Havana. "Do not be afraid," he often said, "You are and should be the protagonists of your own personal and national history." The crowds responded enthusiastically, chanting, "Cuba, with the Pope, renews her hope." The people of Santiago paid him the highest of compliments: "John Paul, brother, you are now a Cuban." Cries of "Freedom! Freedom!" electrified hundreds of thousands at the outdoor masses.[15] John Paul II's visit was historic in another way: During five days, the Cuban government did not occupy center stage.

Afterwards, the Cuban church stood stronger. While carefully keeping within the bounds of religion, its pastoral mission now also carried the civic responsibility of advancing a more tolerant society. How else could priests preach the gospels freely and Catholics give fearless testimony of their faith? Catholics—within the church hierarchy, in their parishes and on their own—began acting more assertively. In July 1999, a group of priests from eastern Cuba issued a critique of the church's pastoral work in which the *curas guajiros* (peasant priests) implicitly chastised the bishops for not forcefully pursuing the opportunities served by the papal visit.[16] The government suspected the hand of Santiago's Archbishop Pedro Meurice, a vigorous critic. A few months later, Castro accused Meurice of conspiring with the U.S. Interests Section, the Cuban American National Foundation and a handful of dissidents to sabotage the Iberoamerican summit. Cardinal Ortega immediately dismissed the allegations: "The Catholic Church in Cuba has never allowed itself to be manipulated. The words, homilies or public declarations of Santiago's archbishop are dictated solely by his conscience."[17] Shortly thereafter, the Vatican, conscious of the delicate dialogue between the Cuban Catholic Church and the government, praised the "improved climate," citing the increased numbers of foreign priests and nuns who had gained entry to serve in Cuba, the authorization of religious processions and the occasional radio broadcast of some church messages. But it also asked Cuba to make greater efforts to promote "a climate of trust that guarantees the fundamental rights of the human person" and to open "new spaces of liberty and participation."[18] Vatican policy and the church–state dialogue in Cuba provide an example of the give-and-take necessary for meaningful engagement and the limited but not inconsequential results that engagement brings. In deference to John Paul II, Havana released some 300 prisoners of conscience.[19]

The Iberoamerican summit in Havana ran on two tracks. The first was a meeting not unlike the previous eight, which had produced emphatic condemnations of the U.S. embargo; the second placed a stronger focus on human rights and democracy given that Cuba hosted the summit. The Cuban government worked hard to host a routine summit that would, as usual, denounce the U.S. embargo. Havana being the seat, however, the ninth Iberoamerican summit could not be more of the same. The presidents of Nicaragua, El Salvador and Costa Rica stayed away in order to register their displeasure with Castro. And for those who did attend the summit, the setting became a test of their democratic resolve. Would they limit themselves to the usual declaration in favor of pluralism, or would they resort to more active affirmations? While also working to make the Havana meeting a success, Madrid pursued the second track relentlessly as the date neared. How could Iberoamerican nations meet in Havana without expressing emphatic support for a democratic Cuba? Prior to the summit, Prime Minister José María Aznar criticized Castro for his stubborn refusal to change and met with leading opposition figures in Madrid. Spanish–Cuban relations once again soured.[20]

Heads of state or government on official visits to Cuba do not generally meet with dissidents. In this case, however, the dignitaries were not traveling to the island as invited guests, and the foreign ministry—recognizing the inevitable—signaled that attendees would be free to meet with whomever they pleased, although Cuban Foreign Minister Felipe Pérez Roque warned the dissidents: "Those who meet with participants of the Ninth Iberoamerican Summit will have to face charges under Cuban laws should they distort Cuban reality in those meetings." (Pérez Roque also made explicit mention of the March law that had earned the Cuban government international reprove just a few months earlier.)[21] At the Spanish embassy, Aznar welcomed five opposition leaders as well as relatives of the four dissidents who had been sentenced in March. The Portuguese prime minister, the Uruguayan president and the foreign ministers of Mexico, Costa Rica, Nicaragua and Panama likewise met with Cuban dissidents. In his summit address, King Juan Carlos went right to the point: "Only a full democracy, the utmost guarantees of liberties and the scrupulous respect of human rights will allow our peoples to meet successfully the challenges of the twenty-first century."[22] As he left Cuba, the monarch coined a phrase as memorable as the Pope's nearly two years earlier: "May Cuba open itself to Cuba."[23] Most important was Mexican President Ernesto Zedillo's assertion at the summit's closing session: "There cannot be sovereign nations without free men and women who can fully exercise their essential freedoms. Freedom to think and give opinions, freedom to act and participate, freedom to dissent, freedom to choose."[24] Hugo Chávez's emergence as an ally (and the Cuban team's victory over Venezuela's in the post-summit baseball game) probably helped soothe for Castro the sting of some of the visitors' public criticisms. In the days after the summit, the Comandante might have been left mulling over Mexico's symbolic turnabout and the prospect that Iberoamerica might thereafter be more insistent on democracy and human rights. Within two weeks, however, Castro's—and the world's—attention would shift to Cuban Miami and the plight of five-year-old Elián González.

All the World's a Stage

With Helms-Burton in place, Havana lost no time in taking advantage of the uproar in Europe, Canada and Latin America over the law's extraterritoriality. In August 1996, Foreign Minister Roberto Robaina traveled to Paraguay, Chile, Uruguay, Argentina and Ecuador. While in Asunción, Robaina and the Paraguayan foreign minister announced the restoration of diplomatic relations.[25] In October, Great Britain strengthened bilateral cooperation with Havana to combat narcotrafficking, an expression of trust that flew in the face of Helms-Burton's accusation that Cuba was participating in the drug trade.[26] Earlier, Castro had dispatched a large delegation to London to woo British investors. The group had been headed by Carlos Martínez Salsamendi, president of Cuba's Chamber of Commerce and a respected economist, who told the investors: "We are willing to do our utmost to help those foreign companies who think they could be subject to reprisals from this legislation [Helms-Burton]."[27] In November, Castro joined 100 heads of states for the UN World Food Summit in Rome. Afterwards, he met with Pope John Paul II, whose visit to Cuba was now assured. The Italian prime minister and the Comandante also met to discuss trade between their two countries.[28] In January 1997, Canada and Cuba signed a fourteen-point agreement covering economic and political matters. Almost simultaneously, France delivered an aid package for the sugar, food and oil-refining industries and tendered a more generous line of credit. In May, the French trade minister highlighted his government's opposition to Helms-Burton by announcing a new investment accord with Havana.[29] While EU–Cuba talks on a cooperation agreement were stalled, the European Union agreed to Cuba's request to participate as an observer in the Africa, Caribbean, Pacific (ACP) group of states.[30]

In the late 1990s, Cuba's relations with Canada and Spain were again good barometers of Havana's willingness to engage. Lloyd Axworthy, Canadian foreign minister, extended Chrétien's policy of engagement with Cuba. Shortly after he assumed his charge, Cuban MiGs shot down the two unarmed Brothers to the Rescue planes and Helms-Burton became law. While the Canadian government deplored Havana's actions, the extraterritorial measures in Helms-Burton loomed larger with Canadian public opinion. As in Europe and Latin America, opposition to the legislation bridged partisan divides. After Helms-Burton, Canadians only redoubled their support for closer relations with Havana. In sharp relief with the United States, Axworthy's fourteen-point agreement established a framework of dialogue and cooperation without conditionality. Canadian government institutions worked closely with Cuba's economic ministries, the justice system and the National Assembly, and senior-level contacts between government officials became routine on a broad range of topics, including human rights. In April 1998, Chrétien traveled to Havana. As a gesture before his arrival, the Cuban government announced a payment of $12 million to Confederated Life Insurance, a Canadian company, in compensation for properties that had been confiscated in the early 1960s. Chrétien pressed Castro on political-prisoner release, particularly the four from the Internal Dissidence Working Group. Though interested in closer trade and diplomatic ties with Canada, Castro rejected outright any meddling in Cuban domestic affairs.[31] Leaving empty-handed, Chrétien faced questions at home about his unconditional engagement with Havana. In January 1999, Axworthy returned to Cuba in the hope of seeing political prisoners freed and to review Canadian–Cuban relations.[32] In March, Castro answered Canada's interest in the four political prisoners for whose freedom the prime minister had especially interceded by submitting them to a closed trial and condemning them for sedition. Chrétien ordered a policy review that resulted in Canada becoming a "frustrated partner."[33] For a while, Havana even considered Canada "enemy territory."[34]

After winning the 1996 elections, José María Aznar took Spanish relations with the island in a new direction, making a conscious effort to move Spain closer to the U.S. position and thus undermining the notion of a Spanish–Latin American community of nations that had been a *política de Estado* (state policy) since 1977.[35] In June, his government canceled all cooperation except for humanitarian aid until Cuba took meaningful steps toward democracy. Spanish Foreign Minister Abel Matutes gave an official audience to CANF president Mas Canosa, and sometime later, the Popular Party (PP) created the Hispanic Cuban Foundation, which was closely aligned with CANF. It also promoted the Common Position for the EU, which was adopted—though somewhat softened by other EU members as the Spanish draft hewed too closely to U.S. position for European comfort. The Common Position still called for dialogue with Havana, supported its modest reforms and harshly criticized U.S. policy. Still, Aznar pursued a path of confrontation with Havana that brought frequent barrages of verbal assaults from Cuba. In 1998, however, in light of the pope's visit to Cuba and opposition at home, Aznar began to reconsider. Cuba, looking ahead to the Iberoamerican summit in Havana, also changed its stance. At the Oporto, Portugal summit, Aznar and Castro toned down their rhetoric. Afterwards the Comandante traveled to Madrid on a "private visit" that, nevertheless, brought him and Aznar together in marathon meetings. For a while, Spanish–Cuban relations regained a modicum of stability.

The Clinton Administration II

Throughout his second term, Clinton dealt with Cuban matters more than he could ever have anticipated. Helms-Burton thrust Cuba into the heart of U.S. relations with its closest allies and trading partners, all of whom protested profusely over the extraterritorial provisions in Title III and Title IV. NAFTA partners Canada and Mexico enacted antidote laws that barred their citizens and corporations from complying with the U.S. legislation. In June 1996, the OAS General Assembly issued a resolution calling on the Inter-American Juridical Committee (IAJC)—charged with advising the OAS on legal matters—to determine whether Helms-Burton adhered to international norms. Department of State spokesperson Nicholas Burns dismissed the OAS resolution: "The countries that are teeing off on us now ought to sit back and cool it and understand that we're going to implement this law."[36] U.S. Ambassador Harriet C. Babbit charged the OAS with "diplomatic cowardice" and asked why "the hemisphere will flex its muscles to defend illegal expropriations, but remain silent while our brothers and sisters remain subject to the caprices of a brutal dictator? Where is our sense of perspective?"[37] On point, Chilean Foreign Minister José Miguel Insulza noted: "This is not a resolution about Cuba. It is a resolution about freedom of trade and about international law. It cannot be interpreted as support for the current reality in Cuba."[38] In August 1996, the IAJC determined that Helms-Burton indeed deviated from international norms.[39] An advisory panel without binding powers, the IAJC ruling still reflected the Western Hemisphere's outrage. Europe, for its part, took its appeal to the World Trade Organization, which did have the power to issue binding decisions.

While Helms-Burton dominated the White House's public attention on Cuba, Washington and Havana continued their behind-the-scenes cooperation on concrete issues of mutual interest. The Drug Enforcement Administration (DEA) has had a long-established interest in Cuba. In the late 1970s, the two countries held talks on antidrug cooperation without reaching an agreement, but unofficial cooperation still took place until Reagan ended it in 1982. In the 1990s, Cuban security forces confiscated more than thirty-one tons of drugs, almost all headed for the United States. Nearly 200 foreigners and countless more Cubans were arrested for trying to use the island as a transit point north. By international and, particularly, Latin American standards, Cuba's record of combating drug traffickers is quite respectable, and the DEA gives Cuban security forces due regard for their professionalism and relative honesty. Given the tensions between the United States and Cuba, military-to-military relations have also been unusually cooperative. Both sides have had an interest in managing their common land border around the Guantánamo Naval Base to avoid or contain incidents. The American and Cuban commanders in the area maintain computer communication through their staffs and can call face-to-face meetings if necessary.[40] All the same, the positive experience on drug smuggling and Guantánamo had little bearing on the ever-tense relations between the United States and Cuba.

Helms-Burton, the European Union and the World Trade Organization

In a February 1997 interview with the *Economist*, Clinton described the U.S.–Cuba relationship in terms of a family feud that had caught Europe in the middle: "It's like we invited you over for dinner, you walked in and the people that invited you were half drunk and throwing bottles at each other."[41] By signing Helms-Burton, the president had become entangled in a feud of his own: Shortly after his second inauguration, the European Union lodged a complaint against the United States with the World Trade Organization.[42] In February, the WTO convened a panel and gave it six months to decide if Helms-Burton's Title III violated the organization's rules. (Title III allowed American claimants to sue, in U.S. courts, companies that invested in properties that had been expropriated by the Cuban government.) The White House ruled out any cooperation with the panel; Helms-Burton was a national-security matter, it argued, not a trade-policy issue, and the WTO allowed members exceptions "for the protection of its essential security interests." The lack of U.S. cooperation, however, had more to do with a cantankerous Republican-controlled Congress disdainful of all international institutions, particularly when U.S. national sovereignty might be undercut.

On July 15, 1996, fully cognizant of the troubles ahead, the president waived Title III, a prerogative included in Helms-Burton that the White House had negotiated with Congress. In issuing the suspension, Clinton hoped to defuse the most strident attacks by U.S. allies: "By working with our allies—not against them—we will avoid a split that the Cuban regime will be sure to exploit. Forging an international consensus will help maintain our leadership authority in international organizations." The European Union welcomed the suspension, but considered it a temporary measure without future guarantees for European companies. Moreover, EU members would not desist from legislation to forbid European compliance with Helms-Burton. Though it characterized the waiver as "a step in the right direction," the Canadian government reiterated its decision to enact legislation allowing Canadian corporations to countersue U.S. companies that sued them under Title III. Mexico acknowledged Clinton's effort to address U.S. allies' concerns but stood fast on the right to defend its national interests by all domestic and international means necessary.

In Congress, Dan Burton (R-IN) berated Clinton's waiver:

> I am very angry. We had sent a very strong signal to Fidel Castro that we wanted his tyrannical leadership to end. There were a number of companies that have pulled out of Cuba because they were going to be penalized for dealing in stolen American properties. Let's not talk about confiscated; we're talking about stolen American property. And now with the suspension of Title III, President Clinton has caved in to foreign interests. We think this is a terrible message to send.

Lincoln Díaz-Balart (R-FL) expressed his views tersely: "Backbone of Jell-O. That's what President Clinton demonstrated today." Only Democrats like Representative Lee Hamilton (IN) and Senator Christopher Dodd (CT)—both of whom had voted against Helms-Burton—praised the president's prudence. Still, CANF president Francisco Hernández reacted rather mildly: "We're not entirely satisfied, but this is a first positive step. What the president has done today is to give investors another few months to pack their bags and get out of Cuba." Most in the business community, in contrast, sighed in relief. For the time being, American corporations would not face retaliation by EU and NAFTA partners.[43]

Before the Europeans lodged their WTO complaint, the White House deferred the application of Title III a second time. In December 1996, the EU's Common Position allowed Clinton to argue that European and U.S. viewpoints were moving closer. Enforcing Title III would be counterproductive "as long as America's friends and allies continued their stepped-up efforts to promote a transition to democracy in Cuba."[44] However, while the Common Position made economic cooperation conditional on progress on democracy and human rights instead of the looser constructive engagement practiced toward Cuba in the early 1990s, the European Union was not one iota closer to the U.S. position on coercion and sanctions as the best policy. And, the second waiver did not deter the EU from going to the WTO. The Clinton administration's decision to boycott the WTO panel for short-term domestic imperatives threatened to undermine the organization's conflict-resolution procedures and endangered the long-term interests of building a strong world-trade system.[45] That scenario, however, did not come to pass as the United States and the European Union settled their dispute in bilateral negotiations outside the WTO. All the same, the White House surely saw the absurdity of having "the insignificant island of Cuba" put such strain on U.S. relations with its closest allies. Helms-Burton was an "embarrassment" that only a great power, unchallenged in the Cold War's immediate aftermath, could afford.[46]

The World Trade Organization had opened its doors in 1995, after decades of American support for free trade. Under Clinton, the United States had used WTO conflict-resolution panels more than any other member and had won the majority of the cases. From April 1997 to May 1998, Clinton and the Europeans talked. In April 1998, the European Union agreed to allow its WTO Helms-Burton challenge to lapse. On May 18, a U.S.–EU accord was announced around two propositions. First, the European Union would establish "binding disciplines" to prohibit state support for European companies that invested in U.S. properties that had been confiscated by Cuba; investments before May 1998 would be exempt. A registry of claims would also be established to let potential investors know which properties were in dispute. Second, the White House would enter into negotiations with Congress to obtain a waiver for Helms-Burton's Title IV, which denied visas to executives of foreign corporations that invested in American properties seized by Cuba, as well as to the executives' immediate families.[47] In short, the EU would do its part as soon as Clinton obtained the Title IV waiver from Congress. Congress, however, never gave Clinton the authority to waive Title IV neither did the European Union prevent new investments in Cuba. Still, both sides complied in practice: Titles III and IV were not applied against Europeans nor did the EU register other complaints at the WTO.

Senator Helms (R–NC) quickly dismissed U.S.–EU accord:

> For me to accept this agreement offered by the EU would be to condone thievery and dishonesty. It will be a cold day in you-know-where before the EU convinces me to trade the binding restrictions in the Helms-Burton law for an agreement that legitimizes their theft of American property in Cuba.[48]

Not unexpectedly, Congress refused to grant the president the right to waive Title IV. In 1999, Washington briefly considered applying Title IV against executives of Sol Meliá, the Spanish hotel giant, perhaps including France's Club Med and Germany's tour operator, LTU Group Holding GmbH as well. All had built hotels on land once owned by the Sánchez family, U.S. naturalized citizens who had been citizens of Cuba when their properties were seized.[49] Had the Clinton administration applied Title IV to Sol Meliá executives and their families, the de facto truce in place since May 1998 would have collapsed. But the agreement survived, thanks to the common sense that the United States and the European Union exercised. Clinton waived Title III eleven times between July 1996 and January 2001. It applied Title IV only three times and never against European corporations: to Sherritt International, a Canadian mining company; to Grupo Domos, a Mexican telecommunications enterprise; and to BM Group, an Israeli citrus consortium. In 1997, Grupo Domos liquidated its investments in U.S.-claimed properties, which enabled its executives to enter the United States and take their children to Disney World. The Italian telecommunications company STET avoided Title IV sanctions by agreeing to pay ITT Corporation $25 million for a ten-year "lease" of its confiscated properties.[50] Only Sherritt stood defiant and, thus, its executives suffered the consequences of Title IV.

Clinton had, indeed, taken the bite out of Helms-Burton, even if he could not avoid the serial headaches in the process of doing so. The White House frustrated the two titles' intention, which was nothing less than the internationalization of the embargo. When he signed Helms-Burton into law on March 12, 1996, Clinton issued a signing statement that read in part:

> I interpret the Act as not derogating from the President's authority to conduct foreign policy. A number of provisions could be read to state the foreign policy of the United States, or would direct that particular diplomatic initiatives or other courses of action be taken. The President's constitutional authority over foreign policy necessarily entails discretion over these matters.
>
> The President must also be able to respond effectively to rapid changes in Cuba. Section 102(h) concerning the codification of the economic embargo, and the requirements for determining that a transitional or a democratically elected government is in power, could be read to impose overly rigid constraints on the implementation of our foreign policy. I will continue to work with the Congress to obtain the flexibility needed if the United States is to be in a position to advance our shared interest in a rapid and peaceful transition to democracy in Cuba.[51]

Clinton thus signaled a determination not to cede Congress his authority regarding Cuba policy. That he would waive Title III routinely and apply Title IV lightly was perhaps not anticipated by Senator Helms and Representative Burton. By doing so, Clinton set a precedent of presidential authority in spite of Helms-Burton's rigidity. In Clinton's second term, moreover, a bipartisan coalition emerged in Congress in favor of ending the embargo or, at least, rethinking U.S. policy toward the island. Clinton's push back to retain his foreign-policy prerogatives and the rise of this congressional bipartisanship seeking change resulted in a less constraining Helms–Burton law than originally supposed.

Clinton, Congress and Cuba Policy

The U.S. embargo against Cuba is authorized by the Trading with the Enemy Act, which gives the president broad powers to institute and maintain economic sanctions against hostile countries. Since 1962, the Treasury Department's Office of Foreign Assets Control (OFAC) has been responsible for making and enforcing the rules that bind the embargo against Cuba and has thus defined the embargo's reach under executive-branch authority. Though commonly believed to have codified the embargo, Helms–Burton left the president's powers in this matter untouched. Section 102(h) reads:

> Codification of the Economic Embargo. The economic embargo of Cuba, as in effect on March 1, 1996, including all restrictions under part 515 of title 31, Code of Federal Regulations, shall be in effect upon the enactment of this Act.

Unintentionally, however, Helms–Burton also codified OFAC's regulatory powers. The key section in the Code of Federal Regulations reads: "All transactions [involving Cuba] are prohibited except as specifically authorized by the Secretary of the Treasury by means of regulations, rulings [and] licenses."

Herein lies the legal loophole that allowed the Clinton administration to deflect congressional curbs on executive power regarding U.S. policy towards Cuba.[52] Asserting his constitutional right to conduct foreign policy, Clinton crafted a more nuanced Cuba policy than Helms–Burton's authors had intended.

To be sure, some political winds blew in the administration's favor. For the first time, the EU's Common Position explicitly made economic cooperation conditional on Cuba's progress on democracy and human rights, a soft wink toward Washington. And in 1998, Pope John Paul II's visit to Cuba offered up possibilities that the Clinton administration took. The Vatican had long opposed the U.S. embargo so there was no surprise in the Pope's urgings to the United States "to change, to change" and his condemnation of U.S. policy as "unjust and ethically unacceptable."[53] On the contrary, the Pope's words created a golden opportunity to move Cuba policy a bit. Two months after the Pope's visit, the White House reinstated the right of Cuban Americans to send up to $1,200 in annual cash remittances to their families (remittances had been prohibited after the February 1996 shootdown of the Brothers to the Rescue planes). Direct charter flights were also restored for family and humanitarian travel. In making the announcement, Clinton said:

The presence of his Holiness John Paul II in Cuba inspired the Cuban people, providing an important psychological boost to the Cuban Catholic Church and to Cuba's nascent civil society. The measures I have announced today are designed to build upon that visit, to support the Cuban people through the hardships and difficulties ahead, to contribute to the growth of a civil society and to help prepare for a peaceful transition to democracy.

In addition, Clinton expressed interest in congressional proposals for expanding humanitarian assistance. Representative Esteban Torres (D-CA) and Senator Chris Dodd (D-CT) introduced bills to lift all prohibitions on the sale of food and medicine to the island, thus eliminating the cumbersome OFAC licensing requirements. CANF backed an alternate proposal to increase the already allowed humanitarian donations to Cuban NGOs, which aides to Senator Helms drafted. Congressional Republicans and Cuban Miami were wary of efforts to end the embargo on food and medicine, which would encourage the anti-embargo forces to chip away further at U.S. sanctions.

Prior to the president's announcement, Secretary of State Madeleine Albright met with Cuban-American groups in Miami to put their minds at rest. The changes, she told them, signaled only humanitarian concerns, not a change in U.S. policy. She also read a seven-minute message to the Cuban people over Radio Martí reassuring them of the U.S. commitment to a peaceful transition. In addition, Albright met with Pope John Paul II at the Vatican. Though in disagreement over the embargo, she told him that his visit might be "a point of departure" for political change on the island. Cuban-American lawmakers Ileana Ros-Lehtinen and Lincoln Díaz-Balart, however, denounced Clinton's actions: "The pope's visit to Cuba has not deterred the Castro regime from its ongoing and systemic repression of the Cuban people. That visit should not be used as a pretext to soften sanctions on the Cuban tyranny."[54] Ros-Lehtinen and Díaz-Balart also opposed the CANF-backed proposal, claiming it was superfluous since humanitarian donations were already permitted under existing law. It was a rare hint of daylight between the lawmakers and CANF. José Cárdenas, the foundation's representative in Washington, said: "The challenge of U.S. policy following the pope's visit is trying to keep the momentum going without re-energizing the regime." Exiles, too, needed to change in order to meet John Paul II's challenge of openness.[55] Amid the papal afterglow, Havana welcomed Washington's modest changes.

Throughout 1998, the administration continued the political balancing act required of making Cuba policy: mollifying U.S. allies on Helms-Burton; announcing a disbursement of more than $1 million in new grants mandated by Helms-Burton to support "democracy-building"; giving Cuban airliners en route to and from Canada the right to fly over the United States; arresting two Cubans and eight Cuban Americans on charges of infiltrating exile organizations and spying on U.S. military installations in southern Florida.[56] In May, the Pentagon released a long-awaited report on Cuba and U.S. national security. Since the Soviet Union's collapse, the report determined, the island posed a "negligible conventional threat," the Cuban military having been turned into a "stay-at-home force that has minimal fighting ability." In a letter to Strom Thurmond (R-SC), chairman of the Senate's Armed Services Committee, Secretary of Defense William Cohen expressed concern about Cuba's "potential threat" in intelligence matters and the regime's "potential instability." Cohen's caveats did not placate administration critics in Congress and Cuban Miami.[57] In the fall, the administration received a welcome political cover. A group of prestigious Republicans—including former Secretaries of State Henry Kissinger and Lawrence Eagleburger, former Undersecretary of State William Rogers, former Secretary of Defense Frank Carlucci, former Senate Majority Leader Howard Baker and fifteen current members of Congress—sent the president a letter calling for the establishment of a National Bipartisan Commission to review Cuba policy.[58] Not since Ford and Carter had an administration fully reviewed American policy toward the island. The call for a bipartisan commission seconded what had become increasingly palpable since Clinton's first term: Support for changing Cuba policy now came from both parties, just as support for maintaining the embargo traditionally had.

In January 1999, the White House announced a new round of measures: authorizing direct flights between cities other than Miami to cities other than Havana; pledging to establish direct mail service; allowing remittances to independent organizations and individuals as long as they were not affiliated with the government or the PCC; supporting academic exchanges by expanding licensed travel to Cuba and increasing visas for Cubans to visit the United States; granting permission for the Baltimore Orioles and the Cuban national team to play ball in Havana and Baltimore; allowing the licensed sale of food and agricultural products to independent farmers and NGOs, and increasing support for Radio and TV Martí.[59] The restoration of direct mail service had been raised before, but Havana had always argued that international regulations required that mail be carried on commercial flights, and only charter flights flew between the two countries. This time, Cuban officials refused again, alleging that militant exiles might take advantage of the service to send letter bombs. Clinton, however, rejected the Republican suggestion of a bipartisan commission: Not only would it stir controversy among congressional Republicans and Cuban Miami, but some of his most ardent Democratic supporters during his recent impeachment ordeal opposed it as well. Senator John Warner (R-VA) lamented that Clinton's efforts fell "way short" of what a bipartisan commission could have accomplished.[60] In Miami, CANF was relieved that Clinton had not convened the commission. Ordinary Cuban Americans generally welcomed the measures, even if they were still supportive of the embargo. Auxiliary Bishop Thomas Wenski agreed with Senator Warner that the efforts fell short: "The embargo cannot be sustained morally. Lifting the embargo would be both smart policy and a powerful humanitarian effort."[61] Havana dismissed the new measures as "crumbs," "a deceptive maneuver" meant to deflect growing opposition to the embargo and censured the administration's efforts to strengthen Cuba's independent farmers and NGO sector.[62]

Clinton's decision to license the sale of food and agricultural products harbored the greatest potential for change in bilateral relations since the 1970s. Hardline Cuban Americans and their congressional allies lobbied their strongest criticisms against licensed trade. Representative Díaz-Balart told Secretary Albright: "One thing would be for you to seek a change in the law. But if you proceed with this executive order, that would violate the law." The White House proceeded and did so legally as per Helms-Burton's codification of OFAC's rulemaking authority regarding Cuba. Indeed Clinton's new measures gave renewed impetus to the anti-embargo movement, which had been stymied by Helms-Burton but had never gone away. Market forces had, moreover, created a potentially powerful constituency for a change in Cuba policy. Amid the agricultural glut and low prices of the late 1990s, U.S. farm interests turned their hungry eyes to the Cuban market, which represented a potential of $1 billion in annual business.[63] The farm crisis drove the bipartisanship push to exclude food and agricultural products from all trade embargoes, as neither Republicans nor Democrats could afford to lose the support of influential agricultural lobbies and their voters. Unfazed by the fate of earlier bills that his own Republican leadership had derailed, Senator John Ashcroft (R-MO), submitted a new bill, Food and Medicine for the World Act, that included Cuba; Representative George Nethercutt (R-WA) sponsored a similar bill in the House. Though no one predicted easy or quick passage, the medium-term momentum favored ending sanctions on the sale of agricultural products.[64]

In October 1999, the Republican governor of Illinois, George Ryan, became the first U.S. governor to visit Cuba since the triumph of the revolution. Explaining the reasons for his trip, Ryan simply said: "Isolating Cuba is not in the best interests of Illinois or in the best interests of the United States." He led a forty-five-member delegation of state, business, religious and university leaders that included executives from John Deere, Caterpillar, Archer Daniels Midland and the Illinois Corn Growers Association. The Illinois group brought donations worth more than $1 million. In Havana, Ryan bluntly stated: "Basically, the problem with Cuba is Fidel Castro." The Comandante, nonetheless, met with the governor. Though the State Department and many in Miami chided him, going to Cuba turned out to be good local politics: his fellow Illinoisans heartily approved of his trip.[65]

In March 1999, the Cuban regime tried and sentenced the four members of the Internal Dissidence Working Group under a newly enacted sedition law. The crackdown led the Clinton administration to delay issuing the regulations for the measures the president had announced in January; they were eventually issued in May.[66] Neither did Havana's sentencing of the four dissidents slow down the congressional movement to end sanctions on the sale of food and agricultural products. After a July 1999 trip, Thomas J. Donahue, president of the U.S. Chamber of Commerce, noted that Castro delighted in welcoming American executives who criticize U.S. policy but did not have the disposition to create an investment-friendly climate. When the Cuban minister of health complained about the embargo's restrictions on pharmaceuticals, Donahue answered: "The real problem is you don't want to buy that stuff. You want to complain about how you can't buy it."[67] In November, President Clinton expressed his not unfounded frustration:

> Every time we do something, Castro shoots planes down and kills people illegally or puts people in jail because they say something he doesn't like. I almost think he doesn't want us to lift the embargo because it provides him an excuse for the economic failures of his administration.[68]

Cuban officials, in fact, had sent signals regarding their government's view of a partial lifting of the embargo. At the United Nations in September, Foreign Minister Felipe Pérez Roque had warned on what the easing of sanctions on food and medicine might mean: "There's the risk that public opinion will consider the matter of Cuba solved if food and medicine sales are authorized. But that wouldn't be the case. The embargo is much more than that."[69] A few weeks later, National Assembly President Ricardo Alarcón criticized the effort to end these sanctions on similar grounds: As an attempt to portray a softening of the embargo and assuage critics of U.S. policy.[70]

In October 2000, Bill Clinton signed the Trade Sanctions Reform and Export Enhancements Act (TSRA), which authorized U.S. producers to sell agricultural commodities and medical goods to Cuba while barring the Cuban government from receiving U.S. public or private credits; in effect, if it wanted to buy from the United States, Cuba would have to pay cash.[71] The House Republican leadership had given Miami Republicans Ileana Ros-Lehtinen and Lincoln Díaz-Balart the last word on all Cuba-related legislation; the credit prohibition was their doing. So was the codification of the existing travel ban, which they succeeded in inserting into the TSRA. In doing so, they had implicitly recognized the flawed wording in Helms-Burton's section 102(h). Under TSRA, the White House would still have the power to license travel broadly, but it would not be able to lift the ban altogether. Only Congress could do so, which meant that Americans wanting to go to Cuba as tourists would have to wait for Congress to change the law. President Clinton commented:

> It certainly restricts, in a completely unwarranted way, the ability of the United States to make travel decisions on policy that I do not believe should be made, written in law, in stone by the Congress. I think it's wrong.[72]

Havana promptly rejected the change and declared that no food or medicine purchases would be made. For Cuba, the embargo remained the central issue, and TSRA did not address it. On the day the U.S. Senate passed TSRA by an 86–8 vote, Fidel Castro led some 800,000 people in a protest march through Havana.[73]

In his second term, Clinton reclaimed executive prerogatives that the Helms-Burton Act had intended to curtail. (Congress did not do so inadvertently, when it codified OFAC's rulemaking authority along with the embargo.)[74] He made Cuba policy more flexible, setting a precedent that his successor could build on. First, he routinely invoked the Title III waiver allowed by Helms-Burton. Second, he largely disregarded Title IV, which barred foreigners who had "trafficked" in confiscated properties, and their family members, from entering the United States. Third, the White House made liberal use of Helms-Burton's codification of OFAC regulations to revise some sanctions. Upon leaving office in 2001, Clinton bequeathed his successor a policy that mobilized trade and soft power to pry Cuba open. Without abandoning the goal of a democratic Cuba, the White House had started down a path of limited engagement.

Cuban Miami on the Eve of the New Century

Over the 1990s, exile organizations established or widened links with opposition and human-rights groups in Cuba. Frequent communication with anti-regime activists had a salutary influence on Cuban Miami, as more exiles committed themselves to nonviolence. In the mid-1970s, dissidents inside the island had embraced a nonviolent, human-rights agenda, which was a breakthrough in Cuban political culture. Simultaneously in exile, the Washington, DC-based Of Human Rights had raised the UN Universal Declaration as its lodestar, and from within Cuban Miami, voices promoting dialogue as the best strategy toward Havana began to emerge. But old habits die hard. Between July and September 1997, several bombs exploded at hotels in Havana. An Italian tourist was killed while having a drink at the Copacabana Hotel, the single fatality of a bombing streak that otherwise caused minor material damages and human injuries. In early September, Cuban authorities arrested a Salvadoran who claimed that individuals tied to CANF had paid him $4,500 for each bomb he placed in Cuba.[75] A year later, the *New York Times* published a 10,000-word series based on a six-hour audiotaped interview with the well-known anti-Castro militant and terrorism suspect Luis Posada Carriles. Though he later recanted, Posada told the *Times* that CANF had been involved in the bombings.[76] The foundation vehemently denied all accusations.[77] Exiles also plotted to assassinate Castro at the Iberoamerican summits in Margarita Island, Venezuela (1997) and in Panama (2000).

At the same time, younger Cuban Americans had begun to break from the traditional political culture. In the 1980s, Ramón Saúl Sánchez—born in Cuba in the mid-1950s—spent four years in jail for refusing to testify before a grand jury that had been convened to investigate exile violence. Upon his release, Sánchez said:

> When I left prison, I made the commitment to myself and my brethren in this struggle to disseminate a philosophy of nonviolent civic struggle, to work according to its ideas, not just as a matter of strategy, but as a principle for living and struggling.[78]

On the anniversaries of the 1994 sinking of a tugboat full of refugees near Havana and the 1996 Cessna shootdown, his Democracy Movement led several flotillas to the edge of Cuba's territorial waters, where participants threw flowers into the ocean to honor the victims. Once, when the flotilla crossed the twelve-mile border into Cuban waters, Cuban gunboats rammed the flotilla's lead boat, *Democracia*, injuring some participants.[79] In 1995, Sánchez had been the leader of a protest against Clinton's wet-foot/dry-foot policy that blocked toll plazas and tied Miami traffic in knots. Most important, his influence weighed heavily on a younger cohort of Cuban Americans—largely born in Miami—whose initiation into anti-Castro militancy involved only civic political activities.[80]

Farewell to CANF's Founder and Chairman

On November 23, 1997, CANF Chairman Jorge Mas Canosa died at the age of fifty-eight. Nearly fifteen months earlier, he had received an unusual recognition: Havana had agreed to a debate between him and Ricardo Alarcón. Taped on August 23, 1996, the encounter was broadcast on September 5 by CBS affiliates throughout Latin America. The moderator, journalist María Elvira Salazar, asked the questions that turned out to be the crux of the debate:

SALAZAR: Would you, Mr. Alarcón, support Mr. Mas Canosa if he gained the presidency in an election, would you support such a government elected by the people?

ALARCÓN: A government elected by the people, yes. But not a North American who would represent a foreign power. My answer is no because he's not Cuban.

MAS CANOSA: My Cuban citizenship doesn't belong to the Cuban revolution or to Fidel Castro or to Ricardo Alarcón. I'm a Cuban citizen and I carry it in my heart. What I'm saying is that the road to power is through free elections, universal suffrage and secret ballots, respect for the popular will, that Cubans can choose the system and the leaders they want.

SALAZAR: If Fidel Castro leaves Cuba's political scene and Ricardo Alarcón becomes the man to lead the transition toward democracy, would you give him your full economic support?

MAS CANOSA: If in a democratic election where the popular will is respected, if political parties can be organized, if we have the opportunity to express our ideas, if we have the same access to the media, if in a democratic election Mr. Alarcón wins, or Mr. Juan Pérez or Mr. José Rodríguez, we would respect him, yes sir.

Though neither man liked the idea of the other winning a free election in a post-Castro Cuba, Mas Canosa finally said yes to Salazar's question. Alarcón, no doubt, was right that his opponent was a naturalized U.S. citizen.[81] But there was historical precedent to Mas Canosa's position. Tomás Estrada Palma had been a U.S. citizen before he became the Cuban republic's first president, and the Cuban people had cheered him wildly as he advanced westward from Oriente to Havana.[82] Mas Canosa's claim to Cuban citizenship made sense to many exiles who, like him, held U.S. documents but still felt emotional ties to the island where they were born. So did his opening remarks, in which he dedicated the debate to "Castro's victims, including my own sons who—because of this tragic political incident in Cuban history—weren't born in the free land of their parents."[83]

Mas Canosa's popularity in Cuban Miami was, in fact, at least partly the result of that emotional connection he had with his fellow exile.[84] Hurt by the separation from the homeland, by so many Nochebuenas in exile, Cuban Miami cheered when CANF wielded its influence in Washington. That the CANF-supported U.S. policy failed to usher in a democratic Cuba did not diminish the sense of empowerment that the exile community felt through the organization's victories in Washington. (Though neither side would likely accept the comparison, there had been similar rejoicing in the island when Cuba's armed forces defeated the South African Army and secured Angolan independence. That the Angolan war cost Cuba mightily in lives and treasure should not expunge from the historical memory the joy that Cubans felt over their military's success in 1975, nor the fact that Havana's foreign policy from the 1970s to the present stands as a real accomplishment.) Long-standing political polarizations such as Cuba's are driven by strong emotional undercurrents. That Mas Canosa's emotions came to the fore so forcefully during the debate says more about his being on the losing side than anything else. Have not similar inklings of loss long simmered in some quarters of the American South? Alarcón clearly understood the depth of feelings he would touch by saying that Mas Canosa was not a *cubano*, and in saying so he gave a grudging nod to Mas Canosa's—and *el exilio*'s—alternate *cubanía* (the Comandante's green-lighting of the debate itself was another nod). His glib negation did not a political reality make. In a 1992 interview, Mas Canosa had said: "I've never been assimilated. I have no intention of doing so. First and foremost I am Cuban. I live here as an extension of Cuba."[85] That reality calls for recognition, not the caricature that Alarcón tried to paint. But by the same token, exiles, too, must recognize the emotional bonds that tied so many Cubans to the revolution and turned *la revolución* into a quasi-mystical symbol.

In the 1980s and 1990s, Mas Canosa and CANF played political hardball: against the *Miami Herald*, against Cuban Americans with different ideas on Cuba policy, against dissidents on the island who did not toe CANF's line. The foundation and its chairman also played smart politics: declaring a win when the Reagan administration's renewed immigration accord included the U.S.-entry rights of Cubans stranded in third countries (even if the accord itself implied dialogue with Havana), securing Clinton's support for the Torricelli bill, making campaign donations to Democrats as well as Republicans, supporting Cuba's opponents in Angola and Nicaragua, forging close ties with the new Central European democracies. CANF, under Mas Canosa, crafted an effective political strategy. Life for Havana certainly became harder after Radio Martí was launched, after the U.S. Congress voted to allow material support to Angolan forces fighting the Havana-backed government, after the UN Commission on Human Rights took up the case of Cuba, all of which happened, in part, thanks to CANF. Mas Canosa and CANF may not have been well liked outside of Cuban Miami, but they were respected and even feared, which in politics constitutes a plus. By accumulating the political victories that slowly sidelined violence as a means against Castro, CANF and its chairman made Cuban Miami a player in national politics.

What direction CANF might have taken had Mas Canosa not died prematurely is unfathomable. Neither CANF nor Mas Canosa in the 1990s had crafted a political style conducive to dialogue. On the contrary, their swaggering ways smacked of confrontation. Reading a transcript of the Alarcón–Mas Canosa debate may, for instance, leave one with a more positive appreciation of the CANF's president answers than actually watching him in action. However, by embracing political action, he was quick to learn the art of compromise in national politics even if Cuban Miami had not. Upon learning of his death in 1997, a former State Department official's comment emphasized the point:

> Over the past five years, Jorge was a moderating influence in exile politics. While Brothers to the Rescue provoked confrontation and the Democracy Movement caused a death, Jorge was the one to debate Ricardo Alarcón. No other exile leader would have accepted that challenge.[86]

(To be fair, the death mentioned in relation to the Democracy Movement referred to a man who suffered a heart attack while participating in one of Sánchez's flotillas.)[87] As the 1990s wore on and Castro's regime remained largely unchanged, Mas Canosa might well have rethought his long-standing advocacy of the hardline. How would he have reacted to Clinton's openings under the Helms-Burton law? Had the 1994 *Maleconazo* uncontrollably spread to other

Havana neighborhoods or to other cities in Cuba, might Mas Canosa have called for a U.S. invasion? Would Mas Canosa's CANF have broken with its past and supported the sale of food and medicine to Cuba as Congress loosened the embargo?

Over the 1990s, Cuban Miami gave indications that its thinking with regards to Cuba was evolving. That is what the results of Florida International University's Cuba Poll suggested. While in March 1991 nearly 80 percent of those polled expected major political change to come to Cuba within five years, by October 2000 a combined 56.1 percent said it would take six years or more. In 1991, about 40 percent had favored a national dialogue inclusive of government, opposition and exile; in 2000, nearly 52 percent did. Early in the 1990s, nearly 87 percent favored the embargo, while in 2000 that support had declined to 62.4 percent. In June 1993, almost 50 percent said U.S. companies should be allowed to sell medicines to Havana; by 2000, over 66 percent did. On the question of U.S. companies selling food to Cuba, just under 25 percent approved in 1993, a proportion that had more than doubled by 2000 to 56.1 percent. Unrestricted travel to the island elicited similar responses: in 1991, over 44 percent approved while nearly 53 percent did in 2000. Support for a U.S. invasion of Cuba, however, remained constant (63 percent versus 60 percent). On the embargo, poll results were contradictory; Cuban Miami seemed to favor it, even though an overwhelming majority thought it worked badly or not at all, and a majority favored allowing food and medicine sales as well as unrestricted travel, measures that would weaken the embargo. The embargo's only advantage seems to have been that it was the sole club available to brandish at Castro. Substantial majorities favored U.S. military action to overthrow the Castro government. However, Cuban Americans polled over the 1990s also expressed increasing support for a national dialogue, until support for it became a majority position in 2000.[88]

Might Mas Canosa have responded to these changes or, as so many of his exile compatriots, would he have clung to his support of the embargo even as he might have started to doubt its efficacy? At any rate, nearly two years after Mas Canosa's death, an immigration incident revealed the leadership void in the Cuban-American community. On June 29, 1999, the U.S. Coast Guard stopped a small boat carrying six Cubans in sight of North Miami Beach, that is, within U.S. territorial waters ("wet-foot") but not on U.S. soil ("dry-foot"). When the Cubans refused to turn around, the Coast Guard overpowered them with water and pepper spray. Television helicopters hovering over the scene filmed the confrontation, which ended with the men's detention. In Miami and Washington, Cuban-American leaders worked the media and the proper federal channels to try to set the Cubans free. In the meantime, Ramón Saúl Sánchez walked unto the MacArthur Causeway—one of the access points between Miami Beach and the mainland—and sat down. Hundreds of people joined him, effectively closing down the causeway and creating a traffic nightmare. The sit-in, Sánchez claimed, pressured federal authorities to release the men.[89] Had Mas Canosa been alive, he might have simply called the White House and perhaps achieved the same result.

Two other men had also been gaining influence as exile leaders since Mas Canosa's death: Jorge Mas Santos and José Basulto. None of the three—Sánchez, Mas Santos and Basulto—quite reached Mas Canosa's stature. Sánchez had Mas Canosa's common touch if not his money or his wealthy followers. Mas Santos inherited his father's organization and wealth, but he had yet to show leadership abilities. Basulto had saved thousands of *balseros* and put his life on the line against Castro, but he was less interested in a Miami power base than in looking south for Cubans on the island to rise up and overthrow the regime. All three men would soon be caught in the middle of the custody fight over a little boy.

Elián González in Miami

Nine days after the European and Latin-American dignitaries had returned home from the Havana Iberoamerican summit, five-year-old Elián González was found floating on an inner tube in waters near South Florida. The world's attention, which had been focused on the Cuban regime's human-rights violations and dictatorial ways since the Havana summit, suddenly shifted to the little boy's plight. Had Elián been a Mexican child found north of the Rio Grande, it is unlikely that the Immigration and Naturalization Service would have handed him over to his relatives in the United States. But he was Cuban, and so immigration officials released him to his Miami relatives in Little Havana. Elián's mother had perished in the passage; his father lived in Cuba. Though the mother had had full custody of the boy, upon her death, custody rights reverted to the father. But for seven months, a custody battle raged between the boy's U.S. family and his remaining parent. Almost immediately, Havana mounted a campaign to have Elián returned. Just as defiantly, Cuban Miami engaged in an effort to keep him in the United States. Throughout the ordeal, the Clinton administration and the Cuban government stayed in constant contact. In early April 2000, Elián's father, stepmother and infant half-brother traveled to the United States. On April 22, INS officials forcefully took the boy from his grand-uncle's Little Havana home and reunited him with his father in Maryland. Upon learning of the father–son reunion, Castro remarked: "Today is a day of truce, perhaps the only one in the course of these 41 years of confrontation with the United States."[90] Three months later Elián and his family returned to Cuba.

The saga over Elián brought unintended—and enduring—consequences. In Cuba, the custody battle afforded Castro an ideal opportunity to reignite the mobilizational campaigns that best suited his style of leadership. For once, many Cubans appeared to respond genuinely to official calls for demonstrations:

Elián's father elicited widespread sympathy in his quest to get his son back. By July, the Comandante had embarked on what he called the Battle of Ideas, an ideological campaign to reaffirm the revolution's spirit. From 2000 until his illness in 2006, Castro practically marginalized the government's institutions in favor of his hand-selected support group and prevented the Communist Party from calling its Congress. Instead, there were weekly gatherings in town after town, nightly roundtable discussions on television, loyalty pledges and newly created brigades of revolutionary vigilance. In the years after Elián, Castro required an almost nonstop performance from ordinary Cubans, which he then read as evidence that the revolution lived on. In November 2005, he gave an address at the University of Havana in which he cautioned against the revolution's self-destruction. As antidotes, he offered familiar remedies: upholding correct ideas, championing social justice, keeping markets at bay and never yielding to the United States on matters of principle.[91] Ironically, the mobilizational opportunities that Elián offered the elder Castro would complicate the succession for his brother. In 2006 Raúl Castro's first order of business would be to restore *la institucionalidad* and bring order to the chaos that his charismatic brother so often created.

In Miami, the struggle over Elián crystallized changes that were already underway toward a more politically diverse community. During the 1990s, the Cuban American National Foundation had been the strongest Cuban voice in Washington. Mas Canosa and other CANF leaders often met with White House officials on Cuba-related matters. Mas Canosa's death, however, had left the foundation without strong leadership while younger members grumbled in private about the resistance to modify the long-held hardline. In 1998, many Cuban-American Catholics had traveled to Cuba to support Pope John Paul II's historic visit, strengthening ties between island and Cuban-American Catholics that would continue to flourish. For Cuban Miami, which had almost monolithically clamored for Elián to stay in the United States, the episode proved to be a fiasco in almost every sense. U.S. and international public opinion stood fast against taking away parental rights for political reasons.[92] In not granting him U.S. citizenship or residency, as Senator Connie Mack (R-FL), and Representatives Ros-Lehtinen and Díaz-Balart had hoped, the Republican-controlled Congress sent a strong signal that, this time, the exile community could not win.

José Basulto, Jorge Mas Santos and Ramón Saúl Sánchez were all involved front and center in the Elián controversy. At first, Basulto expressed the opinion that the child should be returned to his father. Once Castro vociferously demanded the child's return, however, he quickly changed his mind: If Fidel wanted something, it couldn't be good. For Basulto and many others in Cuban Miami, anti-Castro politics overshadowed parental rights: If the boy were returned to Cuba, it would be tantamount to appeasing the Comandante. Basulto had, moreover, been swayed by the myth that Elián had been found clinging to an inner tube surrounded by dolphins. God, he believed, had sent the dolphins to protect Elián; how then could the boy be handed over to Castro? (Neither the two South Florida boaters who rescued the boy nor the Coast Guard officer who came to their help saw any dolphins nearby.) Basulto, who became an advisor to Elián's Miami relatives, proposed peaceful mass resistance to prevent the Clinton administration from sending the boy back to the island.[93] Since Mas Canosa's death, CANF had been somewhat rudderless. At first, CANF was but one of many groups who stood by Elián. By January 2000, Mas Santos had assumed an active, pivotal role. He was rarely absent when the boy's family or their attorneys gave a press conference. When Elián went to meet his grandmothers, who had traveled from Cuba to see him in Miami, Mas Santos drove him. And he took Elián's relatives to Washington in his private jet to lobby Members of Congress for residency or U.S. citizenship for the boy.[94] Still, the setting did not favor Mas Santos, the American-born scion of privilege who had no first-hand memories of what it was like to have fled Castro's Cuba. So Sánchez emerged as the leader of the Save Elián movement. Described as "part urban Thoreau, part Cuban Gandhi and part populist Caudillo," Ramoncito—as the crowds who gathered daily at the Miami relatives' home called Sánchez—was the voice and heart of working-class Cuban Miami, making sure that the anger at Castro, the Clinton administration and Attorney General Janet Reno did not lead to violence. In early April, Sánchez told the demonstrators:

> The moment of truth has arrived. Listen well. We are always going to be with you. And we are going to be forming [human] chains when we have to and going to jail when we have to. It is very important to know where we are going and that we have a direction. This is not chaos or a riot. This is about the dignity of a people who have decided that the civil rights of its children are respected, and who are tired of 41 years of oppression. But anyone who raises a stone or a fist in hatred is raising them against [Elián].[95]

The Elián saga let loose unstoppable emotions in Little Havana. Cuban Miami lost its bearings. Exiles demanded an act of Congress to make him an American citizen; they demanded that the case be decided in family court; they closed Cuban businesses for a day; they tied up traffic with demonstrations; they flew American flags upside down. Just when international momentum was building for human rights in Cuba, the custody battle put the exile community under the klieg lights, and the exiles' actions seldom drew sympathy outside South Florida. The media and public opinion all over the world had a field day.[96] Yet, the controversy would also lead to positive outcomes, such as the creation of the Cuba Study Group—an organization made up of Cuban-American businessmen supportive of a new U.S.–Cuba policy. It also resulted in a split within CANF that led hardliners to form the Cuban Liberty Council (CLC), and left CANF to take a more moderate line. Elián had proved cathartic for the exile community.

The ill-fated fight to keep Elián in the United States soured Cuban Miami's mood towards the Democratic Party. Some called it a new Bay of Pigs, recalling the time when Kennedy had failed to give the invasion the promised air cover. Others felt betrayed by the Clinton administration for sending the INS to forcibly remove Elián from Little Havana even as a committee of Cuban Americans was completing negotiations to hand the boy to the authorities.[97] Even though Democratic presidential candidate Al Gore supported the exiles during the Elián controversy, more than 80 percent of Cuban-American voters cast their ballots for George W. Bush in the 2000 elections. The marked increase from the 65 percent that Bob Dole had garnered in 1996 was a factor in the Republican's winning Florida. Without the butterfly ballot in Palm Beach County or the 96,000 Floridians who voted for Ralph Nader, Cuban Miami would not have mattered. But it did and not just on Election Day. Cuban Americans relentlessly supported the Bush campaign over the five weeks before the Supreme Court tendered the ruling that finally gave the Republican the presidency. Thus, once in the White House, Bush owed Cuban Americans a debt of gratitude, one that the community did not let him forget.

4

"WE NEED TO DE-AMERICANIZE THE PROBLEM OF CUBA"

On January 20, 2001, George W. Bush began his first term. An accidental president of sorts, he won the White House after losing the popular vote. Only two other presidents—Rutherford B. Hayes (1876) and Benjamin Harrison (1888)—had earned that distinction. Though neither Hayes nor Harrison left much of a mark, Bush's legacy will be long remembered. After September 11, 2001, the president found his calling as a wartime Commander-in-Chief and the American people rewarded him with sky-high approval. Later that month, Al Gore, the Democrat he had defeated in the 2000 election, delivered the keynote address at the Iowa Democratic Party's annual Jefferson-Jackson Day dinner in Des Moines. He shelved the hard-hitting speech he had been preparing and simply said: "George W. Bush is my commander in chief."[1] Across the Atlantic, Europeans seconded *Le Monde*'s oversized headline that shouted off the page: "We Are All Americans Now!" In the West, most applauded the war in Afghanistan where Al Qaeda had found safe harbor under the Taliban. At home and abroad, however, Bush's fortunes slowly began to turn with the decision to launch the Iraq War, the occupation's subsequent mismanagement and the revelations of prisoner abuse in Abu Ghraib. All the same the president won reelection outright, even if his victory margins in Electoral College and popular votes were the tightest since Woodrow Wilson's reelection in 1916.[2] Though down 10 percentage points from 2000, Cuban Americans gave him a hefty 72 percent of their votes. Hardliners in particular hoped Bush would find an Iraq-like resolve to rid the Western Hemisphere of its last dictator.

In Havana, Fidel Castro never looked back after Elián González. Castro was an old-fashioned Stalinist, especially regarding the economy. While the Soviet Union, China and Vietnam advanced market reforms in the mid-1980s, the Comandante had reversed the mild market socialism that Cuba had adopted a decade earlier. In the early 1990s, he had accepted limited market openings, but only because Cuba's economic collapse amid the demise of its erstwhile patrons had forced him to do it. Even more distasteful to Castro were the debates within the elite that advocated more thorough market reforms and minor political liberalization. The Elián saga gave Castro the opportunity to restore the mobilizational politics that suited him best. Venezuela, moreover, provided Cuba with an economic backing that relieved the urgency for further reforms. The Comandante and Chávez shared an aversion to markets and a worldview against U.S. imperialism that other populist leaders would soon brandish in Bolivia, Ecuador, Nicaragua and Honduras under Manuel Zelaya. Still, Castro failed to take full advantage of Bush's mounting unpopularity. In 2003, he unleashed a Black Spring of fury against peaceful opponents on the island that earned him widespread international rebuke.

Well before becoming a presidential candidate, Bush had strongly backed the embargo. Cuban Miami, moreover, had been an important player in the post-election drama that eventually led to his presidency. All the same, not until 2003 would the White House move to stiffen U.S. policy to the satisfaction of hardliners in Washington and Miami. During Bush's first two years, the United States and Cuba stayed on the tracks the Clinton administration had laid down in 1999–2000. By July 2006, however, when Fidel Castro fell ill and seemed on his deathbed, the United States and Cuba were communicating mostly through public recriminations. In January 2004, the Bush administration had suspended the migration talks that had been held every six months since 1995.

A Harder-line Policy in Slow Motion

It could have been an easy, quick U-turn: Reject Bill Clinton's under-the-radar reading of Helms–Burton; curtail student, research and other professional travel, and issue export licenses more sparingly. Hardline Cuban Americans in Miami would have been happy and felt rewarded for their role in the 2000 presidential election. But no such U-turn happened at first. In the late 1990s, the drive to reconsider U.S. policy toward Cuba had come from both sides of the aisle. A high-level Republican group of former secretaries of state and defense as well as prominent senators and representatives had called on Clinton to convene a bipartisan, blue-ribbon commission to review Cuba policy. When Clinton did not heed the luminaries' advice, Republicans loudly protested and bemoaned the missed opportunity. In addition, prominent Bush cabinet members—for example, Vice President Richard B. Cheney and Attorney General John D. Ashcroft—opposed embargos in general, as Wall Streeters usually do, or the Cuban embargo in particular, as Ashcroft did when he was a senator. Then again, the 2000 Trade Sanctions Reform and Export Enhancements Act (TSRA) stood to benefit agricultural exporters in the electorally competitive Midwest and the solid Republican South. There was Cuban Miami to consider, but it could wait: The president's and Florida Governor Jeb Bush's bona fides on Cuban matters were beyond reproach. Bush, moreover, toughened the rhetoric on Cuba from the start.

After Bush's inauguration, Washington and Havana kept the Clinton momentum going. In July 2001, the president waived Helm-Burton's Title III. Like Clinton, Bush went on to waive said title throughout his presidency. In contrast to their response to Clinton's waivers, hardline Republicans did not berate their own president, whom they knew to be a staunch embargo supporter. Lincoln Díaz-Balart issued a sober statement:

> During the first six months of his presidency, President Bush has intervened decisively to derail anti-Cuban embargo efforts in Congress. I support the implementation of all titles of Helms-Burton. Despite that, President Bush reached the conclusion that a trade war with Europe at the WTO over a single title of Helms-Burton at this time would dangerously strengthen the coalition of those seeking to eliminate the entire embargo.

Ileana Ros-Lehtinen called the president's waiver "regrettable," while taking note of his support for programs that "will help bring freedom to the Cuban people." Representative Bob Menéndez, a democrat, bristled: "On his first opportunity to show his true colors, the president was dishonest and weak. His bait and switch is insulting to Cuban Americans and will continue to hurt Cubans suffering under the Castro dictatorship."[3] Senator Helms said the difference between his rebuking Clinton and muting criticism of Bush lay in the latter's "very tough line" on Cuba in contrast to the former president's "fuzzy, wishy-washy posture."[4]

On Title III, President Bush had yielded to realism: Cuba was not important enough to declare an all-out trade war with the European Union. His decision followed Clinton's precedent and all but annulled Title III for the lifetime of Helms-Burton. The waiver overshadowed the fact that, a few days earlier, Bush had directed the Treasury Department's Office of Foreign Assets Control to enforce the embargo on travel and remittances more strictly and had promised increased support of pro-democracy activists. The president said:

> It is wrong to prop up a regime that routinely stifles all the freedoms that make us human. The United States stands opposed to such tyranny and will oppose any attempt to weaken sanctions against the Castro regime until it respects the basic human rights of its citizens, frees political prisoners, holds democratic free elections, and allows free speech.[5]

Shortly thereafter the House of Representatives voted 240–186 to lift the travel ban in clear defiance of the White House's call to enforce OFAC travel regulations without quarter. Sixty-seven Republicans—forty-four from farm states—joined 173 Democrats in voting Yea, a bit of an embarrassment for the White House.

In early 2002, the Cuban government signaled an interest in improving relations with the United States. The Bush administration had given Havana advance notice that it would be sending Taliban and Al Qaeda prisoners to the Guantánamo Naval Base; Cuba, in turn, issued a respectful acknowledgment.[6] At the sixth meeting of the U.S.–Cuba Sister Cities Association, held in Havana, Ricardo Alarcón told the audience that Cuba wanted "a civilized relationship" and was ready to talk even with the embargo in place. He added: "Cuba is willing to discuss, negotiate and forge a joint cooperation in areas such as the struggle against terrorism, narcotrafficking and human smuggling." More than 100 Americans from thirty-one cities and seventeen states participated in the meeting. In January alone, more than 2,000 Americans had traveled to Cuba, a number Alarcón termed unprecedented.[7] (In 2000, some 3,400 Americans had visited Cuba to explore business opportunities, a sevenfold increase since 1994.)[8] Between 1999 and early 2002, eight U.S. senators, eighteen U.S. representatives and the governor of Illinois had visited the island.[9] Cuba nonetheless looked askance at the Bush administration's close ties with Cuban Miami and the appointment of two hardline Cuban Americans to high-level positions in the administration.[10]

Over the course of 2002, the Bush administration began to set Cuba policy on a track of its own, a hard line spurred by ideological conviction and political expediency. While many Republicans favored a change in Cuba policy, Bush backed the Republican leadership's determination to block the efforts in Congress to loosen the embargo. His brother Jeb Bush, moreover, faced reelection to Florida's governorship and needed Cuban Miami's unstinting support. With domestic politics on his mind, presidential advisor Karl Rove met with anti-embargo Republican legislators who wanted the travel ban lifted and trade restrictions eased further. Rove read them the "riot act" and dismissed the notion that farm-state interests would ever best Florida politics on Cuba.[11] For now, farm states would have to make do with the Trade Sanctions and Reform Act.

During the Bush years, one-way trade from the United States to Cuba flourished. In January 1999, the Clinton administration had authorized licensed exports by American farmers and agribusiness to independent farmers and nongovernmental organizations on the island; in 1999–2000, food sales to Cuba hovered at a modest $11 million.[12] The TSRA had modified the embargo so that the Cuban government could make purchases, yet Castro and other Cuban officials vowed never to make any purchases under the strict TSRA conditions (they were particularly upset by the ban on financing by U.S. public and private institutions). After Hurricane Michelle battered Cuba in November 2001, however, the Comandante changed his mind. Declining the humanitarian aid offered by the Bush administration, he announced: "We are ready, just for this once, to acquire certain quantities of food and medicine from the United States, paying them in cash."[13] In December 2001, Havana put in a modest order for $4.3 million. The purchases continued, and between 2001 and 2008, U.S. agricultural exports to Cuba totaled just under $2.6 billion.[14] In February 2005, the Bush administration imposed a new restriction by requiring Havana to pay for purchases before the vessels bearing the cargo departed for Cuba.[15] At times, farm groups and agribusiness lobbied Congress to soften the TSRA restrictions on trade with Cuba, which were harsher than those on trade with Iran, Libya, North Korea and Sudan. Their efforts came to naught, blocked by the Republican leadership's unyielding opposition and the president's veto threat.[16] Havana's support of terrorism, administration officials contended, merited the iron-fisted restrictions. Even so, since 2003, the United States has been Havana's first supplier of farm products.[17] Cuba, in turn, ranked twenty-fourth out of 212 markets for American agro-exports.[18]

Whatever the continuities from Clinton to Bush on Cuba policy, there was no gainsaying the political and ideological sea change that the Bush administration represented. During the 1990s, neoconservative Republicans had issued a critique of George H.W. Bush's and, especially, Clinton's foreign policy. They promulgated a Ronald Reagan-like appreciation of moral clarity and military might, though they did so without the Gipper's sense of realism. Before September 11, 2001, the realists and neoconservatives competed for the president's attention. Afterwards, neoconservatives brought most of the realists to their side and held sway for the remainder of Bush's first term.[19] Throughout the Bush presidency, hardline Cuban Miami also had a direct line to the Oval Office. If Bush I and the Senate Republicans in the late 1990s had no longer considered Cuba a threat, hardliners in Washington and Miami now argued to the contrary. Havana posed a national-security threat, they said, whether it take the form of unleashing another wave of uncontrolled migration, supporting terrorism, developing biological warfare capabilities or placing spies in the United States. On September 20, 2001, the FBI arrested Ana Belén Montes—an analyst at the Defense Intelligence Agency—for being a Cuban agent. For seventeen years, Montes had delivered sensitive information to Havana, perhaps the highest publicly known breach of U.S. national security by Cuba's intelligence services. In October 2002, she received a twenty-five-year sentence.[20] In 1998, the FBI arrested ten men—dubbed the Wasp Network by Cuban intelligence—on charges of spying in South Florida. Havana claims their charge was to prevent exile terrorism. Five of the men—known in Cuba as the Five Heroes—were convicted in 2001; the other five turned state's evidence.[21] Other known cases of American citizens working with Cuban intelligence included a U.S. immigration official, a Florida International University professor and his wife, and a former State Department official and his wife.[22]

Between May 12 and 17 of 2002, former President Jimmy Carter traveled to Cuba. The private trip had been in the works since the mid-1990s, but

Carter had never received the Clinton White House's blessing, which made Bush's consent all the more significant. A few days before Carter's arrival in Havana, Oswaldo Payá Sardiñas and other dissidents had presented the National Assembly with a petition signed by 11,000 Cubans. Known as the Varela Project, the petition called for a referendum on political liberties, entrepreneurial rights, free elections and the release of political prisoners. Under the Cuban Constitution's Article 88, citizens can introduce a petition for the assembly's consideration if it bears at least 10,000 valid signatures. Once in Cuba, Carter met with Payá and other opposition figures. In his address at the University of Havana, which was broadcast live, Carter called on the U.S. Congress to lift the travel ban, open trade and repeal the embargo. But he added: "These restraints are not the source of Cuba's economic problems." Neither did he mince words on human rights, asking Cuba "to meet universally accepted standards in civil liberties, permit the International Red Cross to visit prisons and to receive the U.N. Human Rights Commissioner." Carter praised the Cuban Constitution for Article 88 and the Varela Project for making use of it. "When Cubans exercise this freedom to change laws peacefully by a direct vote, the world will see that Cubans, and not foreigners, will decide the future of this country," Carter noted.[23]

In the meantime, the Bush administration finished its review of Cuba policy. On May 20, 2002, the 100th anniversary of Cuban independence, the president announced an Initiative for a New Cuba.[24] It proposed easing restrictions on humanitarian and entrepreneurial assistance to independent groups, offering U.S. scholarships to students and professionals committed to building autonomous institutions, modernizing Radio and TV Martí, and working with world leaders to empower Cuban civil society. Noticeably absent were tighter restrictions on family travel and remittances, both of which remained on the same terms as in the late 1990s: once-a-year family visits and an annual $1200 limit on remittances. Most noteworthy were Bush's comments on Cuba's upcoming round of Popular Power elections:

> If Cuba's government takes all the necessary steps to ensure that the 2003 elections are certifiably free and fair and if Cuba also begins to adopt meaningful market-based reforms, then—and only then—I will work with the United States Congress to ease the ban on trade and travel between our two countries.

While recognizing that "freedom sometimes grows step by step," Bush asked Havana to invite "objective outside observers" to certify the election. Though his tone and most of his remarks hewed to Helms-Burton, his mention of the 2003 elections tacitly accepted the Cuban Constitution as a starting point for change. His offer of "a meaningful American response" to "meaningful reform on Cuba's part," moreover, echoed the Cuban Democracy Act's "carefully calibrated steps," and an approach that Secretary of State Warren Christopher had often proposed in the first Clinton administration. A strict reading of Helms-Burton would not allow for the recognition of the Cuban Constitution as a legitimate document, nor would it permit a step-by-step strategy for U.S.–Cuba relations, particularly with Fidel or Raúl Castro still in charge. Perhaps Carter's visit had persuaded Bush to appreciate the potential in the Varela Project and the Cuban Constitution if Havana ever demonstrated the political will to change.[25]

Bush's May 20 speech was immediately rebuffed by hardcore sectors in the administration and Cuban Miami. Neoconservatives had already tried to derail Carter's visit. In early May, John Bolton, undersecretary of state for arms control, had stated: "The United States believes that Cuba has at least a limited offensive biological warfare research and development effort. Cuba has provided dual-use biotechnology to other rogue states."[26] Carter labeled the undersecretary's accusations, issued six days before his departure for Havana, "a suspicious coincidence." In his briefings by U.S. intelligence, the former president had been assured that Cuba was not involved in terrorist or biological-warfare activities.[27] On May 13, Secretary of State Colin L. Powell distanced himself from Bolton: "We do believe Cuba has a biological offensive research capability. We didn't say it actually had some weapons."[28] After the intelligence fiasco in Iraq, the Bush administration had scaled back claims on the dangers allegedly posed by Cuba and, at the State Department's behest, the intelligence community revised earlier assessments. While expressing concern that Cuba "has the technical capability to pursue some aspects of an offensive biological weapons program," it added: "it is unclear whether it has an active, offensive biological weapons effort under way."[29] (Cuba does have a major medical and biotechnology program and sells some of its products to other countries.)

Only a few months later, by the end of 2002, Bush's Initiative for a New Cuba had shed most pretense of moderation. The president's May 20 speech with the heterodox passages implicitly accepting the Cuban Constitution had long been forgotten. In early 2003, James Cason, chief of the U.S. Interests Section in Havana, visited opposition groups throughout the island, offered journalism workshops at his home and in general increased contacts with dissidents, since Washington wanted to gauge the state of independent civil society in order to structure a more effective aid program. Not surprisingly, Havana labeled his actions "repeated provocations." As a matter of course, diplomats everywhere establish communication with representatives from the government, the opposition and civil society. The Cuban government, however, does not accept universal standards of civil liberties and, therefore, takes offense at overtures toward what it calls *grupúsculos* (minuscule groups), which it dismisses as mercenaries beholden to the United States.

In mid-March, Castro responded by arresting seventy-five peaceful opponents who were quickly convicted and sentenced to prison terms ranging from six to twenty-eight years. On April 2, the government intercepted three men who had hijacked a fifty-passenger ferry to cross the Florida Straits. Tried and convicted of terrorism, the men were executed on April 11, 2003. Even though it called Cuba's actions "brutal," the administration still issued new rules to allow Cuban Americans visiting relatives to carry up to $3,000 when visiting relatives on the island. After the worst Cuban crackdown in years, Bush looked to extend contact and increase cash flow to all but senior-level Cuban Communist Party and government officials.[30] Underlying the White House's response was the president's determination to support independent civil society more forcefully than ever before.[31] Two years later, Cason lent his support to the Assembly to Promote Civil Society, an unusual closeness between the U.S. Interests Section and an opposition group. The assembly was an umbrella of dissident organizations led by Martha Beatriz Roque, one of the seventy-five activists arrested during the Black Spring, who had been released from prison in July 2004 for health reasons. On May 20–21, 2005, the Assembly convened 200 Cuban delegates plus a smattering of Western diplomats and foreign media. Cason attended the meeting and took along a videotaped message from President Bush. "We are working for the day of Cuban freedom," Bush told the delegates. "We are confident that Cuba *será libre pronto*." Some delegates shouted "*¡Viva Bush!*"[32]

The political crackdown and the hijackers' swift execution brought Cuba a wave of international condemnation, including sanctions from the European Union.[33] Finally Cuban Miami and world public opinion agreed: Havana's actions were inexcusable. Still, the Iraq War, which had started on March 19, 2003 elicited mixed reactions from Cuban Americans. While strongly behind the president, many asked, Why only Iraq? And migration matters stirred their concern with some of Bush's decisions on Cuba. In July, two more boats were hijacked. One hijacking ended violently, with three fatalities. The other concluded when the U.S. Coast Guard picked up twelve hijackers, whom Washington agreed to return on the condition that Havana punish them with prison, not execution. Before July was out, the Coast Guard intercepted another twelve Cubans "driving" a retrofitted 1951 Chevy truck in the Florida Straits; the men were sent back to Cuba and their ingenious contraption destroyed. In mid-August, thirteen state legislators from South Florida—ten Cuban Americans—wrote Bush a letter expressing "great disappointment and outrage" and noting the damage already inflicted on "the historic and intense support from Cuban American voters for Republican federal candidates, including yourself."[34]

The White House at last understood that Cuban Miami's patience was wearing thin. On October 10, 2003, the president announced the creation of a Commission for Assistance to a Free Cuba co-chaired by Secretary of State Powell and Secretary of Housing and Urban Development Mel Martínez. Over several months, the commission mobilized 100 federal employees in seventeen agencies. An administration official underscored its purpose: "There will be change in Cuba, and it will come under George Bush!"[35] In May 2004, the commission issued its "Report to the President," a 423-page document that called for the "expeditious end of the Castro dictatorship" without the customary adjective "peaceful."[36] The report reads like an occupation manual. Some recommendations for a hypothetical post-Castro government included disbanding Cuba's security institutions and prosecuting former regime officials, the type of measures that would almost certainly prompt violence and social unrest. In fact, at the time the report was published, the U.S. occupation of Iraq was already mired in violence, in part, the result of the precipitous disbanding of the Iraqi Army. The commission's staff wrote as if someone other than the people of Cuba would determine the island's future. The report's obsessive guidance on technical, economic, political and social issues largely ignored the island's reservoir of human capital—talented individuals whose potential contribution the report never acknowledged.

The Bush administration also created an office in the State Department to promote and oversee a Cuban transition. In July 2006, Secretary of State Condoleezza Rice and Secretary of Commerce Carlos Gutiérrez issued a ninety-three-page sequel report on behalf of the Commission for Assistance to a Free Cuba.[37] Many opponents of the Castro regime had chafed at the notion of direct U.S. involvement in a transition in Cuba. After meeting with Powell in early 2003, for example, Oswaldo Payá, the leader of the Varela Project, had said: "We need to de-Americanize the problem of Cuba."[38] Like Bush's May 20, 2002 speech, Payá's sound advice vanished into thin air. Be that as it may, the United States needed a plan to support a Cuba in transition. In 1997 the Clinton administration had issued a nineteen-page report on how the United States would back Cuba's democratic transition once it started. Though largely forgotten, the Clinton-era effort offers a more appropriate template than the reports submitted to President Bush.[39] In addition, the Bush administration's attempts to speed up a transition were particularly heavy-handed. On June 16, 2004, the administration announced draconian restrictions on family travel and remittances, disposing of the more liberal policies adopted after the Black Spring of 2003.[40] As a result, family visits to the island by Cuban Americans—now defined as visits to grandparents, parents, spouses, siblings, children and grandchildren only—were limited to once every three years from the last trip taken prior to the new regulations. Thus an individual who visited his parents in Matanzas in December 2003 could not travel again until December 2006. Rarely if at all did the administration grant waivers for emergencies such as the imminent death of a parent or sibling on the island. Although the amount of money Cuban Americans could send to the island remained the same ($300 per quarter per household), their remittances were now limited to direct-line kin. Under the new guidelines, aunts, uncles, cousins, nieces and nephews were not considered family worthy of visiting or helping. A niece concerned about her ninety-six-year-old aunt could neither travel to Cuba to visit her nor send her money. Like other Latin Americans, most Cubans—in the diaspora and on the island—cherish their extended families.

The Regime Sails on

By the end of the 1990s, the Cuban leadership had achieved a normalcy that deflated expectations of its quick demise. With the Comandante at the helm, the Communist Party could not fully function as the Soviet and Eastern European parties had, that is, providing the bureaucracy through which decision-making took place. Yet, Castro grasped that he needed the PCC—not just the military and state security—to navigate the uncertain seas of the post-Cold War years. Had Havana embraced bold market reforms, Cuban leaders would have had to change their governance blueprint. Castro, of course, stood in the way of the first and, therefore, there was little change in the country's politics. Rather than focusing on improving the material well-being of ordinary citizens as the Chinese and the Vietnamese had done, the PCC acquiesced to the Comandante's insistence on mass mobilizations and the primacy of revolutionary values and national sovereignty.

While these mass mobilizations were low key at first, everything changed with the Elián González saga. Castro could not resist the opportunity to mobilize millions to wave flags and demand the little boy's return. In July 2000 he proclaimed a battle of ideas to save the revolution, which unleashed daily television roundtables and weekly open forums in cities and towns throughout the island. There were frequent mass demonstrations on behalf of the five WASP-network spies—dubbed the *cinco héroes*, or the five heroes—who had been arrested in 1998 and eventually convicted in 2001. Revolutionary vigilance brigades went to work everywhere, and workers were made to take loyalty oaths in factories, hospitals, schools, agricultural cooperatives and government offices. In short, the frenzied trappings of Castro's leadership style tipped the precarious balance between the Comandante and the PCC against the party. Though its statutes do not specify a time frame between congresses, the PCC had been holding them every five or six years since 1975. By that precedent, the next congress should have been called in 2002 or 2003, but Castro refused, perhaps due to his adamantine rejection of market reforms. Beginning in 2003, a partial economic recentralization had met some resistance among elite and rank-and-file sectors. Calling a congress could have exposed these potential fissures, so it was better for the Comandante to keep all discussion at bay. Unwittingly or not, he was making life harder for his successors than if he had fostered his symbiosis with the PCC. (Before he was sidelined by ill health in 2006, Castro had given his less-than-equal cohorts three scares: in 1997 when he disappeared from the public eye for nearly five months, in 2001 when he fainted at a weekly open forum in El Cotorro and in 2004 when he suffered multiple fractures after falling in Santa Clara.[41] After the maladies that kept him out of the limelight in

1997, Castro and his brother Raúl likely drew up a succession roadmap in earnest.)

In 2002, the confluence of Carter's visit and Payá's Varela Project piqued Castro intensely. Payá had read the Constitution's Article 88 as a means to change the regime's basic pillars: unchecked state power, imprisonment of peaceful opponents, a command economy and politically uncompetitive elections. Submitted to the National Assembly days before Carter's arrival, the Varela Project petitioned a referendum on five questions: whether or not to allow freedom of expression, freedom of association, an amnesty for prisoners of conscience, entrepreneurial rights and electoral-law reform, all of which struck at the regime's heart. Carter had then held up the Varela petition as a laudable example of ordinary Cubans seeking peaceful change under the Constitution. In response, in June 2002, hundreds of marches were summoned island-wide, millions of citizens signed a petition for amending the Constitution to safeguard the revolution forever, and the National Assembly declared socialism an irrevocable fixture of Cuban politics in a live, three-day television broadcast.[42] In November 2002 the assembly denied the Varela Project's petition.[43]

Some 11,000 signatures freely given in a society without freedom, and their endorsement by a former American president so threatened the regime that the Comandante felt compelled to stage an unparalleled, over-the-top response. Never before had there been such dissonance between official Cuba and ordinary Cubans. When Castro asked citizens to sign a petition to declare socialism irrevocable, most people did so perfunctorily, as just another public performance that the regime demanded. Still, the campaign in support of the revolution embodied Castro's leadership and praetorian governance. A visionary, he generally prized the callings of history over the mundane needs of ordinary Cubans.

In February 2003, Castro visited China. While in Beijing, he told Li Peng, then chairman of the National People's Congress:

> I can't really be sure just now what kind of China I am visiting. The first time [in 1995] I visited your country appeared one way and now when I visit it appears another way. You can say that every so often your country undergoes great changes.[44]

By all accounts, Castro went home admiring Chinese leaders for their political tenacity but determined that Cuba not undergo "great changes." In a speech delivered at the University of Havana in November 2005, Castro warned his successors: If revolutionaries forsake correct ideas, betray social justice, embrace markets and lower their guard against U.S. imperialism, then and only then would the revolution perish. "We have a different type of nuclear weapon," Castro said then. "It's our ideas. We possess a weapon as powerful as nuclear power and it is the immense justice for which we are struggling. Our nuclear weapon is the invincible power of moral weapons."[45] In his waning years, the

Comandante remained true to his lifelong convictions. In June 1960, when the revolution shone bright in the eyes of most ordinary Cubans, he had said:

> The revolution shows that ideals are more powerful than gold! If gold were more powerful than ideals, those large foreign interests would have swept us off the map. If gold had more power than ideals, our *patria* would be lost because our enemies have plenty of gold to buy *conciencia* and yet all our enemies' gold is not enough to buy the *conciencia* of a revolutionary. Cubans of dignity have conquered their revolutionary *conciencia*. They will not trade their revolution, their *patria* for gold.[46]

The campaign to make socialism irrevocable and the November 2005 speech are the Comandante's political testament.

The Black Spring of 2003 earned Havana a surprisingly intense international rebuke. The United States had just launched the invasion of Iraq when seventy-five pro-democracy activists were rounded up by state-security officers island-wide. Nearly half were from the Varela Project in the provinces. All received harsh sentences—from six to twenty-eight years—for daring to exercise their conscience in public. Castro had reportedly considered closing down the U.S. Interests Section in Havana, which would have meant that Cuba's in Washington would suffer the same fate, but decided on the dragnet instead. Calling Cason "a bizarre official" and accusing him of fomenting "internal counterrevolution," Havana further restricted the movements of American diplomats.[47] Though the Iraq war held the world's attention, Havana's repressive wave—which also included the summary trial and execution of three hijackers—did not go unnoticed.

In April, the European Commission deferred discussion on Cuba's joining the Cotonou Convention, a cooperation agreement with the Africa, Caribbean and Pacific group.[48] Two months later, the European Union announced diplomatic sanctions that restricted high-ranking official visits and reduced EU participation in cultural events. EU representatives also began inviting dissidents to embassy receptions on national holidays.[49] In Washington, every member of the board of directors of the Cuba Policy Foundation—a group of prominent business leaders and former U.S. government officials that had spent $1 million since 2001 to bridge U.S.–Cuba differences—resigned in protest.[50] Leftist intellectuals such as the Portuguese Nobel laureate José Saramago and the Uruguayan writer Eduardo Galeano deplored Havana's actions. The Cultural Platform against the War, which represented Spanish filmmakers and actors opposed to the Iraq War, similarly upbraided Havana.[51] While the major newspapers in Latin America censured the executions and arrests, the region's governments had more subdued responses.[52] The Catholic Bishops' Conference of Cuba lamented the deaths by firing squad of the three hijackers and the long prison terms imposed on the dissidents.[53] The Vatican issued an unusually harsh statement against Castro saying that he was "filling the Gulag with bodies," while conveying Pope John Paul II's disheartenment over the arrests and executions.[54]

As usual, Castro put the onus for his actions on the United States. In late April 2003, he made a long presentation on the nightly television roundtable on Cason's outreach to pro-democracy activists. His exposition is useful in understanding official Cuba's mind-set at the time. The Comandante argued that Cason's principal objective was to hasten the transition to a democratic Cuba. He offered as proof the many encounters the U.S. Interests Section chief had held with numerous activists in Havana and the provinces. With a series of hijackings between August 2002 and April 2003 as backdrop, Cason's outreach, Castro said, was a clear indication that the Bush administration, Assistant Secretary of State for Western Hemisphere Affairs Otto Reich and the Miami mafia were striving to destabilize the revolutionary government and create the conditions for a U.S. military intervention to "liquidate the revolution."[55] The United States, in short, sought to impose a "fascist world order" through U.S. military might. Castro also brought to bear the ill treatment of Cuba's "five heroes" in American prisons, the hotel bombings in the late 1990s, the Cuban Adjustment Act, NATO's war in Kosovo, the Iraq War and the suppression of African-American votes in the 2000 presidential election. Such were the official justifications for the Black Spring of 2003, actions taken to stave off U.S. aggression and defend Cuban national sovereignty, which, in Castro's view, trumped all other considerations. His government, Castro claimed, had averted a migration crisis and war with the United States, saving an untold number of lives.[56] Might Castro have been pondering a new mass exodus even though Helms-Burton's Title I warns that "any further political manipulation of the desire of Cubans to escape that results in mass migration to the United States will be considered an act of aggression"?

International rebuke of Havana did not result in the release of the seventy-five activists, nor did it lead the regime to accept human rights without adjectives, that is, as the UN Universal Declaration defined them: human rights are inseparable from our common humanity whatever our political views or differences by race, ethnicity, religion or gender. From the start, the European Union's sanctions proved ineffective. Inviting pro-democracy activists to embassy receptions, which was tantamount to putting them on equal footing with Cuban officials, most irritated the regime. The foreign ministry's response came quickly: Embassies that invited the activists would be barred from sending their diplomats to official functions and would have to conduct all communication with the Cuban government via postal mail, European embassies would have no access to government ministries and Cuban officials would not set foot on any European embassy. A European diplomat from one of the offending embassies said:

> This is ridiculous. If we have no communication with the authorities, if Cuban officials don't come to our receptions and dinners, if there are no

official European visits and we meet only with journalists, diplomats and dissidents, what are we doing here?

Such was the Crisis of the Hors D'Oeuvres with the European Union.[57] In March 2004, the Spanish Socialist Workers' Party (PSOE) won the election, José Luis Rodríguez Zapatero became prime minister of Spain, and the PSOE government almost immediately began to nudge the EU from the 2003 sanctions on Cuba. By April 2005, Havana had reestablished official contacts with the Spanish and eight other EU embassies. Tensions did not dissipate altogether, though, as EU countries continued to vote against Cuba in the old UN Commission on Human Rights.

In April 2003, the UNCHR met in Geneva and considered a resolution on Cuba as it had every spring for twenty-five years. Costa Rica proposed a text condemning the Black Spring crackdown, demanding the release of the seventy-five activists and calling on Havana to allow a UN human-rights monitor to visit the island. Cuba's UNCHR ambassador reacted bluntly:

> Our position is clear: We will not accept even a comma in that resolution should it be adopted. We will not accept the monitoring of Cuba. It's unjust; it's immoral. We will never permit a visit from an inspector.[58]

Cuba then offered a counterproposal lambasting the United States for the embargo and for allowing terrorists to launch attacks against the island from its territory. Neither proposal made it into the final resolution, which soft-balled the issue by simply asking Cuba to accept a visit by a UN human-rights monitor. Cuban Foreign Minister Felipe Pérez Roque boasted that the final resolution did not condemn Cuba for the crackdown and consequently was a "resonant victory." Still, he said his government would not comply with the UNCHR request.[59] Two weeks later, Cuba was reelected to the UNCHR without a single Latin-American government objecting.[60] In 2006, a new UN Human Rights Council (UNHRC) took the place of the UNCHR. Cuba was elected as a founding member, serving for a three-year term through 2009. In principle, the UNHRC offered a less politicized process whereby all UN member states were to be evaluated and therefore Cuba would not be singled out as it had been in the UNCHR. Procedures, moreover, required all members to cooperate with the UNHRC when their turn came up. Cuba's evaluation was set for February 2009.

Cuban Miami in the New Century

In early 2001, Michael Greene, president of the National Academy of Recording Arts and Sciences (NARAS), received a letter signed by South Florida mayors Alex Penelas of Miami-Dade, Joe Carollo of Miami and Neisen Kasdin of Miami Beach, plus Cuban American National Foundation chairman Jorge Mas Santos and William Talbert representing the Greater Miami Convention & Vistors Bureau. The men made a pitch for Miami's American Airlines Arena as the place to hold the second Latin Grammy Awards.[61] In 2000, South Florida had lost out on the inaugural ceremony: An ordinance banned Miami-Dade County from doing business with companies or people having commercial ties with Havana.[62] Since Cuban artists could be nominated and therefore might attend the awards ceremony, Miami could not contend as the Latin Grammy host city. In June 2000, however, the U.S. Supreme Court issued a decision that effectively invalidated the Miami-Dade ordinance when it struck down a Massachusetts statute that denied state contracts to companies that did business with Burma. In the court's unanimous decision, Justice David H. Souter wrote: "The state act undermines the president's capacity in this instance for effective diplomacy."[63] The ruling voided all state and local government measures that infringed upon the executive branch's foreign-policy prerogative. With Miami-Dade's ordinance thus annulled, NARAS made plans to bring the 2001 Latin Grammys to Miami.

Hardline Cuban exiles, however, scuttled those plans. They sought a permit from the City of Miami to protest the ceremony. The city granted it, but limited the protestors to a "safety zone" far from where the attendees would step off their limousines and walk the red-carpeted path into the arena. The American Civil Liberties Union, which had actively defended the right of Cuban artists to perform in Miami, joined the exiles in appealing to City Hall for closer access, and Mayor Carollo granted it. In August, the National Academy pulled out and returned the show to Los Angeles. In explaining the move, Greene cited the security of 10,000 attendees: "Having to run that gauntlet is demeaning at best and dangerous at worst."[64] South Florida's economy lost an anticipated $35 million in revenues and the city an opportunity to burnish its image. In 2003, the Latin Grammys were held in Miami without incidents. While Cuban artists never received their U.S. visas, the Latin Academy of Recording Arts and Sciences gave awards to Cuban singer Ibrahim Ferrer of Buena Vista Social Club, to the Paris-based rap group Orishas, who frequently performs on the island, and to expatriate saxophonist Paquito d'Rivera.[65] Music producer Emilio Stefan said:

> It's a victory for the city. My heart is always divided in two: One part feels the pain of my country and my people and the other half refuses to do what Castro does. I have to support freedom of expression in all its manifestations.[66]

The fracas over the Grammys exposed the tensions within the CANF. Mas Santos's signature on the NARAS letter raised quite a few eyebrows among hardliners in CANF and in Cuban Miami at large. Having presented an ironclad front for so long, CANF now showed itself vulnerable to dissension. Many veterans chafed under the young men who had assumed positions of leadership, Mas Santos and Joe García, CANF's newly appointed executive director. Banker and CANF elder Luis J. Botifoll (1908–2003), then ninety-two, said about the Grammys: "I don't give a damn if they come or not. But I don't promote them to come. The foundation was created to liberate Cuba, not to promote business in Miami." Mas Santos, however, was promoting something else: "If the Grammys are held in Los Angeles or New York, this community cannot show itself as the bastion of freedom of expression that it is." Earlier, Mas Santos had delivered an address in Washington in which he discussed the possibility of creating a micro-loan program to promote already existing independent projects in Cuba, such as soup kitchens, restaurants, day-care centers and church-run clinics. His audience had been the Inter-American Dialogue, long an advocate for a change in U.S. policy toward Cuba. Though CANF had been sending aid to dissidents and the families of political prisoners since 1998, some in the old guard balked at the micro-loan proposal even if it had little chance of becoming reality due to Havana's lack of cooperation. "Theoretically, it looks great. But any equipment would fall into the hands of the government," said Diego Suárez, a heavy-machinery industrialist and part of Mas Canosa's inner circle. Botifoll just said: "We don't support making loans to Castro."[67]

In July 2001, the foundation had reelected Mas Santos chairman at its annual meeting. Shortly thereafter nearly two dozen board members resigned. After Elián González's custody case, some within CANF had pressed for rethinking their strategy. Lombardo Pérez Sr., an auto dealer, pointed out that the boy's saga had turned American public opinion against the exiles: "The Cuban community suffered greatly; a lot of people were ready to bury us."[68] Thus, the Latin Grammys was to be a showcase for Cuban Miami's tolerance of island artists performing in its midst. But more conservative directors shunned all hint of compromise and cringed at the idea of tolerance with Fidel or Raúl Castro. In their view, Cuban artists represented the dictatorship. Supporting the Varela Project was likewise anathema to the hardliners because it legitimized the Cuban Constitution and used it as stepping-stone for change. The appointment of García, a Democrat, as CANF's executive director had also rankled with the old guard. While the foundation had made campaign contributions across the aisle, loyal Republicans well outnumbered Democrats in its ranks. Still, most CANF members sided with the new proposals, while the die-hard Republicans among them resigned. There was no denying the consequences of the generational change embodied by Mas Santos and García. Both had been born in Miami and were truly hyphenated in their outlook. To CANF breakaways, neither was Cuban nor knowledgeable enough to mark CANF's direction. Mas Santos and García, however, stressed the urgency of reaching other Cuban Americans like themselves and most of CANF's veterans took their side. Botifoll, who stayed with CANF until his death, noted: "We should all feel proud of this new generation, most of whom haven't been to Cuba, weren't born in Cuba and feel as we feel. I'm sorry this [the split] has occurred but we have to pass the torch."[69] In October, claiming the mantle of Mas Canosa's legacy, a group of CANF breakaways founded the Cuban Liberty Council. While the CLC remained within the hardliners' fold, CANF moved on to join the moderates' rank in Cuban Miami.

In the early 2000s, two organizations, the Cuba Study Group and the Cuba Democracy Advocates, came into being. Founded by wealthy businessmen, they stand on opposite sides of the exile divide.[70] The Cuba Democracy Advocates took up the old CANF mission: lobbying Washington to keep or harden the embargo and the travel ban. Its founders, Madrid-based magnate Leopoldo Fernández-Pujals and Miami auto-dealer Gus Machado, were set on reaffirming the hardline profile of the Cuban-American community and rejected the Varela Project.[71] Loosely connected with the Cuba Democracy Advocates is the U.S. Cuba Democracy Political Action Committee, which has raised about $2.4 million since 2004. "We simply believe economic engagement with the Cuban dictatorship should be conditioned on the release of political prisoners and respect for the fundamental human rights of the Cuban people," said Mauricio Claver-Carone, executive director of Cuba Democracy Advocates and a U.S.–Cuba PAC director.[72]

The Cuban Study Group (CSG) set out to rehabilitate the exile community's image, which had suffered during the out-of-kilter Elián months. "Exiles can't appear like barbarians at the gate waiting to attack," said its co-chair, Carlos Saladrigas. "We have always concentrated on urgency but forgotten that there are two other sides of change: a message of reconciliation and increasing the rewards of change." Polls commissioned by the CSG among the Cuban-American community revealed a more open-minded, reasonable and diverse spectrum of opinion than usually assumed. The CSG is committed to peaceful change spurred by Cubans on the island and has wholeheartedly supported the Varela Project. The group maintains an active network of congressional, business, academic, international and community contacts on behalf of changing U.S. policy to promote regular contacts between Americans and Cubans on the island.[73] Unwavering anti-Castro militants have dismissed the group's members as regime appeasers, looking askance at its leaders, the successful businessmen who came so late to *la lucha*, the struggle for a free Cuba. An incident in early 2003 further soured hardliners towards the Cuba Study Group. On March 29, militant Cuban Miami called a rally against Castro as a way to show the community's unity in its determination to continue *la lucha*, despite polls that indicated otherwise.[74] Miami police estimated the crowd that marched in Little Havana at 40,000; some enthusiasts put the number twice as high. The Cuba Study Group hired a firm from Santa Clara, California, which specializes in the use of aerial photographs to count anything from the number of trees in orchards and fish in rivers to the number of people in crowds. The company said the actual number of demonstrators in Calle Ocho on March 29 had been closer to 5,400.[75] What started out as an affirmation of the struggle against Castro proved to be an embarrassment for hardline Cuban Miami.

In 2003, the Cuban American National Foundation publicly distanced itself from the Bush administration and, especially, from Representative Lincoln Díaz-Balart. In February Jorge Mas Santos underscored the need for dialogue among all Cubans in order to jointly find a solution to Cuba's problems.

> Cuba and its destiny belong to all Cubans with the will to be free, to take off existing chains, and to walk towards the light. We need to walk down that road together, those who are in Cuba and those abroad, young and old people, the intransigent and the benevolent. Let's not be afraid of talking to each other, of a conversation among Cubans, of looking for the road to peace, freedom, and progress together.[76]

Though his offer did not include Fidel and Raúl Castro, Mas Santos committed CANF to a national dialogue, something that ran counter to all that hardline Cuban Miami represented. The rift, however, did not surface until the Bush administration's decision in July to repatriate a dozen Cubans who had hijacked a boat to reach Florida. The White House and Havana had come to an agreement: If the United States returned the men, Cuba would spare their lives and limit their prison sentences to less than ten years. Though the three South Florida Cuban-American representatives—Díaz-Balart, his brother Mario, who had been elected in 2002, and Ileana Ros-Lehtinen—had also slammed the administration, CANF broke with the White House over the repatriation. Mas Santos warned: "This will cost them. They can't count on the support of our community if they don't fulfill their promises. We will not give unconditional support to a political party or to any individuals."[77] CANF executive director Joe García and Lincoln Díaz-Balart exchanged fusillades. García said: "The repatriation shows that this administration has lied to us. It's been three years of lies, and it shows even more the impotence of our Republican representatives before this Republican administration." Díaz-Balart shot back:

> What's sad is that at a time when Cuban-American representatives are fighting so forcefully to maintain the only measures in the world that punish the dictatorship, this group is so intent on attacking us and on seeking a dialogue with the dictatorship.[78]

In fits and starts, CANF had reached a point of no return. In its heyday, the foundation embodied an intransigence against the Castro regime that suited Cuban Miami well. Mas Canosa's genius had been to channel exile energies away from terrorism and into the political arena. Often, however, the chairman had shown little patience or tolerance with those who disagreed with him. By wooing the Latin Grammys, Mas Santos sought to showcase Cuban Miami as a "bastion of freedom of expression," an implicit admission of an uncivil past. In 2002 CANF board member Domingo Moreira noted the following about the climate that had long prevailed in Miami:

> For too many years, many of us kept quiet when the motives of our fellow citizens were questioned. To those who suffered because of it, I ask for forgiveness for not having spoken out more forcefully. From now on, I'll refuse to play that game, and will not diminish another person who fights for freedom.[79]

By the early 2000s, CANF was no longer the premier exile organization nor as powerful as it once had been. With the Republicans in control of the White House and Congress, the Díaz-Balart brothers and Ileana Ros-Lehtinen became the most powerful Cuban-American voices in Washington; Florida Senator Mel Martínez joined them in 2004. When the Democrats regained Congress, their influence waned but that of New Jersey Senator Bob Menéndez's rose. All five Cuban-American legislators profess a hardline on the embargo.

Polls conducted by Florida International University continued to show evolving trends in the Cuban-American community. Whereas in October 2000 nearly 52 percent supported a dialogue inclusive of the government, the dissidents and the exiles, in March 2007 a solid 65 percent did. Support for the embargo continued on a slow, downward slide: from 62.4 percent to 57.5 percent. The majority favoring food exports to Cuba increased from 56.3 percent (2000) to 62 percent (2007). The proportion of people supportive of medical sales grew from an already substantial majority of 66 percent to nearly 72 percent. Perhaps because Fidel Castro had transferred power to his brother in July 2006 due to ill health, those expecting major change in Cuba within five years increased from just under 44 percent in October 2000 to nearly 63 percent in March 2007. Support for a U.S. invasion of Cuba declined from 60 percent to 51 percent, a dramatic fall. By 2000 an overwhelming majority already agreed that the embargo did not work very well or not at all and in 2007 it remained at about 75 percent. By 2007, then, it appeared that a hefty majority of exiles would welcome a national dialogue among Cubans on both sides of the Florida Straits, while support for a U.S. invasion had declined nine points, to basically a fifty-fifty split. Even if 57.5 percent favored the embargo, solid majorities approved of U.S. food and medical exports to Cuba. And three-quarters thought the embargo worked badly or not at all, which may account for the modest upward trend in the anti-embargo position into the 40-percent range.[80]

After Hurricane Michelle ravaged the island in November 2001, José Basulto, president of Brothers to the Rescue, expressed his approval of sending humanitarian aid to Cuba:

The material value of our aid, given all that Cuba needs, would not give Castro a single additional day in power. The benefit Castro could draw from the aid sent by exiles carries no real political cost to our cause. We only imagine it so. Showing human solidarity does not imply weakness. If we give generously, we will have achieved a great moral victory before our people and the world, with a small material and insignificant cost as far as helping the regime is concerned. Yet, if we do not provide our assistance, our fellow citizens would judge us indolent, and, in the opinion of third parties, we would again be acting intransigently in the face of a tragedy that should concern us all. We have fallen into this trap before.[81]

In 2008, Cuba was hit by three major hurricanes—Gustav, Ike and Paloma—and by tropical storms Fay and Hanna. The weather-related toll was $10 billion in damages. Though Havana turned down the Bush administration's offer of humanitarian aid, Catholic Relief Services, Caritas Cubana and Miami's Daughters of Charity sent more than $1 million in aid. For its part, CANF sent at least $250,000 in donations.[82]

After Fidel (Sort of)

On July 31, 2006, Fidel Castro ceded power to his brother Raúl.[83] Shortly thereafter, the younger Castro made an offer—albeit couched in militant language—to open a dialogue with the United States:

At this stage of the game, they should understand that impositions and threats will achieve nothing with Cuba. We have always been willing to normalize relations on an equal plane. What we won't admit is an imperious and interventionist policy which the current administration frequently assumes."[84]

In 2001, Raúl had twice advised the United States to normalize relations while his brother was still chief of state. "With our unsolvable differences, it would be more convenient to try to normalize relations while Fidel is alive than in the future," Raúl had said. "Then it will be more difficult."[85] Washington did not heed his advice, and so he is now faced with the task of reducing tensions, if not achieving normalization, with the Comandante still trying to direct U.S.–Cuba relations from the sidelines.

A few days after Raúl offered to open a dialogue with Washington, Assistant Secretary of State for Western Hemisphere Affairs Thomas Shannon said:

In May 2002, President Bush effectively made an offer to the Cuban regime. If Castro were prepared to free political prisoners, respect human rights, if he were prepared to permit the creation of independent organizations, and if he were prepared to create a mechanism and a pathway towards elections, then we would look in consultation with Congress for ways to lift the embargo and begin a deeper engagement with the Cuban state."[86]

The fact that Shannon had mentioned a Bush speech that had once distressed hardliners was significant. Like the end of the Cold War, Castro's illness stoked the anticipation that Cuba would finally change. For the United States, however, Cuba policy remained fixed, untouched by the reappraisal of U.S. foreign policy that the Bush administration carried out in its second term.

Raúl Castro's interim and then official presidency held out the possibility of easing relations with the United States. Lacking his brother's charisma, he had to govern through institutions, especially the military and the PCC. Unlike his brother, Raúl valued the institutions of state socialism. In the 1970s and early 1980s, he led efforts to institutionalize the political system and somewhat loosen central control of the economy. In the early 1990s, Raúl and the generals were likewise instrumental in the modest economic reforms enacted in Cuba. On both occasions the Comandante stopped the reforms and Raúl accepted his decisions. Still, after the power transfer, the new president disbanded the informal networks of loyalists that his brother had used to keep tabs on the party and government bureaucracies. While institutions never stopped Fidel from setting and implementing policy as he saw fit, especially on economic and international matters, since assuming the presidency, Raúl has again emphasized the importance of *la institucionalidad*, the notion that decision-making flows through institutions.

As interim president, Raúl began to make his mark, calling for franker discussions, sidestepping the mass mobilizations that had been his brother's favorite method of governing and loosening some restrictions on the economy. On July 26, 2007, he called for "structural changes" in a speech that was subsequently discussed in work and neighborhood assemblies throughout the island.[87] People's reactions spanned a wide spectrum: "a national catharsis," "exhaustion and skepticism," "people couldn't stop talking," "Cubans under forty were largely disengaged and uninterested."[88] Raúl had raised popular expectations, a politically risky move if living standards did not improve relatively quickly. Most of the changes, however, have done little to overcome the lack of productivity that shackles the Cuban economy. The changes proposed for the agricultural sector held the greatest promise, but their implementation was slow and erratic. In February 2008, Raúl was officially installed as president and he chose José Ramón Machado Ventura, a close ally since the 1950s, as his second in command. No country for young men, many said shaking their heads. The following July 26, before hurricanes Gustav, Ike and Paloma lashed at the island, Raúl signaled that reforms would slow down, blaming the rising costs of food and oil.[89] It was clear that ordinary Cubans would not see their living standards improve anytime soon.

What was behind the change? In March 2007, Fidel Castro had announced that he would begin writing his *Reflexiones*, a column that he has published since then in the PCC daily, *Granma*, and the webpage Cubadebate. Since the power transfer, Castro has not been seen in public, though now and then he meets privately with foreign dignitaries and sometimes the taped encounters are aired on TV. Until early 2007, he seemed to be near death. By March of that year, however, he was well enough to start writing his musings. Raúl has said that he consults his brother on all major decisions, and given the Comandante's outsize persona, it is safe to conclude that Raúl cannot ignore him. In 2008 the elder Castro may have vetoed the slow-paced agricultural reforms, which involved paying the debts long-owed by the state to cooperatives and independent peasants, increasing prices for many agricultural products, selling agricultural tools and other inputs in Cuban convertible pesos (CUCs), leasing state-owned arable land to cooperatives and peasants, and opening agriculture ministry offices in rural municipalities with the authority to make local decisions—all unspoken repudiations of Fidel's policies.[90] The policy reversals that on July 26, 2008 Raul had blamed on the rising cost of oil may in part have been the result of a physically stronger Fidel reasserting his will. The Comandante had always stood fast against markets and local control even as food production declined year after year. That Cuba spends scarce hard currency on food imports—for example, $2.2 billion in 2008, including $800 million from the United States—cannot but be an indictment of long-standing agricultural policies.

All the same, Raúl may have slowed down for his own reasons. His appointment of Machado is reminiscent of Moscow in the early 1980s. After Leonid Brezhnev's passing, two old men—first the more open-minded Yuri Andropov, then the mummified Konstantin Chernenko—ruled the Soviet Union. Not until 1985 did the youthful Mikhail Gorbachev take the reins at the Kremlin. Is Raúl more akin to Andropov than to Chernenko? Although Gorbachev and China's Deng Xiaoping are often mentioned as two role models, the earlier Soviet pair may be a more apt analogy. But if it is to be Gorbachev or Deng, the latter is clearly the more attractive model for Raúl, since the Communist Party still governs China. Yet Raúl cannot quite embrace Deng's wisdom: "It doesn't matter whether the cat is black or white, as long as it can catch mice." Unlike the Comandante, Raúl accepts the market socialism of yore, the reforms introduced in the former Soviet Union and Eastern Europe to counter Stalinism's hypercentralization. After 1970, Cuba's economic institutionalization incorporated market socialism, though not in the more liberal Hungarian version that allowed for small, family-owned businesses. At best, Raúl and his elderly cohort are reformers in this sense, believers in a socialism that history washed away. For the Comandante, however, market socialism is almost as deplorable as capitalism. In addition, Raúl not only always cowered when confronting his brother but also shudders at the thought of undermining his legacy. The elders may hope to hand over a more orderly, less economically strapped country to the next generation. But their task is infinitely complicated by their timidity regarding market reforms and, especially, by Fidel Castro's in-the-flesh presence and the albatross of his legacy. *Après moi le déluge* may be the Comandante's unwitting motto, a self-fulfilling prophecy of his 2005 speech at the University of Havana when he sounded the alarm that the revolution could only be destroyed from within.

What do ordinary Cubans want? Without civil liberties and free elections, the question cannot be answered with an acceptable level of certainty. And even if somehow both were guaranteed, Cuban citizens would likely behave like their counterparts elsewhere, changing their minds on just about anything from one election cycle to the next. Herein lies the fatal weakness of Cuba's current government, which behaves as if the major issues had been decided fifty years ago for all time. In the 2000s, several foreign organizations conducted surveys on the island.[91] Gallup's has the advantage of being both highly regarded and offering comparisons with other polls in Latin America. In September 2006 the Gallup Poll of Cuba was carried out door to door, with face-to-face interviews with 1,000 urban Cubans (600 in Havana, 400 in Santiago). Pollsters selected questions from the template applied in Latin America and other world regions. By near unanimity Cubans agreed that health care and education were available for all regardless of economic situation; only 42 percent (health care) and 52 percent (education) of Latin Americans said the same, on average. Some 78 percent of Cubans were satisfied with the quality of their schools while 59 percent expressed the same in Latin America. In contrast, opinions on the availability of quality health care did not markedly differ: in Cuba 60 percent are satisfied, in Latin America, 57 percent are.

On more subjective expressions of well-being, Cubans scored lower than Latin Americans. When asked whether they had a talent or could do something better than most of their acquaintances, only 23 percent in Cuba answered positively while Latin Americans averaged 32 percent. Urban Cubans said they were less likely to say that they had the opportunity to do their best at work (60 percent versus 84 percent in Latin America), a bit more likely to waste time (30 percent versus 24 percent) and significantly less satisfied with their jobs (68 percent versus 83 percent). Only 26 percent expressed satisfaction with their freedom to choose what to do with their lives while the Latin American average surpassed 80 percent. Cuba ranks at the bottom of the Gallup World Poll on this last question, below the urban populace of Zimbabwe, Chad and Ethiopia, all of which are at around 30 percent. When asked about collective characteristics, urban Cubans tended to rank their fellow nationals higher on questions about optimism, persistence, entrepreneurship and creativity than the average in Latin America. Yet, only 42 percent agreed that hard work leads to a better life and only 32 percent said they had an idea or a plan to improve their living standards (respectively 77 percent and 42 percent of Latin Americans did). Astoundingly more Latin Americans (82 percent) than Cubans (62 percent) said they had smiled or laughed the day before the survey. Overall, 49 percent of urban Cubans said they approved of their leaders, 39 percent said they disapproved and 12 percent did not know or refused to answer.[92] The Gallup poll gives Raúl Castro little comfort. Even his best face—market socialism under PCC control—falls short of relieving ordinary Cubans from the material drudgery of lives lived without freedom.

Cuba in the International Arena

An activist foreign policy has been the Cuban government's best antidote to the U.S. embargo. At first the United States sought to strangle the Cuban economy, isolate Havana and bring down the revolutionary government. It did not work. From the 1970s on, Fidel Castro engineered a foreign policy that undermined U.S. intentions and advanced Cuban interests.[93] During the 1990s, a decade during which the Cuban economy floundered, Castro once again showed his mastery of foreign policy. While the United States and most of its allies brought Cuba to task at the old U.N. Commission on Human Rights, Havana mobilized almost unanimous condemnation of the embargo at the U.N. General Assembly. As much as it deplored Cuba's record on human rights, time after time the world denounced the embargo more forcefully. As the Cuban Democracy and Helms-Burton acts hardened the embargo, Canada, the European Union and Latin America stayed the course of engagement, even if Havana yielded precious little in return. In the 2000s, whether under the Comandante or under Raúl Castro, foreign policy remained an all-important recourse for Cuba. An overview samples the reach of Cuba in the world.

• Brazil. In January 2008, President Luiz Inácio "Lula" da Silva visited Havana. The two countries agreed to increase their economic cooperation, especially in the sugar and oil industries. What else but ethanol production would lead to Brazilian–Cuban cooperation in the sugar industry? The elder Castro is a vehement critic of biofuels. Brazil's oil company, Petrobras, has joined Cupet (Cuba Petroleum) in offshore exploration of oil fields estimated at no less than five billion barrels.[94] In a May 2008 visit to Havana, Foreign Minister Celso Amorim expressed Brazil's desire to become Cuba's principal trading partner. In November, Lula returned to Cuba. Shortly thereafter, the Río Group announced that Cuba was joining its ranks.[95] Improved Brazilian–Cuban relations could lessen Havana's dependence on Caracas for oil.

• Canada. Trade, investments and tourism have been at the center of the relationship between Canada and Cuba. Occasionally, human rights have caused tensions between the two countries. After a lull in relations, Ottawa sent a trade mission led by its secretary of state for Latin America in November 2002. As the Black Spring of 2003 unfolded, however, Canada's foreign affairs minister summoned Havana's ambassador and presented him with a strongly worded protest letter for the Cuban foreign minister. Canada downgraded official exchanges with Cuba.[96] Between 2003 and 2008, Canadians constituted about 35 percent of Cuba's tourists.[97] In the 1990s, Canadians invested $950 million in Cuba.[98] Between 2003 and 2008, trade between the two countries totaled $4.9 billion.[99] Like other U.S. allies, Canada enacted legislation forbidding its citizens to comply with Helms-Burton. In 1997, the Clinton administration brought suit against Canadian citizen James Sabzali for doing business with Cuba, mostly while living in Canada though he later moved to the United States. When a Philadelphia jury found Sabzali guilty in 2002, Ottawa protested the verdict. After considerable legal wrangling, Sabzali was sentenced to a year's probation in 2005; he is the only foreigner ever prosecuted under Helms-Burton.[100] In December 2006, Thomas Shannon, the top U.S. diplomat for Latin America, noted Canada's ties with Cuba: "Canadians have been able to maintain relationships with the regime, Cuban society and Cuban dissidents. That's no small feat."[101]

- China. In the 2000s, China emerged as Cuba's second largest trading partner, with trade totaling $7.8 billion.[102] Chinese buses and locomotives have helped the Cuban government to improve its battered transportation infrastructure. Sinopec, China's state oil company, and Cupet are jointly exploring in the island's western waters. The two countries are also pursuing joint ventures in biotechnology. Economic ties with China are based on economic interests, not political solidarity. China, moreover, does not impose political conditions. Visits by high-ranking officials to Beijing and Havana—including then-Defense Minister Raúl Castro's in April 2005 and Chinese President Hu Jintao's in November 2008—highlighted the political ties between the two countries. Chinese–Cuban relations are rooted in institutions, especially the military, not in the personal ties between their leaders.[103]

- European Union. Cuba's Black Spring in 2003 elicited the EU's condemnation and led to EU sanctions that did not affect humanitarian aid. Castro, however, later rejected all such aid as a matter of "dignity" (during 1993–2002, EU aid had totaled 145 million). After Zapatero's election, Spain continued to lead the EU on Cuban matters but not as Aznar had: Engagement returned to the center of Spanish policy toward Cuba. In September 2006, Madrid came under fire when a high-ranking official from Zapatero's foreign ministry met with dissidents in Havana. While Cuba allows Canada some leeway regarding its approach to civil society and the dissidents, the same is not extended to Spain and the European Union. In March 2009, relations between Cuba and the EU were normalized, even though the Czech Republic, Poland, Sweden and Great Britain still favored a tougher stance. Cuba is the only Latin-American country without an economic cooperation agreement with the European Union. Such an agreement would carry a human-rights clause that Havana rejects.[104]

• Iran. Since the 1979 revolution, Cuban–Iranian relations have been on a strong footing. In the 1990s, Havana and Tehran forged several cooperation agreements in biotechnology. These ties formed the basis for Undersecretary Bolton's claim that Cuba was providing "dual-use technology to rogue states," although no hard proof in that regard was ever put forward. Cuba has had strong political affinities with Iran, from backing the Palestinian cause to supporting Tehran's right to develop nuclear power. During a visit to Iran in May 2001, Fidel Castro said: "Iran and Cuba, in cooperation with each other, can bring America to its knees." After the attacks of September 11, some analysts saw a potential Cuba–Iran axis in the making. After his election in 2005, Mahmoud Ahmadinejad noted: "Iran's relations with Cuba are strategic and deep-seated." In September 2006, when Havana hosted the Non-Aligned Movement's summit, Raúl Castro met privately with Ahmadinejad as he did with other heads of state in attendance. Iran sees Cuba as an important ally in the Americas. In general, the new Cuban president is not prone to take risks, either abroad or at home. While politically siding with Iran against the United States, Raúl Castro is unlikely to engage in perilous behavior.[105]

• Russia. Since 2007, Russian–Cuban relations have noticeably improved from the estrangement that followed the collapse of the Soviet Union. In November 2008, President Dmitry Medvedev visited Cuba, the last leg of a Latin-American trip that also included Brazil, Peru and Venezuela. In early 2009, Raúl Castro spent a week in Russia and returned to Cuba with $354 million in new loans, mostly for purchasing agricultural, construction and transportation equipment. Moscow had already provided generous relief aid after the devastating 2008 hurricane season. Russia's national oil company and Cupet have signed agreements to explore for oil offshore. Moscow sees Cuba as a key ally in the Americas, a region where it seeks to wield some influence. Raúl always had a soft spot for the former Soviet Union, and Vladimir Putin—who called the USSR disintegration "the greatest political catastrophe" of the twentieth century—has partly moved Russia back to authoritarianism. Even if Putin closed the spy center at Lourdes in 2001 and thus ended the annual payment of $200 million, the Castro brothers certainly appreciated the rehabilitation of the Soviet Union's image.[106] Russia, in addition, can supply Cuba with spare parts for military and industrial equipment. After an unnamed Russian Air Force official raised the "hypothetical possibility" that Moscow might place nuclear-capable bombers in Cuba or, at least, refuel them there, Foreign Minister Felipe Pérez Roque responded unequivocally: "The answer is

'No'."[107] Still, Cuba supports Russian positions in Georgia and on U.S. anti-missile defenses in Central Europe. From Soviet days, Cuba owes Russia $20 billion, a matter that will not be resolved soon. Thus far, Cuba refuses to pay and Russia resists any talk of pardoning the debt.[108]

- United Nations. On February 28, 2008, Cuba signed the UN-sponsored International Covenant on Economic, Social and Cultural Rights (ICESCR) and the International Covenant on Civil and Political Rights (ICCPR). The two covenants would only become binding if ratified by the National Assembly, and like other signatories, Cuba has the right to issue future "reservations or interpretive declarations." Still, before ratification can happen, the Cuban government must decide how to amend existing legislation so that it complies with the ICCPR in particular.[109] That the signing took place four days after Raúl Castro formally assumed the presidency was no coincidence. In December 2007 *Granma* had published the transcript of an April 2001 interview with Fidel on the nightly *Mesa Redonda* in which he argued against Cuba signing these treaties.[110]

- The Vatican. In late February 2008 the Vatican's secretary of state, Cardinal Tarcisio Bertone, visited Havana to discuss issues such as building new churches, gaining regular access to the media and establishing Catholic elementary schools. In early May, Pope Benedict XVI himself called for the church "to enjoy normal access to the social communications media" and for parents to exercise "their fundamental right to a religious and moral education for their children."[111] After the hurricanes of 2008, the church and the government engaged in a dialogue to jointly seek humanitarian relief for the victims, though no public agreement was ever reached. In November 2008, Raúl Castro attended a special mass to celebrate the beatification of José Olallo Valdés, a nineteenth-century friar from Camagüey. Diplomatic protocol did not require his presence.

- Venezuela. Hugo Chávez's election tendered Havana a political and economic lifeline. After almost a decade of solitude, the Comandante found a soul mate in the Americas. Venezuelan–Cuban relations were initially established on the strong personal bond between the two men. Between 1999 and 2004, the bilateral relationship blossomed into an enduring partnership rooted in Venezuela's sale of oil at preferential prices and Cuba's dispatch of health-care personnel. Cuba also provides Caracas with military and security advisors. Since the advent of the Bolivarian Alternative for the Americas (ALBA) in 2004, Caracas and Havana have forged a regional network of allies and influence based on Venezuela's oil and Cuba's health-care services. Both countries likewise have military and intelligence ties with some allies—e.g., Bolivia and Nicaragua—though their extent is hard to determine. In 2007, trade in goods and services between Cuba and Venezuela reached $7.1 billion. Up to 65,000 Cubans—some 30,000 in the health sector—were estimated to be in Venezuela.[112] Cuban industries such as oil refineries, construction and metallurgy were recipients of Venezuelan largesse. In December 2008, Raúl Castro paid an official visit to Venezuela before traveling to Brazil.[113] He and Chávez are not soul mates; rather, at best, they are in a marriage of convenience. Raúl's foreign policy, nonetheless, is geared towards diversifying Cuba's international trade partners. Through his reflections, Fidel keeps the ALBA ideals of anti-imperialism and twenty-first century socialism alive. Once the Comandante departs or, even before, if Havana succeeds in broadening commercial and investment ties with Brazil, Canada, China, Russia and the EU while easing tensions with Washington, the relationship between Havana and Caracas could become less intense. Given the intimacy of their current relationship, such a change would be remarkable.

Were it to embrace meaningful economic reforms, Havana would improve living standards, widen its international reach and attract significant foreign investment. Under these hypothetical conditions, the U.S. embargo might well be fatally undermined. Even many Cuban Americans might clamor for the opportunity to open small businesses with their families on the island. Cuban foreign policy has been an exceptional political success, if success is measured by how it has advanced the interests of Cuba's leaders. Havana's foreign policy, however, has utterly failed to put the economy and living standards at the center. That, after all, should be the first charge of a small country so close to such a powerful neighbor.

5

"THE POLICY WE'VE HAD IN PLACE FOR 50 YEARS HASN'T WORKED"

Barack H. Obama assumed the presidency at one of the most critical junctures in American history. At home, a financial crisis lashed at the economy in ways unseen since the Great Depression. In most quarters abroad, the reputation of the United States was diminished. After September 11, 2001, George W. Bush had declared a war on terror, a historic challenge that his administration compared to World War II and the Cold War. For the first time since the Cold War ended, the United States harbored no doubts about how to conduct itself in world affairs. The anti-terrorism paradigm brooked neither limits nor uncertainties. By launching preemptive war against Saddam Hussein's Iraq, the Bush administration surrendered the realism that had been central to U.S. foreign policy since World War II. The White House's attempt to spread democracy in the Middle East might have been mistaken for Wilsonian but for its dismissal of the international institutions and agreements so cherished by President Woodrow Wilson. Though stepping back from unilateralism in his second term, Bush still considered countries like Iran, Syria and Cuba pariahs and, consequently, pursued confrontational policies without diplomatic respite.

Early in his administration, Obama made overtures to Tehran, Damascus and Havana. The difference was that Cuba lacked strategic importance while Iran and Syria held key pieces in the Middle Eastern puzzle; in addition, Iran's evident if undeclared intention to acquire nuclear weaponry commanded the White House's attention. In terms of Cuba, Obama changed the tone and some elements of U.S. policy, such as eliminating all restrictions on Cuban-American family travel and remittances; allowing U.S. telecommunications companies to do business with Havana; making it easier for U.S. agricultural interests to sell their goods; opening talks with Havana on immigration and other topics; issuing many more visas for Cubans to travel to the United States; and authorizing

many more Americans to travel to Cuba. Still, the administration was no closer
to the fundamental overhaul that a group of Republican luminaries had asked of
Bill Clinton in 1998, one based on the assumption that Havana no longer posed
a national-security threat. Upon accepting the Nobel Peace Prize in Oslo,
Obama—without mentioning Havana—referred to the complexities of dealing
with dictatorial regimes:

> The promotion of human rights cannot be about exhortation alone. At
> times, it must be coupled with painstaking diplomacy. I know that
> engagement with repressive regimes lacks the satisfying purity of indigna-
> tion. But I also know that sanctions without outreach—condemnation
> without discussion—can carry forward only a crippling status quo.[1]

Striking the right balance between realism and principle on Cuba would not
come easily.

Meanwhile Raúl Castro was caught in a bind, trapped between his own
modest reformism and his brother's behind-the-scenes vigilance and frequent,
widely diffused columns. In late December 2009, Raúl acknowledged the
"expectations and honest concerns" regarding the limited, slow-moving changes
he was attempting to put in place: "In updating Cuba's economic model, we
cannot run the risk of improvisation and haste. We must walk toward the future
in firm and certain steps because we simply do not have the right to make mistakes."[2] So spoke a cautious leader well aware of what was better left unsaid:
that over five decades too many mistakes had been made and that this time everything was on the line. While ordinary Cubans bore the brunt of the country's
economic stagnation, Raúl's timidity on reforms also had repercussions for the
island's standing in the world. He rightly boasted that forty-one heads of state or
government and seventy-eight foreign ministers had visited Cuba in 2009.
Their presence confirmed the "support and solidarity that our just cause commands," he claimed. Most dignitaries, however, visited Cuba in the routine
course of diplomacy, not necessarily to embrace Havana's "just cause," though
all expressed opposition to the U.S. embargo. Still, without some movement on
human rights and more purposeful reforms, Havana was not likely to receive
the kind of support it really needed—for instance, an economic cooperation
agreement with the European Union—or to help build momentum in the
United States for ending the embargo. Cuba had managed without either in the
past and might do so again. All the same, dire economic conditions could yet
prompt Cuban leaders to embrace a meaningful opening to the market or ordinary Cubans to take their frustrations to the streets, a particularly dreaded scenario for the leadership. Much to Havana's chagrin, Cuban domestic affairs
mattered, sometimes decisively, for its foreign relations.

Take Havana's relations with the European Union. After the Black Spring of
2003, Europe had placed sanctions on Havana, which strained relations without

bringing about any noticeable improvements in the regime's human rights record. By the end of 2009, EU-Cuban relations had all but normalized. The last step would be the lifting of the Common Position—an EU measure adopted after the 1996 shootdown of two Brothers to the Rescue planes over the Florida Straits—which had made an improvement in relations to Havana conditional on Cuba making progress on human rights. With Spain assuming the rotating EU presidency during the first semester of 2010, Madrid had intended to make the case for the elimination of the Common Position. As of June 2010, however, the Common Position was still in effect. On New Year's Day weekend, Havana had expelled Luis Yáñez, a senior member of Spain's Socialist Party, and his wife shortly after they landed at José Martí International Airport. The couple had hoped for a brief vacation but Cuban authorities deemed their motives suspect. Most damning, however, was the death of Orlando Zapata Tamayo on February 23, 2010, after eighty-five days on a hunger strike he undertook to press for the release of twenty-six ailing political prisoners. The next day, Guillermo Fariñas Hernández declared himself on a hunger strike in his house in Santa Clara, both to protest Zapata's death and to second his demand for the prisoners' freedom. In the meantime, the regime intensified the harassment of *Las Damas de Blanco*—mothers, wives and relatives of those imprisoned for their beliefs and peaceful activities during the Black Spring. The women received their name for the white dresses they wore as they walked in peaceful protest after Sunday Mass, coral gladioli in their hands, demanding freedom for their loved ones. As the harassment increased, the international community rained opprobrium on the regime while the Ladies in White became the object of a campaign to nominate them for the Nobel Peace Prize. Still, unprecedented talks between Cuban authorities and the Catholic Church held in May 2010 opened the possibility of easing the tensions with the international community over human rights.

In the Age of Obama

On May 23, 2008, Obama—not yet the Democratic Party's presidential candidate—delivered a speech in Miami at a luncheon sponsored by the Cuban American National Foundation to mark the 106th anniversary of Cuban independence. Speaking on the need to renew U.S. leadership in Latin America, Obama made news only for his stance on Cuba. He said then:

> It's time for more than tough talk that never yields results. It's time for a new strategy. There are no better ambassadors for freedom than Cuban Americans. That's why I will immediately allow unlimited family travel and remittances to the island. It's time to let Cuban Americans see their mothers and fathers, their sisters and brothers. It's time to let Cuban-American money make their families less dependent upon the Castro regime.[3]

CANF, too, grabbed some headlines for hosting the senator. U.S. policy toward Cuba could not change without some support in the Cuban-American community. CANF—once the bastion of hardline Cuban Miami—stood along-side Obama in the campaign and later in the White House on the basis of his promise to change Cuba policy. Supporting dissidents on the island and pro-moting the elimination of all restrictions on Cuban-American family travel and remittances were now the foundation's primary missions.

In the 2008 election, leading CANF and Cuba Study Group members endorsed the efforts to unseat South Florida's three Cuban-American Republi-can members of Congress, Lincoln Díaz-Balart, Mario Díaz-Balart and Ileana Ros-Lehtinen. The challengers—former Hialeah mayor Raúl Martínez (who ran against Lincoln Díaz-Balart), former CANF executive director Joe García (Mario Díaz-Balart) and Colombian-American businesswoman Annette Taddeo (Ros-Lehtinen)—were defeated by the incumbents, Taddeo and Martínez losing by 16 percentage points and García by 6. For the first time, the three Cuban-American Republicans had faced well-funded challengers and had to work for reelection. Lincoln Díaz-Balart and Ros-Lehtinen won by their small-est, albeit still lopsided, margins ever; Mario's was the smallest since his 2002 election.[4] Even at a time when Congress had meager approval ratings, constitu-ents seemed to like their representatives enough to reelect them time after time, and the three Miamians were no exception. In September 2008, the financial collapse thrust the economy center stage. While the crisis helped Obama make strong inroads with South Florida voters, it did nothing of the kind for the three Democratic challengers. Even young Cuban Americans who solidly went for Obama split their votes to support the three South Florida incumbents.[5] In Feb-ruary 2010, Lincoln Díaz-Balart announced that he would not seek reelection to the seat in Florida's 21st Congressional District he had held for eighteen years. Mario Díaz-Balart, in turn, made it known that he would forfeit his seat in the 25th District and run for the safer seat his brother was vacating. Two months later, Joe García announced that he would again try to become the U.S. Representative from the now-open 25th District, an unexpected opportunity for the Democrat.

While the Republicans controlled Congress, South Florida's Cuban-American representatives had the last word on Cuban issues. The Democrats regained the majority in 2006, but the Cuban Americans' ascendance has remained strong inasmuch as support for—or rejection of—the status quo in Cuba policy does not split along party lines in Congress. In 2008, South Florida representatives Debbie Wasserman-Schultz and Kendrick Meek—fiercely loyal Democrats—did not endorse the challengers to Ros-Lehtinen and the Díaz-Balarts.[6] In late February 2009, the House of Representatives passed a $410-billion spending bill to fund the federal government through September 30. In the Senate debate over the bill, heated objections were raised against three Cuba-related provisions: issuing a general travel license for Americans selling agricultural products to the island; allowing Havana to pay for goods on arrival instead of before ships left American ports; and defunding enforcement of the 2004 family travel restrictions. Democratic senators Robert Menéndez (NJ) and Bill Nelson (FL) voted for the bill only after receiving written assurances from Obama and Treasury Secretary Timothy Geithner that the provisions would not fundamentally alter Cuba policy.[7] Earlier Menéndez had delivered a stinging statement on life in Cuba and blocked two presidential nominees in protest. The offending provisions and a staff report issued by a senior aide to Senator Richard G. Lugar (R-IN) that recommended a change in U.S. policy stoked Menéndez's anger.[8] In November, a group of fifty-three House Democrats that included South Florida's Wasserman-Schultz and Meek sent Speaker Nancy Pelosi a letter in opposition to lifting the travel ban.[9] Since 2003, the U.S.–Cuba Democracy Political Action Committee (PAC) has given more than $10 million to congressional campaigns. Like CANF in its heyday, the new PAC supports Republicans and Democrats.[10] In December 2009, the four leading candidates for Florida's open Senate seat, Republicans and Democrats, addressed the PAC's annual luncheon in Miami.[11]

The Cuban Democracy and Helms-Burton laws took away the president's power to lift the embargo by executive action. Change, if it came from the president, would have to be piecemeal. In its last two years, the Clinton administration loosened some restrictions while reinforcing others. Most important were broadening travel licenses for humanitarian, professional and academic exchanges, opening up limited agricultural exports and increasing support for democratic activists on the island. In October 2000, Clinton signed the Trade Sanctions Reform and Export Enhancements Act which authorized licensed agricultural exports, the most significant crack in the embargo since Jimmy Carter ended the travel ban (later reinstated by Ronald Reagan). The TSRA, moreover, established a congressional blueprint for step-by-step reform in which legislators for and against the status quo in Cuba policy compromised: In exchange for the codification of the travel ban, pro-embargo forces signed off on agricultural exports. While bills seeking to overturn the embargo have been routinely introduced, these have no chance of passing for the foreseeable future. Other proposals in the 2009–2011 Congress follow the TSRA piece-by-piece approach and include ending the travel ban altogether; authorizing U.S. companies to explore and drill for oil off Cuba's northern coast; and allowing Cuban financial institutions to make direct transfers to American banks instead of having to use banks in third countries.[12] Though these bills advance U.S. national and specific industry or regional interests, they are not popular in Congress. An example from the 2007–2009 Congress—the first after the Democrats regained control—illustrates the difficulties.

In September 2007, a farm bill amendment introduced by Representative Charles Rangel (D-NY) authorizing Cuba to make direct payments to U.S. banks went down to embarrassing defeat (245–182) when sixty-six Democrats voted against it. Rangel had hoped a Democratic Congress would make it easier to change Cuba policy: "I was blindsided. I don't think we really put up much of a fight," he said. Not one of the Democrats intending to oppose his amendment warned Rangel that defeat was imminent. Then again, neither did the Congressman rally and count the votes for passage. In the 2007–2008 election cycle, the U.S.–Cuba Democracy PAC bipartisan political donations amounted to $322,500. Of the sixty-six Democrats who voted against the Rangel amendment, fifty-two—seventeen of whom were freshmen—had received one or more PAC contributions. Mauricio Claver-Carone, a U.S. Cuba Democracy PAC director, noted:

> From about 2000 to 2003, everything was going downhill in terms of maintaining current Cuba policy. A coalition of liberal Democrats, free-trade Republicans and agriculture state lawmakers interested in opening travel and trade restrictions to Cuba seemed to be gaining ground.

As a result, the PAC decided to target Congress and put up a "bipartisan wall of support" for sanctions.[13] Coming after the 2006 Republican rout, the U.S.–Cuba Democracy PAC's success is all the more significant. In the case of the Rangel amendment, the pro-embargo forces were ready to fight and asked for a roll-call vote, which meant that a solid minority of Democrats went on the record against easing the hardline policy on Cuba. Most worrisome for the advocates of change were the newly elected Democrats. Changing a legislator's vote once she or he has gone on the record is no easy—or cheap—task.

Nonetheless, Cuban Miami offered encouragement for those seeking to change Cuba policy. While an estimated 65 percent of Cuban Americans in Miami-Dade County voted for John McCain in 2008, an exit poll of voters showed movement in the Cuban-American electorate.

- Only 31 percent of those born in Cuba voted for the Democrat, but 61 percent of those born in the United States sided with Obama.
- Some 65 percent in the 18-to-29 age group preferred Obama.
- Cubans who arrived in the 1990s were split 49 percent for Obama and 51 percent for McCain, whereas those who arrived after 2000 broke 58 percent for Obama.
- Post-1990 arrivals and U.S.-born Cuban Americans are trending toward the Democratic Party.
- Obama's 35 percent of the Cuban American vote is comparable to Bill Clinton's share in 1996, 16 points better than Al Gore's in 2000 and 10 points higher than Kerry's in 2004.[14]

Simply put, Cuban Miami was changing. A Cuba/U.S. Transition Poll released in December 2008, further highlighted the community's evolving views: 67 percent favored unrestricted travel to Cuba and 55 percent opposed the U.S. embargo.[15] A poll conducted after the Obama administration lifted all restrictions on family-related travel and remittances underscored ongoing trends.

- Some 64 percent favored the measures; nearly three-quarters of those between the ages of 18 and 49 did so while those arriving in the 1980s and 1990s (82 percent) and after 2000 (91 percent) overwhelmingly applauded the change. In all questions, responses by age and arrival decade were similarly lopsided toward openness.
- When asked whether they favored or opposed allowing all U.S. citizens to travel to Cuba, 67 percent responded in favor of ending the travel ban.
- On the U.S. embargo, there was a virtual tie: 42 percent for continuing it, 43 percent for ending it, with 15 percent answering don't know or saying nothing at all.[16]

On September 20, 2009, Colombian rock star Juanes gave a concert in Havana as part of his Peace without Borders project. Accompanying him were fifteen artists from six countries including the United States. Juanes received Secretary of State Hillary Clinton's personal good wishes for the event.[17] A survey taken a month before the concert found Cuban Miami divided: 47 percent opposed it, 27 percent supported it, 26 percent said they weren't aware of the concert or had no opinion about it. Of those opposing Peace without Borders, 40 percent said Juanes "was ignorant of Cuban reality" and 25 percent thought it "helps Castro." Among those supporting it, 60 percent said Juanes would bring much-needed happiness and music to Cubans. After the concert, which was televised in Miami, Cuban-American public opinion did a volte-face: 53 percent had a favorable opinion of the concert, 29 percent saw it unfavorably, 18 percent answered don't know/no opinion. Of those supporting Juanes, 51 percent said the concert "uplifted the Cuban people"; 21 percent of those opposed thought the concert "helped the Cuban government, not the people."[18] The irresistible images of Peace without Borders seen on television or on the web probably softened many Cuban Americans who watched. María Elvira Salazar, whose nightly Spanish-language *María Elvira Live* commands a large audience, said: "This was different than we expected. Lots of exiles are crying inside. I think the concert got us closer, the Cubans in Miami and the Cubans on the island."[19]

For the first time, Cuban Americans are expressing opinions that are trending—in some cases, strongly so—away from the familiar positions of traditional exiles. With generational turnover and newer arrivals from Cuba, change was bound to come. These trends, however, have no immediate bearing on congressional votes, which have been skillfully harnessed by the Cuban-American legislators and the U.S.–Cuba Democracy PAC. Even though there are Republicans and Democrats on each side of the policy debate, the pro-embargo forces have organization, legislators, funds and intensity on their side. While it is easy to bemoan that a relatively small interest group has Cuba policy in its grip, that is the way the American legislative process works. It behooves the pro-change forces to revive the coalition they forged in the early 2000s and enlist the votes in Congress. Doing so would require significant efforts by free-trade Republicans, farm-state legislators and liberal democrats. Success would take time, money and a dedicated intensity. This time, however, Cuban Americans are joining the effort: In 2009, the New Cuban+American Majority PAC (NCAM), which supports a more open policy towards Cuba, was launched in Washington, DC.[20]

In contrast to the situation in the early 2000s, Cuban-American public opinion is now more diverse. A prospective national coalition for changing Cuba policy could, therefore, include sectors of Cuban Miami. Still, these trends are not fully established. Unforeseen events—for example, a Tiananmen-like confrontation with demonstrators or a radical economic transformation in Cuba—could stall, revert or accelerate them. In Congress, Cuban-American legislators largely oppose the Obama administration's overture toward Havana. Public opinion and the Cuban-American political establishment are then seemingly at odds, in part because traditional exiles still constitute a majority of Cuban-American voters. If these public-opinion trends continue and if post-1990 arrivals become citizens, register and vote, the Democratic Party stands to benefit, although newer Cuban Americans may not vote solely on the issue of Cuba policy and enough may be swayed to back Republican incumbents for their record on local issues. At any rate, unless organized and funded to make their case before Congress, Cuban Americans in favor of change will remain no more than interesting trends in public opinion.

A Softer-Line Policy in Slow Motion

On April 13, 2009, the Obama administration announced a package of measures that might have been considered slight but for the context. In 2004, the Bush administration had scaled back official contacts with Havana and drastically limited travel between the United States and Cuba. So the White House's press release announcing the end of all restrictions on family travel and remittances, authorizing U.S. telecommunications companies to do business in Cuba and expanding the scope of humanitarian donations via licensed exports was significant.[21] Twelve hours after the White House announced the changes, the Cuban government reported them on television in measured language.[22] In March, when Congress passed the spending bill with the controversial Cuba provisions, Havana had been dismissive. A Cuban official had called them "a minuscule gesture" and added that Cuba expected "the unjust blockade to be lifted."[23] But as recently as May 2008, then-Senator Obama had warned that there would be no such thing were he to become president:

I will maintain the embargo. It provides us with the leverage to present the regime with a clear choice: If you take significant steps toward democracy, beginning with the freeing of all political prisoners, we will take steps to begin normalizing relations. That's the way to bring about real change in Cuba—through strong, smart and principled diplomacy.[24]

Nor could Obama lift the embargo without the consent of Congress. When the Obama White House announced the changes, it framed them in terms reminiscent of the Cuban Democracy Act ("calibrated steps") and avoided Helms-Burton's confrontational tone.

At the Summit of the Americas held April 17–19, 2009, at Port of Spain, Trinidad and Tobago, Barack Obama said: "The United States seeks a new beginning with Cuba. I know that there is a longer journey that must be traveled to overcome decades of mistrust, but there are critical steps we can take toward a new day."[25] The administration was prepared to engage the Cuban government, he said, on "a wide range of issues—from drugs, migration and economic issues to human rights, free speech and democratic reform." At a post-summit press conference, Obama acknowledged that "the policy we've had in place for 50 years hasn't worked," while stating that "the Cuban people are not free, and that's our lodestone, our North Star."[26] After he listened to several leaders in Port of Spain on the excellent work Cuban doctors do in their countries, the president paid Havana a compliment:

It's a reminder for us in the United States that if our only interaction with many of these countries is drug interdiction, if our only interaction is military, then we may not be developing the connections that can, over time, increase our influence and have a beneficial effect.

A month later, the Department of State delivered a note to the Cuban Interests Section in Washington proposing that the two countries resume talks on migration.[27] On April 30, however, when the United States released the annual list of state sponsors of terrorism, Cuba was still included along with Iran, Sudan and Syria.[28] Cuban Foreign Minister Bruno Rodríguez retorted that the United States lacked the "moral authority" to pass judgment on others given its status as an "international delinquent."[29]

At a Bolivarian Alternative for the Americas meeting in Cumaná, Venezuela, held before the Summit of the Americas, Raúl Castro publicly took notice of Obama's policy overture:

We have conveyed to the U.S. government that we are open to discuss everything, human rights, press freedom, political prisoners, everything they want to discuss. But it should be on the condition of equality, without the slightest shadow over our sovereignty.[30]

Raúl's statement and Obama's subsequent suggestion that Havana should make a gesture, such as freeing political prisoners, prompted a barbed response from Fidel Castro. "Without a doubt," he wrote on April 21, "the president misinterpreted Raúl's declaration. It was a manifestation of courage and trust in the Revolution's principles."[31] A State Department official observed off the record: "Cuba's president hasn't told us we misinterpreted him." On April 29, Raúl Castro told a meeting of Non-Aligned Movement foreign ministers in Havana:

> President Obama's recent measures, while positive, aren't far-reaching. The blockade remains intact. No political or moral pretext can justify continuing with that policy. Cuba doesn't have to make gestures. As I said recently in Venezuela: We're ready to discuss everything, everything, everything, what pertains to us but also to them, on the condition of equality.[32]

Clearly, Raúl was taking into account his brother's continuing hardline position regarding the United States. Still, his repetition of the word "everything" three times was significant given his earlier mention of "human rights, press freedom, political prisoners" as specific topics for discussion with the United States. On May 30, the Cuban Interests Section delivered a note to the Department of State accepting the Obama administration's proposal to resume migration talks. Havana also signaled a willingness to discuss direct mail service and cooperation on terrorism, drug trafficking and hurricane disaster preparedness.[33]

By the end of 2009, the United States and Cuba had resumed migration talks (July 14 in New York City) and held a meeting on reinstating direct mail (September 16 in Havana). Other than protocol press releases, little of substance about the talks was made public.[34] Travel between the two countries increased: between October 2008 and August 2009, 16,317 Cubans visited the United States in contrast to 10,661 in 2007–2008.[35] According to Cuban government figures released in January 2010, nearly 300,000 Cubans living abroad visited the island in 2009.[36] Though not broken down by country of residence, Cuban Americans almost certainly made up a substantial majority, probably well over 200,000. Cultural, academic and scientific exchanges were also on the rise.[37] On a five-day visit in late August, New Mexico Governor Bill Richardson explored agricultural trade opportunities for his state and met with high-ranking officials.[38] In September, Bisa Williams—U.S. deputy assistant secretary of state for Western Hemisphere Affairs—traveled to Cuba for the postal talks and stayed for five days. She met with Cuban Deputy Foreign Minister Dagoberto Rodríguez, toured a region in Pinar del Río devastated in the 2008 hurricane season and met with American medical students studying on the island. Williams also had lunch with dissidents Elizardo Sánchez, Martha Beatriz Roque and Vladimiro Roca.[39] Havana also allowed her to visit dual U.S.–Cuban citizens jailed in Cuba who must surely have appreciated seeing a friendly face.

Robert Pastor, who was Jimmy Carter's top Latin American advisor, noted: "The prison visits reflect the benefits that could accrue to both countries as a result of better communications and, conversely, how our interests are poorly served when we don't communicate."[40]

U.S. Policy and Human Rights in Cuba

On December 4, 2009, Cuban state security arrested an American contractor—later identified as Alan Gross, a computer expert—at José Martí International Airport as he waited for his return flight home. Development Alternatives Incorporated (DAI), a Bethesda, Maryland consultancy firm, had sent Gross to Cuba on a tourist visa that allowed only leisure activities.[41] Instead, he distributed laptops, cellular telephones and satellite communications equipment.[42] (In 2008, Raúl Castro's government had legalized the sale of laptops and mobile phones which constituted a loosening of sorts, even if few Cubans can actually afford to buy a computer or a phone.) During his stay, Gross helped "members of a community group" access the internet, an illegal activity in Cuba if not done through official channels. Havana sees tight control over information as a *sine qua non* of regime stability. Under the 1999 Law 88 for the Protection of National Independence and the Economy of Cuba, anyone found advancing Helms-Burton's objectives of "breaking the internal order, destabilizing the country and liquidating the socialist state and Cuba's independence" can be arrested, tried and sentenced to up to twenty years.[43] On December 28, Cuban authorities finally allowed U.S. diplomats to visit Alan Gross.[44] A week later, National Assembly President Ricardo Alarcón accused him of working for U.S. intelligence, a charge vehemently denied by the State Department. DAI's president said Gross was "working with a peaceful, non-dissident civic group—a religious and cultural group recognized by the Cuban government—to improve its ability to communicate with its members across the island and overseas."[45] Subsequently, the group was identified as part of Cuba's small Jewish community. Whether Alan Gross is charged under Law 88 or another statute, his arrest underscored Havana's willingness to stand up to Washington. Whether the Castro government intended to force an exchange for the "five heroes," signal a disposition to play hardball against U.S. democracy promotion or, in general, disrupt any prospect of an ease in tensions with the United States, the White House now had to react on Cuba's terms.

From 1996 to 2008, the United States Agency for International Development's (USAID) Cuba program—mandated by Helms-Burton—disbursed $83 million to support human rights, promote civil society and encourage non-violent democratic change. Weakening the "information blockade" is one of its objectives and DAI had received a grant in 2008 to help do just that. In most countries, Gross's actions would have been considered innocuous but not in Cuba for two reasons: The Cuban government is a dictatorship and

Helms-Burton's aim is to achieve regime change. An overhaul of U.S. Cuba policy would need to grapple with this glaring contradiction: Why would Havana's dictatorial regime cooperate with Washington to bring about its own demise? Under Obama, the budget for promoting democracy in Cuba has remained at $20 million a year.[46]

USAID's Cuba program has, moreover, suffered from poor management and oversight of its grantees. In 2006, the U.S. Government Accountability Office (GAO) reviewed ten grantees that had received more than $50 million over the years. Of these, seven—awarded $47.2 million—relied on proper procedures to document, track and report grant expenditures. The other three—awarded $4.7 million—manifested numerous irregularities. Among these were large checks paid without adequate documentation and improper purchases—Godiva chocolates, leather coats, cashmere sweaters, Nintendo Gameboys and Sony Playstations—made with USAID funds. In 2008, the two largest USAID grantees—Center for a Free Cuba (CFC) and the Group to Support Democracy (GAD, *Grupo de Apoyo a la Democracia*)—were suspended and eventually their funding withdrawn, pending the outcome of Department of Justice investigations. After the GAO audit, USAID took constructive steps such as awarding all 2006–2008 grants competitively (only 5 percent of the grants had been issued competitively during 1996–2005). Nonetheless, the Cuba program had yet to fully put in place an airtight oversight structure to monitor and train grantees to manage taxpayer monies with due diligence.[47] Most of the USAID monies, moreover, has gone to organizations in Miami and Washington.[48] After the Gross arrest, Senator John Kerry (D-MA), chairman of the Senate Foreign Relations Committee, called for a review of USAID's Cuba program.[49] In March 2010, Kerry placed a new hold on U.S. programs to promote democracy in Cuba while the Obama administration conducted a thorough review and the committee carried out its own investigations.[50]

Obama was steering American foreign policy away from Bush's confrontational rhetoric and practices. In that sense, he was returning to the realism that had underpinned U.S. leadership in the world since 1945. Unlike previous presidents, however, Obama faced new challenges and limits. A multipolar international community required the United States to stay finely attuned to the rise of new powers, China first and foremost but also India, Russia and Brazil. In addition, the U.S. economy was under extraordinary stress from the financial crisis and the burdens of the recovery program, two wars, an explosive deficit and a growing foreign debt. Obama's speeches announcing his Afghanistan strategy and accepting the Nobel Peace Prize well conveyed an understanding of these challenges and limits while making the case for the uniqueness of American leadership in the world.[51] At the same time, democracy and human rights have always been quintessential, if not exclusively, American values that have also guided U.S. foreign policy. In Oslo, the president said:

There has long been a tension between those who describe themselves as realists or idealists—a tension that suggests a stark choice between the narrow pursuit of interests or an endless campaign to impose our values around the world. I reject these choices.

In an address at Georgetown University a few days later, Secretary of State Hillary Clinton laid out the administration's agenda on human rights. She emphasized the mutually reinforcing connections among human rights, democracy and development:

> Our human rights agenda for the 21st century is to make human rights a human reality, and the first step is to see human rights in a broad context. Of course, people must be free from the oppression of tyranny, from torture, from the fear of leaders who will imprison or "disappear" them. But they also must be free from the oppression of want—want of food, want of health, want of education, and want of equality in law and in fact.[52]

Obama and Clinton outlined an approach based on upholding the core American principles of human freedom and dignity, restoring U.S. credibility on human rights, demanding that rules and treaties be followed and, especially, staying flexible.[53]

The Obama White House moved quickly to restore American credibility. On his second full day in office, Obama banned torture and announced his intent to close the prison at Guantánamo. The administration also strengthened U.S. accountability on human rights. For the first time, the 2010 State Department report on human trafficking in the world included the United States, noting that every year thousands of men, women and children—largely from Mexico and South Asia—are trafficked into the United States for sexual and labor exploitation.[54] Obama reversed Bush's decision to keep the United States off the UN Human Rights Council. By joining, the administration said it hoped to exert "constructive influence" from within rather than stand dismissively on the side. In December 2010, the United States was set to cooperate with its scheduled Universal Periodic Review (UPR), scheduled for December 2010, that all UN member states undergo. On a related matter, Stephen Rapp, U.S. ambassador-at-large for war-crimes issues, addressed the assembly that oversees the International Criminal Court, a first by an American diplomat.[55]

"Principled pragmatism informs our approach on human rights with all countries," Secretary Clinton said in December 2009. Cooperation with Russia and China is vitally important on the global economy, nonproliferation, climate change and security issues like North Korea and Iran. On human rights, the United States needs to engage "in tough negotiations behind closed doors" with these two countries as the best way "to help the oppressed." On Iran, Washington has negotiated directly with Tehran on nuclear matters while expressing solidarity with those Iranians who struggle for democratic change. Clinton gave three other examples of U.S. "tools and tactics" on human rights.

1   Governments, such as Africa's nascent democracies, that are willing but unable without external support to establish or consolidate strong institutions and the rule of law. To them, the United States "can extend our hand as partner."
2   Cases like Cuba and Nigeria where governments could bring about the changes their citizens deserve but are unwilling. The United States "must vigorously press leaders to end repression" in those countries, while supporting citizens in those societies who stand for change.
3   In places like the eastern Congo, where governments are unwilling to respect their citizens, the United States must support individuals and organizations who "try to protect people and battle against the odds to plant seeds for a more hopeful future."

The U.S. government works best with the first group of countries, which have cooperative relations with Washington and welcome American help. In sub-Saharan Africa, USAID has twenty-three bilateral field missions and three regional missions. In Central America, which also belongs in this group, USAID has missions in El Salvador, Guatemala, Nicaragua and Honduras plus a regional program. The third category involves the most egregious violations of human rights: genocide and/or crimes against humanity. In eastern Congo but also in Sudan, the United Nations has intervened to protect civilians without much success. In both cases, USAID has provided humanitarian, security and development assistance.[56]

Pairing Cuba and Nigeria was unusual. Nigeria—a regional power and major oil producer—has normal relations with the United States. In 2004, USAID and the Nigerian government signed five-year, strategic grant agreements on democratic governance, economic growth, social services and HIV/AIDS.[57] Pervasive government corruption is a fundamental reason for entrenched poverty and unemployment, all the more glaring given the country's oil wealth. Since 2000, intercommunal and political violence has taken at least 10,000 lives. State security forces regularly perpetrate extrajudicial killings, torture and extortion without, thus far, being held accountable. At the same time, freedom of expression is generally respected. Civil society and independent media criticize the government and promote vigorous public debate. The judiciary, moreover, functions with a modicum of independence. Regarding human rights, the United States, the United Kingdom and other Western powers have issued strong protests through diplomatic channels, which the Nigerian government has largely disregarded. The country's strategic importance translates into private reproaches without redress for aggrieved civilians or consequences for relations with the United States.[58]

Cuba and Nigeria have little in common. U.S.–Cuban relations have been adversarial for more than five decades. First in the early 1960s and then since the passage of the Cuban Democracy and Helms-Burton acts, the focus of U.S. policy has been to bring regime change to the island. The embargo prohibits USAID or any other federal agency from establishing programs with the Cuban government. Particularly during the Bush years but also under Clinton and now Obama, democracy promotion has been the central tenet of U.S. policy. Since the Cold War ended, the United States has linked normalization of relations to a democratic transition without any indication from Havana that it intends to change. Human rights are no more respected in 2010 than they were in 1990. After taking over in 2006, Raúl Castro dismantled the informal networks of loyalists that his brother employed to bypass institutions, but the regime's indispensable "repressive machinery" is still in place.[59] Cuban laws criminalize dissent, penalize expressions of contempt for the government or its representatives, punish insubordination to authorities and allow imprisonment for "dangerousness," defined by the Criminal Code as "the special proclivity of a person to commit crimes, demonstrated by conduct that is observed to be in manifest contradiction with the norms of socialist morality."[60] The Cuban Constitution does not contemplate civil liberties, freedom of expression or an independent judiciary. State security is ever-present, violating the citizenry's right to privacy, sending mobs to harass, intimidate and assault citizens, and overseeing a prison system of abominable conditions that further penalizes political prisoners by holding them in facilities far away from their families. However, the type of "intercommunal and political violence" with military and police involvement that took 10,000 lives in Nigeria in the past decade has not been seen in twenty-first-century Cuba.

U.S. policy lacks a sense of proportion and this undermines its efforts toward the goal of a democratic Cuba, a goal shared with many ordinary Cubans and unknown numbers within the Cuban government. Not that lives lost, freedom denied and dignity trampled in Cuba are any less significant than anywhere else. Still, the political realities of Cuba's international standing and the continued ineffectiveness of U.S. efforts to prompt either regime change or an improvement in the human-rights situation should give the Obama administration pause. Without a Tiananmen-like massacre or some other horrific action on the part of the Cuban regime, however, the United States will not succeed in mobilizing the world's outrage against Cuba's dictatorship. Neither is it likely that—without a thoughtful reconsideration of what has not worked in two decades—human rights in Cuba will improve as a consequence of U.S. policy. Secretary Clinton put it well:

> We must be pragmatic and agile in pursuit of our human rights agenda—not compromising on our principles, but doing what is most likely to make them real. And we will use all the tools at our disposal, and when

we run up against a wall, we will not retreat with resignation or recriminations, or repeatedly run against the same wall, but respond with strategic resolve to find another way to effect change and improve people's
lives.[61]

After the Cold War ended, American policy has "repeatedly run against the
same wall" without bringing to bear either "strategic resolve" or pragmatism
and agility on behalf of human rights in Cuba.

The International Community

The UN Human Rights Council

On February 5, 2009, the UN Human Rights Council reviewed Cuba. Unlike
the old UN Commission on Human Rights, the UNHRC mandates a Universal Periodic Review for all member states every four years. The current cycle
began in 2008 and will conclude in 2011.[62] The UPR consists of three principal
documents: 1) a national report; 2) a UN report that follows the same protocol
for all countries; and 3) a summary report of NGO submissions drawn by the
Office of the High Commissioner for Human Rights that similarly adheres to
uniform guidelines. The UNHRC holds a three-hour discussion for each UPR:
the country under scrutiny has up to an hour to present its case; the remaining
two hours are alloted among interested UN member states. Subsequently, the
country being reviewed submits written responses to the recommendations
made. On June 10, 2009, the Human Rights Council issued its final report on
Cuba.

Controversies swirled before the UNHRC called Cuba's three-hour session
to order. The summary report of NGO submissions in particular prompted a
bevy of complaints from Havana and its supporters. In their view, the UN-
drawn summary did not do justice to Cuba's achievements nor address the harm
perpetrated by the U.S. embargo. Three-hundred and twenty-six NGOs had
submitted 2,000, mostly Havana-friendly pages. A spokesman for the UN High
Commissioner for Human Rights expressed surprise at the number: "Normally,
they come in dozens, not hundreds." The High Commissioner responded that
"the drafting procedure was rigorously the same as the one used for all countries."[63] Approximately 300 of the NGO submissions came from either official
or semi-official Cuban organizations or international solidarity groups. The UN
document summarizes their presentations as well as those by groups critical of
Havana's record, which had the effect of giving the latter a qualitative presence
amid the repetitive plaudits of the former. Thus, for example, Amnesty International's concern "that human-rights monitoring in Cuba continues to be very
restricted;" the Inter-American Juridical Committee on Human Rights' reference to multiple international reports shedding light on brutal prison conditions;

Christian Solidarity Worldwide's calling attention to rising violations of religious liberty; or Reporters without Borders's pointing out that journalists cannot exercise their profession freely in the face of the government's monopoly of information, among others, stand out in the summary if only for their dissonance from the monotony of so much praise. (Groups critical of Cuba, too, sometimes praised the government, highlighting Cuba's welcoming the UN Special Rapporteur on the right to food in November 2007 and its signing the International Covenant on Economic, Social and Cultural Rights and the International Covenant on Civil and Political Rights in February 2008. Cuba's supporters refrained from criticism.[64])

More than 100 countries signed up to speak at Cuba's review, but only sixty were able to take the floor. Chile, Mexico and Brazil asked Havana to respect the rights of political opponents as well as for an "effective guarantee" of freedom of expression and the right to travel. Other countries in the region— e.g., Colombia, Panama, Jamaica and the Dominican Republic—chose to focus only on Cuba's record on education and health care. A group of eight countries—Austria, Canada, the Czech Republic, Holland, Israel, Italy, Slovakia and the United Kingdom—called on Havana to free human-rights activists and other prisoners of conscience. Afterwards Ricardo Alarcón commented: "In this country, there are no political prisoners. People are in jail for crimes against the law, for being paid agents of a foreign power."[65] Cuba *has* taken some steps in the right direction. It had signed but not ratified the ICCPR and the ICESCR as of June 2010. In 2009, Havana ratified the Convention on Enforced Disappearances and invited a Special Rapporteur from the Convention on Torture and Other Cruel or Inhuman Treatment or Punishment—signed by Cuba in 1986 and ratified in 1995—to visit the island. Though expected in 2010, Havana announced in June that the visit would not be possible before the rapporteur's mandate expired.[66] Cuba also presented periodic reports to the Committee on the Rights of the Child and the Committee on the Elimination of Racial Discrimination. At the time of its Universal Periodic Review, Cuba reported having begun to draft the report for the Committee on Torture and Other Cruel or Inhuman Treatment or Punishment; it was delivered in January 2010.[67]

Cuba's national report to the Human Rights Council made clear its understanding of human rights: "With the triumph of the Revolution on 1 January 1959, the Cuban people achieved true independence and were able to create the conditions for full and universal enjoyment of all human rights." The account highlighted the constitutional protection of civil and political rights: "Chapter V of the Constitution sets forth the principles and guarantees of human rights and fundamental freedoms, which are in line with the rights contained in the Universal Declaration of Human Rights and the other international human rights instruments."[68] Only Havana does not—or cannot—acknowledge that today's human-rights activists and peaceful opponents—a good many once within the revolution's ranks—changed their minds and turned against the government. While a few may well be paid U.S. agents, the overwhelming majority are not. Havana, therefore, does a self-serving reading of the Universal Declaration of Human Rights, the keynote document from which all other treaties and covenants flow. Its country report claims compliance, but its record belies it. The declaration is written in pristine language that leaves no room for interpretation. For example: "Everyone has the right to freedom of opinion and expression" and "to freedom of peaceful assembly and association." The declaration does not say that only citizens who agree with those in power have these rights, nor that meeting basic needs in health and education mitigate the complete disregard of civil liberties.

The Organization of American States

On June 2–3, 2009, the OAS General Assembly met in San Pedro Sula, Honduras. Cuba was the sole item on the agenda. After much debate, the assembly revoked the 1962 sanctions excluding the Cuban government from its ranks. The new resolution—which passed unanimously—states:

1   That Resolution VI, adopted on January 31, 1962, at the Eighth Meeting of Ministers of Foreign Affairs, which excluded the Government of Cuba from its participation in the Inter-American System, hereby ceases to have effect in the OAS.
2   That the participation of the Republic of Cuba in the OAS will be the result of a process of dialogue initiated at the request of the Government of Cuba, and in accordance with the practices, purposes and principles of the OAS.[69]

Except for the United States, all countries in the region now have normal relations with Cuba. In 2009, ten Latin-American presidents traveled to Cuba on official visits. Without Obama's proclamation of "a new beginning," however, rescinding Cuba's OAS exclusion would have been unthinkable.

In 1962, the resolution excluding the Cuban government was approved after Havana sided with the Soviet Union and began lending support to guerrillas in Latin America. Under the Río Treaty (1947), conduct that imperiled hemispheric security merited expulsion from the inter-American system. At the time, the Cold War was at its height. In 1964, the OAS called on member states to break diplomatic and commercial ties with Havana; all but Mexico complied. Eleven years later, however, the General Assembly resolved to end collective sanctions against Cuba and set member states free to restore relations with Havana. The Ford administration, which had opened a discreet dialogue with Havana, green-lighted the OAS move. Still, the 1975 resolution passed with only the requisite two-thirds majority. Chile, Paraguay and Uruguay, then military dictatorships, voted No; military-led Brazil and Anastasio Somoza's Nicaragua abstained.

"What is the next step for us? Nothing," OAS Secretary General José Miguel Insulza said after the annulment of the 1962 expulsion. National Assembly President Ricardo Alarcón called the move "a major victory," but quickly added that Cuba had no plans to rejoin the OAS. In Honduras for the OAS meeting, Dan Restrepo, senior director for Western Hemisphere Affairs at the National Security Council, noted: "We did exactly what we stated we would do here, which was stand up for the core values of democracy and human rights." Senator Robert Menéndez (D-NJ) warned:

> If the OAS allowed Cuba back in the fold without the government in Havana demonstrating a commitment to democracy, then I seriously would have to question why the U.S. government would want to pay 60 percent of an organization that is not committed to democracy, human rights and the rule of law.

Ecuadorean Foreign Minister Fender Falconi lauded the resolution for being free of "conditions of any kind, which is a good sign, because a historic error has been corrected." Honduran President Manuel Zelaya declared: "We begin a new era of fraternity and tolerance."[70] The resolution's meaning was, indeed, in the eye of the beholder.

At first glance, the discussion in San Pedro Sula was about revoking Cuba's suspension. While conditions were not directly imposed, the resolution established a process that only Havana can trigger. If and when it does, the OAS would host a dialogue based on its own "practices, purposes, and principles"— democracy, human rights and the rule of law—to bring about the "participation of the Republic of Cuba." A close reading of Article 3 of the Inter-American Democratic Charter (2001), however, reveals a more complex issue:

> Essential elements of representative democracy include, *inter alia*, respect for human rights and fundamental freedoms, access to and the exercise of power in accordance with the rule of law, the holding of periodic, free and fair elections based on secret balloting and universal suffrage as an expression of the sovereignty of the people, the pluralistic system of political parties and organizations, and the separation of powers and independence of the branches of government.

In the 2000s, some governments—Venezuela, Bolivia, Ecuador, Nicaragua and Honduras under Zelaya—have, in practice, rejected representative democracy and put forward an alternative model of participatory democracy. Should Havana take the initiative to open a dialogue as per the resolution's second point, the OAS would be in a bind that might well bury it. Discussing the character of Cuban politics—dictatorial or simply another variant of participatory democracy—would force into the open the challenges that the Chavista model in Venezuela—winning elections only to subvert democracy from within—has lobbed at the Democratic Charter.

In lifting the 1962 expulsion, the OAS gave Cuba the power to provoke what almost certainly would be a major crisis. But while Hugo Chávez and his allies may well have relished that fight, Havana was not likely to ask to be readmitted to the OAS anytime soon. While sparing no epithet against the OAS, the Cuban government was unlikely to force a debate that almost certainly would tear it asunder. Havana's most important relationship—whether in enmity or friendship—is with Washington. There was no reason to derail the fledgling improvement in relations by forcing the issue on the OAS floor. Arresting Alan Gross, allowing Orlando Zapata to die on a hunger strike, blaming the United States for Guillermo Fariñas's hunger strike and harassing *Las Damas de Blanco* were, however, altogether different matters. Having Gross in custody signaled Havana's determination to stop democracy-promotion programs. Havana's actions regarding Zapata, Fariñas and the Ladies in White undermined a process of rapprochement with the United States and full normalization of relations with the European Union that would have required concessions the regime loathed to make. The Cuban government hunkered down whenever the heart of the matter was the U.S. objective of regime change or the EU's engagement that also aimed for a democratic transition. The church–state dialogue initiated in May 2010 may, however, have represented a small step back from the official Cuba standard response on human rights.

Spain

After the Socialist Party's electoral upset in 2004, Spain's course regarding Cuba changed. José Luis Rodríguez Zapatero, who irritated the Bush administration when he recalled 1,300 combat troops from Iraq, a decision that registered 78 percent approval in Spanish opinion polls, also parted ways with the United States regarding Cuba.[71] Just as the Bush administration fine-tuned a harder-line policy toward Cuba in his first term, Zapatero backtracked from José María Aznar's confrontational rhetoric with Havana.

Obama's White House and the Moncloa Palace were now rebuilding the U.S.–Spanish relationship. Obama and Zapatero shared a similar worldview, particularly with respect to the need of resetting international relations and reaching out to the Muslim world. In October 2009, Zapatero paid his first official visit to the White House. He promised Obama a significant contribution in Afghanistan while agreeing to accept three Guantánamo detainees.[72] Nonetheless, the Moncloa Palace was chagrined at Obama's decision to skip the summit between the European Union and the United States in May 2010, a summit that was later cancelled.[73] On Cuba, Obama reportedly said to

Zapatero: "We're taking steps, but if they don't take steps too, it'd be very hard for us to continue."[74] A few days later, Spanish Foreign Minister Miguel Ángel Moratinos traveled to Havana. On October 27, Cuba's ambassador to Spain reminded Madrid and Washington of Havana's long-standing position: the Cuban government is willing "to discuss directly on an equal basis" with the United States and does not need "intermediaries."[75] Be that as it may, Spain and the United States were again having friendly conversations on Cuba, although with dialogue, not confrontation, as a goal. (Under Aznar and Bush, Spain and the United States had pursued a path of confrontation with one crucial difference: Madrid and Havana had full diplomatic and commercial relations.) Zapatero applauded Obama's "new beginning," his lifting of restrictions on family travel and remittances as well as the American disposition to start a dialogue on issues such as migration and drug-trafficking. "Now the Cuban government has to carry out reforms and, in my opinion, these should start with the economy," the Spanish prime minister said. "Cuba has to move some chips. We have to have that expectation."[76]

Upon landing at José Martí International Airport for a two-day visit to Havana in October 2009, Foreign Minister Moratinos emphasized that the purpose of his trip was to strengthen Spanish and EU bilateral relations with Cuba. It was his second visit to Havana. The purpose of his first trip, in April 2007, had been to mend fences a few months after a high-ranking foreign-ministry official had met with Cuban dissidents, an act that set back Madrid's effort to normalize relations. After his departure then, the Spanish embassy invited a group of dissidents to meet with a senior Spanish foreign-ministry official, though most spurned the invitation. In 2009, Moratinos had initially sounded out Havana on the prospect of a Spanish senior official again meeting with dissidents after Moratinos's departure. Once in Havana, however, he ruled it out.[77] When asked why he did not meet with the dissidents, Moratinos said: "I didn't come to Cuba to meet with any particular segment of Cuban society."[78] A group of thirty-seven political prisoners—all imprisoned in 2003 for their peaceful activities—sent the foreign minister a scathing letter criticizing Spanish "complacency with totalitarianism" and his "contempt" for the dissidents. Madrid's policy was supported by a minority of dissidents inside Cuba.[79]

Was Spain simply coddling the Cuban dictatorship? Of course not. Zapatero followed a realist policy toward Havana. Spain had traditionally maintained normal ties with Cuba: Franco never broke relations with Fidel Castro, a fellow Galician. Even as Aznar dramatically changed the tone, diplomatic and commercial ties continued. Socialist Felipe González never hesitated to be sharp with Cuba either, but he remained committed to engagement. From 1996 to 2004, Aznar placed Spain's relations with Washington on a par with his relations with the rest of Europe and Latin America, areas that democratic Spain had established as foreign-policy mainstays. Particularly after Iraq but even without it, a new Socialist government was bound to retake the post-Franco directions. Since 2004, Spain has been set on strengthening EU-Latin-American ties. While holding the European Union's rotating presidency during the first semester of 2010, Madrid hoped to conclude the long-pending association agreements with Central America and Mercosur.[80]

Normalizing relations with Cuba was an integral part of Spanish policy toward Latin America. Aznar's closeness to Washington and his militancy against Havana had not sat well in the region. Until Orlando Zapata's death, Spain under the Socialists and the EU had refrained from using acerbic language with the Cuban government. Since 1996, Havana had been smarting over the EU's Common Position, a policy that it claimed exerted unique and discriminatory pressure on the island (the EU had, in fact, issued similar positions against Belarus, Libya, Myanmar and North Korea).[81] In 2010, Spain's first-semester presidency of the European Union seemed to present an ideal opportunity to revisit the Common Position with the goal of revoking it or at least significantly diluting it. During his October 2009 visit, Moratinos pressed upon Raúl Castro the importance of making humanitarian gestures of consequence to bolster Spain's case before the European Union.[82] He also invited Castro to the EU summit with Latin America and the Caribbean scheduled for May 18, 2010 in Madrid. Subsequently, Havana freed a political prisoner from the Black Spring of 2003, authorized another—previously released for health reasons—to leave the country, granted a temporary exit permit to the wife of a prominent prisoner of conscience and released from jail a Spanish citizen accused of bribing public officials while he awaited trial.[83] Earlier, Zapatero's government had been instrumental in gaining freedom for other political prisoners.[84]

In late November 2009, *Der Spiegel*, the German weekly magazine, interviewed Zapatero on Spain's upcoming EU presidency. Asked about Spain's special relation with Cuba, Zapatero noted that many Cubans—including the large Castro family—are descended from Spaniards and called ties with the island "a biological imperative." Economic matters and human rights lay at the center of the "exigent dialogue" that Spain expected to have with the Cuban government. "We have to evaluate the steps that Raúl Castro's government takes to launch a period of economic reforms," said Zapatero, adding that these could be "levers" for broader changes. "In the medium term, I think something will move in the regime," he concluded.[85] Were it not that Felipe González walked down the same path and achieved little, the prime minister's logic would be flawless. Still, Cuba's circumstances in 2010 were not those of the early 1990s. Two decades of the special period had exhausted ordinary Cubans. After a nearly three-hour meeting with Raúl Castro, Moratinos said: "I have found in President Castro a commitment to reform, to advance the process of reform in the whole country, to improve the economic situation of Cuba. Today he reiterated his will to continue the process."[86] Were it not that the modest reforms launched in 2007 have been largely stalled since mid-2008, the foreign minister's assessment of Raúl's intentions might have been significant.

At issue were the two models of dealing with Cuba: confrontation or engagement. Spain and the other twenty-six EU member states rejected confrontation, particularly as expressed by the U.S. embargo. Differences within the EU arise on how closely to engage the Cuban government should it fail to make noticeable progress on human rights. Neither the Common Position nor the 2003 EU sanctions prodded Havana into modifying the legal arsenal of repression used against the dissidents but also against the population at large. The regime released political prisoners when it needed to demonstrate goodwill, as it did in 1998 after Pope John Paul II's visit or, more recently, when it reduced the number of political prisoners from about 300 to 208.[87] By ending the 2003 sanctions and establishing a political dialogue with Havana, the European Union moved away from its version of a hardline. Only the Common Position remained.

For Spain to have persuaded the EU to rescind or dilute the Common Position, Madrid needed to have worked out a roadmap with Cuban and EU officials that included the steps Havana should take on human rights if it wanted to partake fully of European cooperation. In February 2010, the Spanish and Cuban foreign ministers and two high-ranking EU officials were to have met in Madrid but Zapata's worsening condition and finally his death derailed the encounter. Cuba's reaction to Luis Yáñez's attempt to visit Cuba in January 2010 foreshadowed this outcome. On the first weekend of the New Year, Yáñez—the Spanish Socialist Member of the European Parliament—traveled to Havana with his wife expecting to spend a few vacation days under the Havana sun.[88] Instead, the couple was unceremoniously expelled without any explanations. Upon learning of the incident, Moratinos said: "This is not good news. I think the Cubans made a mistake."[89] The secretary of state for Iberoamerica, Juan Pablo de Laiglesia, immediately summoned Cuban Ambassador Alejandro González, who declared that Cuba was well aware of what Yáñez had planned to do on the island, and that his trip threatened Cuban sovereignty and national security. Before his departure from Madrid, Yáñez had said that he had "thought" about calling his friends, the social-democratic dissidents Manuel Cuesta Morúa and Elizardo Sánchez.[90] The Spanish foreign ministry issued a statement condemning the Yáñez expulsion and expressing the hope that "similar incidents—which don't help relations between the two countries—don't recur." Ambassador González simply noted that Cuba was "ready to assume the consequences."[91] Cuban sovereignty and national security—which his government claimed Yáñez endangered—would be upheld no matter the costs.

On December 22, 2009, Moratinos testified before the Spanish parliament's Commission on Foreign Affairs. Regarding Cuba and what Spain hoped to accomplish during its EU presidency, he said: "The Spanish government will confine itself to open a debate on the advisability of trying to reach an agreement so that relations with Havana are based on a bilateral juridical instrument."[92] Even as he insisted that it would be a mistake to retain the Common Position, Moratinos emphasized that an EU economic cooperation agreement with Cuba would also be conditioned by the EU's standard clauses on human rights and the rule of law. At the inauguration of the Spanish EU presidency, Zapatero acknowledged that, while Cuba was "always an important topic for Spain," it was "not a priority" for the European Union. In a joint press conference with Zapatero and European Commission chief José Manuel Durão Barroso, Herman van Rumpuy—the EU's first permanent president—said that he had not had "time to think about Cuba." Moreover, Cuba had not been on the agenda of the Zapatero, Rumpuy and Barroso meeting in Madrid. Given the myriad problems confronting Europe, Spain certainly did not want its presidency to ride on Cuba. German Chancellor Angela Merkel, moreover, had pressed upon Zapatero her opposition to discarding or even modifying the Common Position unless Cuba showed serious progress on human rights. Sweden and Great Britain were similarly resistant. From within his own government, Zapatero faced dissent on making Cuba central to Spain's EU presidency.[93] In 2008, the Spanish prime minister had accepted Raúl Castro's invitation to visit Cuba without a date being set.[94] After Zapata's death, his trip seemed likely to be indefinitely delayed. Raúl, for his part, did not go to Madrid for the EU–Latin America summit in May 2010; instead, Foreign Minister Rodríguez represented the island at the gathering. In March, the European Parliament had passed a strongly worded resolution condemning the "avoidable and cruel death of the dissident political prisoner Orlando Zapata Tamayo" and calling for "the immediate and unconditional release of all political prisoners and prisoners of conscience."[95]

Cuba's Crossroads

At the beginning of 2010, the Cuban government continued to move slowly on domestic matters. The disastrous 2008 hurricane season only served to heighten the leadership's indecisiveness on economic reforms, which in any case never lived up to the expectations raised by Raúl Castro's earlier call for "structural changes." Still, throughout 2009, ordinary Cubans heard hints of change. There were calls to increase productivity and warnings that some subsidies would be reduced or eliminated. There was talk of doing away with the ration book, and there was a new slogan, ¡ahorro o muerte! (saving or death!), along with critiques of the "paternalistic state."[96] The latter, of course, followed naturally from the revolution's socialist turn as well as the Comandante's aversion to decentralization and the market. In keeping with his emphasis on la institucionalidad, Raúl Castro led a whirlwind of meetings in mid-2009: the National Defense Council, the Council of Ministers, the Cuban Communist Party's Central Committee (CC) and the National Assembly. The CC meeting postponed the Party Congress, which had been scheduled for the second half of 2009. In Castro's words, "identifying our principal problems will take us some more time."[97] Cuba's "principal problems," however, had long been identified. In 1970, Fidel Castro acknowledged them, and *Granma* reprinted an excerpt of his speech in November 2009:

> Lack of productivity is an abyss that threatens to swallow our human resources and the country's wealth. We have to become aware, the workers need to raise their *conciencia* about this problem. We need to overcome bottlenecks, be more organized, work diligently every day with more discipline, rationality, common sense.[98]

From the mid-1970s to the mid-1980s the Cuban economy registered modest growth only after the government received large increases in Soviet subsidies and applied the post-Stalinist model of relative decentralization and material incentives. Unlike his brother, Raúl Castro embraced market socialism and remained more open to economic reforms, except he favored a failed model over the model that has yielded economic success for China and Vietnam. More than three years after succeeding the Comandante, Raúl had thwarted popular expectations that his government might create "a breathing space and perhaps a turning point in the nation's economic environment," and opted instead to prolong the status quo "in spite of its manifest inefficiency."[99] As a result, the Cuban economy tottered, its fragility no doubt aggravated by the global financial crisis. Still, in good or bad times, the regime never put forward an economic program that placed living standards and individual initiatives at the center. Instead, it preferred token measures such as allowing beauticians to take over Havana beauty shops by paying a $45 monthly tax or piloting a program that permitted taxi drivers to use their vehicles as their own if they assumed responsibility for maintenance. In the meantime, the state sector was bloated by at least a million excess workers.[100]

In part, Cuban leaders had failed to grapple with the country's economic woes due to their military mindset. At the Central Committee gathering in late July 2009, Raúl Castro repeatedly mentioned the party's failure to replicate in the economy the strength it had achieved with its armed forces. Both, he added, were equally essential to national security.[101] In the early 1990s, when he was defense minister, he had said something similar: "Beans are more important than cannons."[102] Each sector, however, thrives on different principles: A strong military depends on an inviolable discipline down the chain of command; a strong economy needs entrepreneurship, innovation, competition and, yes, self-interest. At the CC meeting, Raúl brought up "false unanimity," a pernicious practice that he said stifled "debate and a healthy discrepancy." His words harked back to the *Llamamiento*, the convocation of the 1992 party congress that decried *la doble moral*—saying one thing in public while believing another—and called on the citizenry to speak out without *el afán de unanimidad*, the zeal of unanimity.[103] A few years later, Raúl said it differently: "We need to learn to disagree with those in charge. We don't say anything in meetings but we talk endlessly in hallways."[104] Raúl was, nonetheless, not inviting disagreements with the Comandante, himself or the PCC. How else but under constitutionally guaranteed civil liberties could citizens feel safe to freely express healthy discrepancies?

In March 2009, the regime's purge of Carlos Lage and Felipe Pérez-Roque was but the latest example of how political elites fall precipitously for criticizing the policies of "those in charge."[105] Ordinary Cubans likewise suffered the consequences of living in a closed society: in a 2006 Gallup poll, nearly 75 percent had said they lacked the freedom to decide what to do with their lives. Amid the country's economic frailty and the citizenry's sense of helplessness, the regime conducted a nationwide military maneuver, *Bastión 2009*, in November.[106] The government's rationale was that it needed to be ready to defend the homeland from the empire. On the nightly program, Roundtable, the chairman of the joint chiefs of staff, Division General Leonardo Andollo, said that the goal of the maneuver was "to confront the enemy's subversive activity, directed at provoking social unrest and ungovernability," an unusual acknowledgment of potential troubles from within.[107] In December, Raúl told the National Assembly that *Bastión 2009* had met its principal goals. The next exercise would take place in 2012 and subsequently continue on a four-year cycle.[108] Cuban leaders had a clearly defined military strategy, but they could not muster the political will to redress the nation's dire economic troubles.

How Cuban leaders have chosen to govern has had consequences for the island's foreign relations. Since the 1970s, Cuban foreign policy has had impressive success. After pursuing a strategy of guerrilla warfare in Africa and Latin America in the 1960s, Havana developed a largely diplomatic approach to break through the isolation that the United States intended to create with the embargo. Its program of "international solidarity," which involved sending tens of thousands of civilians to serve abroad, bolstered the island's international standing. After the Cold War ended, Havana again demonstrated first-rate foreign-policy skills to deflect the regime change that the United States hoped to achieve with the Cuban Democracy and Helms-Burton acts. Even when rebuked by the international community for the shootdown of the Brothers to the Rescue planes over the Florida Straits in 1996 and the Black Spring of 2003, the regime stood fast, without making what it judged to be unacceptable concessions on the domestic front.

As the second decade of the twenty-first century begins, the Cuban government's foreign-policy template might not be as useful for advancing its interests as it had been in the past. To begin with, the Obama administration has changed the tone of U.S.–Cuba policy and taken small steps, such as reopening immigration talks with Havana and allowing unrestricted family travel and remittances. At the United Nations General Assembly, Cuban Foreign Minister

Bruno Rodríguez expressed his government's position, which left no room for interpretation:

> The blockade against Cuba is a unilateral and criminal policy that also has to be lifted unilaterally. It is not reasonable, just, or possible to wait for gestures from Cuba for an end to the criminal application of measures against the Cuban people.[109]

As the UN General Assembly again voted overwhelmingly in favor of lifting the U.S. embargo in October 2009, many delegates expressed optimism that U.S.–Cuban relations would improve under the Obama administration.[110] Cuba's position, however, left little margin for a gradual easing of tensions. The Cuban government was fully cognizant of the politics surrounding the embargo in Washington and, if it truly wanted to change the status quo, crafting a policy that allowed for an incremental process of change in U.S.–Cuban relations would be in order.

In the first semester of 2010, Havana would have faced a test with the European Union. Under its presidency, Spain had intended to negotiate the Common Position's end or dilution. After Orlando Zapata's death, however, a meeting of Spanish, Cuban and EU officials scheduled for February was cancelled. In mid-March, Spain admitted that it would be impossible to modify, let alone lift, the Common Position.[111] The twenty-seven-country consensus would remain a goal for another day when Havana might be willing to show some goodwill on human rights.[112] Even before Zapata's demise, Zapatero was grappling with dissent from within: Moratinos clearly wanted to lift the Common Position, while other Socialists balked at sacrificing Spain's EU presidency to the controversy over Cuba. In the late 1990s, Havana had been somewhat pragmatic regarding the Common Position. Despite official policy to the contrary, then the regime sometimes welcomed visits by EU ministers and the European Commission.[113] Whether in the future it would be able to show a flexible disposition on human rights—for example, by eliminating the "dangerousness" clause from the penal code or allowing the Red Cross to visit some prisons—was an open question. Havana was certainly cognizant of the centrality that the EU accords democracy and human rights:

> The EU fosters the universality and indivisibility of all human rights—civil, political, economic, social and cultural—as stipulated in the Universal Declaration of Human Rights and reaffirmed by the World Conference on Human Rights (Vienna, 1993). The Treaty on European Union (article 11) defines that one of the objectives of the EU's Common Foreign and Security Policy is the development and consolidation of democracy, and the rule of law, and respect for human rights and fundamental freedoms.[114]

The European Instrument for Democracy and Human Rights (EIDHR) supports civil society in non-EU countries.[115] Since 1995, EU economic cooperation agreements have included the following sentence: "Respect for human rights and democratic principles is the basis for the cooperation between the Parties and for the provisions of this Agreement, and it constitutes an essential element of the Agreement."[116] In the event the Common Position were lifted, Havana would still have to come to terms with the European Union's insistence on democracy and human rights as the basis for peace, development and security. Without such an acceptance, an economic cooperation agreement would be impossible.

Regarding relations with the European Union, the United Nations and the United States, Vietnam could serve as a model for Cuba. The citation above—standard language for EU agreements—is from the EU–Vietnam economic cooperation accord that went into effect in 1996. Since the mid-1990s, the European Community–Vietnam Joint Commission has provided a forum for biannual, high-level discussions. Two working groups—on cooperation and on trade and investment—and two sub-groups—one on institution building, administrative reform, governance and human rights, the other on science and technology—created opportunities for annual consultations. Though non-binding, the democratic clause requires a dialogue on sensitive domestic matters. Even if resistant to making political concessions, Vietnam sometimes offers gestures. In 2005, for example, Hanoi softened its stance on at least three occasions. After repeated requests, the British ambassador and the head of the EU delegation were permitted to visit a prominent dissident in prison. The UN High Commissioner for Refugees (UNHCR) visited the Central Highlands to check on the Montagnards, Christians from the Degar ethnic group who were returning to Vietnam from Cambodia. (A Memorandum of Understanding between the UNCHR and the Vietnamese government committed Hanoi not to punish the returnees for having illegally left the country.[117] The U.S. embassy lauded the Vietnamese government for freeing religious prisoners and enacting less restrictive religious laws.)[118] Vietnam signed and ratified the UN International Covenant on Civil and Political Rights. Unlikely to meet universal and indivisible standards on human rights, Vietnamese leaders nonetheless go through the motions. Unlike Cuba's leadership, Vietnam's has focused its efforts on economic growth and on improving the living standards of its people. The 2005 concessions came about as a result of Vietnam's interest in joining the World Trade Organization, which it did in 2006. Regarding U.S.–Vietnamese relations, the United States has largely focused on trade, investment and security issues while urging Hanoi to do better on human rights.[119]

Vietnam is an authoritarian regime that "respects" human rights if it serves official purposes while trampling them more often than not. Neither Vietnam nor Cuba accept the universal and indivisible character of human rights: that, for example, freedom of speech applies equally to government supporters and opponents. Hanoi has long faced criticism for its persecution of the Montagnards for practicing their faith or expressing their political opinions, and it has never committed to altering that behavior. Havana's troubles lie largely with stifling political dissent and jailing peaceful activists. Related to this is a more recent development: The rising numbers of Cubans of African descent in the opposition, drawing attention to the still pervasive prejudices and discriminatory practices in Cuban society. In December 2009, sixty African Americans called on Havana to release Darsi Ferrer, a black physician who was on a hunger strike to denounce Cuban racism. Two months earlier, Abdias Nascimento, the historical leader of the Black Movement of Brazil, had written a letter to Raúl Castro urging him to free Ferrer and stop the harassment of civil-rights activists. Havana responded swiftly to the African Americans, accusing them of contributing to a "campaign that is attempting to suffocate our sovereignty and national identity."[120] Should Cuba face a future challenge in international forums for alleged racism and discrimination, Havana's present attitude would not serve it well.

From Cuba's perspective, the crux of the matter with the European Union was whether to accept the EU system on human rights and democracy, which would neither be like the old UN Commission on Human Rights (hostile since the early 1990s) nor the new council (mostly friendly). Havana would be obliged to face uncomfortable but diplomatic questions from the EU on subjects Cuban leaders consider their business and no one else's. If it moved meaningfully on human rights and the EU lifted the Common Position, the Cuban government would have entered uncharted terrain and a new foreign-policy paradigm. As long as it stalled or resisted substantive economic reforms, however, the regime would not find a Vietnam-like *modus vivendi* on human rights with the European Union while benefiting from economic cooperation, trade and investment. In the end, of course, Vietnam is strategically important for many international actors; Cuba simply is not. The Cuban leadership had yet to grasp that the island no longer had a significant role in international affairs. Neither had it admitted to the connection between improving living standards and the formulation of a new foreign-policy template.

What's Next?

As *Las Damas de Blanco* gathered on December 10, 2009, Human Rights Day, and handed out copies of the UN Declaration of Human Rights, some 200 individuals encircled them, shouting insults and occasionally delivering blows.[121] Since the Black Spring of 2003, the ladies dressed in white had made it a habit to attend Sunday Mass at the Church of Santa Rita. Afterwards, they would stroll down the stately Fifth Avenue in the Havana suburb of Miramar, raising their coral gladioli in a silent plea for their loved ones' freedom. State security had not usually interfered with their Sunday walks and the December 10 assault proved to be a preview of what was to come on the seventh anniversary of the Black Spring. Beginning on March 15, 2010, *Las Damas* marched every day for seven days straight, a day for every year their loved ones had been in jail. State security staged an all-out effort to dissuade them from walking, to no avail. Agents dressed in civilian clothes "protected" the women as deputized mobs followed them, hurling verbal abuse. Every day, *Las Damas* went to Mass at a different parish in Havana and then walked to government buildings such as the Union of Cuban Journalists and the National Assembly, demanding freedom for their relatives. Pedestrians, drivers, people in their front porches or balconies, shoppers at open-air markets, all watched, with only a few joining the mob chants.[122] On March 21, the last day of that week of protests, diplomats from Germany, Sweden, Italy, United Kingdom, Czech Republic, Poland, Hungary, the United States and Spain joined the women for Mass at Santa Rita.[123] In Miami, Gloria Estefan led tens of thousands through the heart of Little Havana in support of the Ladies in White.[124]

Palm and Easter Sundays provided *Las Damas* with a respite from state security. Afterwards, the harassment resumed in force. For three consecutive Sundays, pro-government women kept them from walking on Fifth Avenue. Government agents told the ladies to apply for a permit but they refused. Though sometimes *Las Damas* answered official slogans—*¡La calle es de Fidel!* (The Street Belongs to Fidel!)—with their own *¡Libertad!* or *¡Viva Zapata!*—they mostly kept silent, raising their arms in a V or making an L with their thumbs and index fingers. On April 25, after *Las Damas* had been hounded for six hours at a park across the street from Santa Rita, Jaime Ortega Alamino—Cuba's cardinal and the archbishop of Havana—decided to approach the authorities. Three days later the government responded: "Tell the women that they can walk wherever they see fit without applying for a permit." On May 2, Ortega officiated Mass in Santa Rita—with *Las Damas* in attendance—to, in his words, "make sure the agreement was kept." The ladies resumed their walks without contretemps. One of them said: "We are thankful for the church's intervention because we were stubborn—the government and we—we [*Las Damas de Blanco*] admit it."[125] At least through May, there would be no "incidents," the authorities said.[126] It was a rare hand extended in moderation, which Ortega firmly shook, a "novel step."[127]

More followed. On May 19, Raúl Castro met with Cardinal Ortega and Dionisio García Ibáñez, archbishop of Santiago de Cuba and president of the Conference of Cuban Bishops. The four-and-a-half-hour meeting was another sign of something afoot. Over the years the church had interceded with Cuban authorities on humanitarian cases, usually without success. A noteworthy exception had been the release of nearly 300 political prisoners after Pope John Paul II's visit in 1998, though in that case it was a gesture made to His Holiness himself.[128] In a press conference on May 20, the cardinal emphasized:

> We didn't go to discuss church issues, what we need to carry out its mission. No, that wasn't the topic. We went to talk about Cuba, the current moment and our future. It should be clear that the president understands well that the relationship is with the Cuban church.[129]

A few days later, the government agreed to move political prisoners closer to their hometowns: The practice had been to hold them in far-away jails, making family visits difficult. The twenty-six prisoners in frail health—for whose freedom Zapata gave his life and Guillermo Fariñas launched a hunger strike— were to be transferred to hospitals for proper care.[130] During May, church officials also visited Fariñas twice. Though adamant about sacrificing his life if no relief came for the ailing prisoners, he offered to end his hunger strike under certain conditions. "If they free the 10 or 12 prisoners most in need of medical care, I would abandon my protest so that the government can negotiate with the church the release of the rest on another timetable and without pressure," Fariñas told *El País*, a Spanish daily.[131]

The Cuban government was stepping on uncharted ground. After an unprecedented international clamor over Orlando Zapata's death and Raúl Castro's words in early April—"We will never yield to blackmail from any country or group of countries, no matter how powerful they might be, and regardless of the consequences"—that held out no hope of compromise, the authorities answered Ortega's call to dialogue.[132] In so doing, Castro recognized the Catholic Church as an interlocutor at a time of international backlash. On May 20, *Granma* published a brief note on the president's meeting with Cardinal Ortega and Archbishop García reporting that "topics of common interest" had been discussed. On May 21, *Granma* took note of the cardinal's press conference in an article that included the church's press release on the June 15–20 visit of the Vatican's foreign minister, Monsignor Dominique Mamberti. Ortega emphasized that Mamberti's long-planned visit was not a topic of conversation with Castro. The meeting was strictly a Cuban initiative to deal with Cuban matters.[133] Unlike the negotiation that gained freedom for the Bay of Pigs invaders and the dialogue of 1978, the United States was not at all involved in the talks between the church and the government. While too early to consider the church–state dialogue a turning point, the May events opened up possibilities that had long seemed inconceivable. By engaging with the church, the government temporarily halted the world's condemnation over Zapata's death and *Las Damas de Blanco*'s harassment. All the same, Havana could not publicly admit that the "colossal campaign" of rebuke had worked. Without the uproar, Raúl Castro may not have been so willing to meet with Ortega and García. Were this kind of moderation to take hold, Havana would have inched closer to a modus operandi on human rights that might bear fruits in the international arena.

The Catholic Church has often been criticized for not confronting the government. Once again the heart of the matter lay in how best to relate to Cuban authorities: The bishops, well aware of the government's resistance to compromise on domestic matters, have long opted for engagement.[134] The fledgling dialogue, moreover, held out the possibility of improving the living conditions of political prisoners, getting proper care for those in ill health and, perhaps, gaining their freedom. At the same time, the Cuban church became more insistent about the urgency for change as the government delayed making meaningful economic reforms. *Palabra Nueva*, the magazine of the Havana archdiocese, published a biting critique of the economy that echoed what many in official Cuba advocated: self-employment, decentralization, liberalization, in short, respect for the economic rights of citizens. Cardinal Ortega reiterated the church's commitment to "dialogue and reconciliation among all Cubans", a phrase that included the diaspora in all its factions as an integral part of Cuba.[135] In March, the church declined an invitation to participate in a meeting to develop a "strategic alliance" between the state and all religious denominations. Ortega explained the inappropriateness of such an alliance:

> I have never accepted these terms… because of their military or political resonances that are not appropriate in the church's relations with the state…serving the men and women who live in our country does not depend on a pact—open or implicit—with the state.[136]

Neither ally nor enemy: that was the Catholic Church that was engaging with Cuban authorities.

For its part, the Obama administration's "new beginning" with Havana had not yet found a sustained momentum in the summer of 2010. Neither the White House nor Congress felt pressed to alter Cuba policy rapidly: Changing the tone and lifting some travel restrictions were significant enough, particularly if contrasted with the state of U.S.–Cuban relations during the Bush administration. Havana, however answered Washington's call to make a conciliatory gesture by arresting Alan Gross and intensifying repression. Still, the president responded with prudence. On March 24, 2010, the White House issued a statement on recent events in Cuba:

> The tragic death of Orlando Zapata Tamayo, the repression visited upon *Las Damas de Blanco*, and the intensified harassment of those who dare to give voice to the desires of their fellow Cubans, are deeply disturbing. These events underscore that instead of embracing an opportunity to enter a new era, Cuban authorities continue to respond to the aspirations of the Cuban people with a clenched fist. Today, I join my voice with brave individuals across Cuba and a growing chorus around the world in calling for an end to the repression, for the immediate, unconditional release of all political prisoners in Cuba, and for respect for the basic rights of the Cuban people.[137]

The European Union had taken the lead in censuring the regime's appalling behavior, and de-Americanizing the problem of Cuba served American interests well. Washington still talked to Havana on concrete matters such as Gross's release and immigration.[138] Two-way travel between the United States and Cuba also continued unaffected by regime repression. Most important, the two countries opened communication on two topics of mutual interest: humanitarian aid to Haiti and BP's catastrophic spill in the Gulf of Mexico.[139]

The United States, however, seemed unwilling or unable to abandon the strict condition that any improvement in relations depended on Havana making progress on human rights and democracy. After the early 1960s, Washington slowly accepted the Cuban government as a fixture of the Cold War. With détente in the 1970s, the Ford and Carter administrations both concluded that normalizing relations and ending the "perpetual antagonism" was the best way to advance American national interests. Flawless as that argument was, Cuban actions in Africa, a renewed Cold War after the Soviet invasion of Afghanistan and the election of Ronald Reagan eventually derailed that process. Nonetheless, in the early 1980s, the Reagan administration twice dispatched high-ranking officials to meet with Cuban officials over Havana's support of Central American revolutionary movements.[140] Subsequently, it negotiated an immigration accord. At the end of Reagan's presidency, Cuban and American diplomats crafted an agreement that ended the wars in southern Africa. For Havana's foreign policy, it was a stellar moment that brought Cuba well-deserved satisfaction: for once the United States dealt with Cuba on an equal footing.

But then Berliners tore down the wall, Eastern European Communism ceased to be and the Soviet Union disintegrated. How could Cuba survive without Soviet subsidies? The Cuban Democracy and Helms–Burton acts tightened the embargo on the assumption that Havana would crumble as well. Two decades later, another Castro presides over Cuba, and the Cuban government's ability to survive without the Soviet Union had defied expectations of a quick democratic transition in Cuba. In addition, the strict conditionality inherent in these two acts carried perverse consequences for both countries. The United States, in effect, turned over control of American policy to Cuba: If Havana did not change, neither would Washington. And Havana, for all its bravado on national sovereignty, held off making domestic changes that would benefit the Cuban people until the United States lifted the embargo. Secretary Clinton was right when she said:

> It is my personal belief that the Castros do not want to see an end to the embargo and do not want to see normalization with the United States, because they would lose all of their excuses for what hasn't happened in Cuba in the last 50 years.[141]

No stronger argument was needed to move U.S. policy away from the conditionality of the past twenty years.[142] If the embargo served the regime with a scapegoat for its failures, would it not be wise for the Obama administration to challenge Cuba through dialogue and openness?

Any attempt to engage the Cuban government is fraught with frustrations. On June 1, the Catholic Church announced that six prisoners of conscience were being transferred to prisons closer to their homes. Though three were among the twenty-six in frail health, none had yet been taken to civilian hospitals, let alone freed.[143] Still, church authorities remained optimistic that progress would be made, if at official Cuba's glacial tempo. Then, amid the hopes that recent events had fanned, on June 3–4, state security arrested thirty-eight dissidents who had been planning to attend a meeting called by two leading opposition organizations.[144] Even if these women and men were only briefly held, the roundup underscored how difficult any dialogue with Havana could be. But the course of non-engagement had proven no more efficient. Tightening the embargo in the 1990s yielded no benefits, nor did the Bush administration's confrontational stance move Havana any closer to respecting human rights or launching a democratic transition.[145] Since the Cold War ended but especially during the Bush years, the United States has dwelled "in the satisfying purity of indignation" at the Cuban regime's behavior without duly considering how its policy may have contributed to "a crippling status quo" in relations with Cuba.[146]

And so *The United States and Cuba: Intimate Enemies* ends where it began: Normal relations between the two countries—which will require that the United States take into account Cuban sensibilities and that Cuba turn geographic proximity into an asset—are nowhere in the offing. With Obama, the United States has taken small steps in the right direction. Havana might be willing to do the same on matters of immigration or combating the drug trade, common interests that could help build mutual trust.[147] Cuban leaders, however, should come to terms with the reality that Cuban domestic politics matter in their relations with the United States. Washington, Cuban Miami, the European Union, most of Latin America and, indeed, the Cuban people would happily welcome a democratic Cuba; Havana, however, might not need to call free elections immediately to improve its relations with the democratic world. The dialogue started between Raúl Castro and Cuba's Catholic bishops could serve as a model for state authorities in crafting an acceptable approach to human rights. Or Cuba could follow the model of China and Vietnam, where the ruling Communist parties have fully embraced economic reforms and have sometimes found ways to address Western concerns on human rights. Cuba's elderly leaders may hesitate to improve living standards out of ideological concerns or, more likely, for fear of losing control. However, many others—perhaps most—in middle-level positions in the party and the ministries are aware that current policies are leading nowhere and that the economic rights of ordinary Cubans must be restored for the economy to recover. Staying the course against the clamor from within official ranks and from the Cuban people might well bring dire consequences for the leadership. A peaceful transformation—whether to market reforms under the Communist Party or democracy and a market economy—is a matter of mutual interest for the United States and Cuba. For five decades, both the United States and Cuba have failed: Washington in overturning the Cuban revolution and Havana in improving the material well-being of the Cuban people. Doing things differently might finally put the great power and its weaker neighbor on the right path towards achieving normal relations for the first time ever.

MEXICO AND CUBA

THE END OF A CONVENIENT PARTNERSHIP

Ana Covarrubias

In June 2010, the Organization of American States General Assembly met in San Pedro Sula, Honduras, to revoke the suspension that had been imposed on the Cuban government, preventing its participation in the activities of the regional organization. Cuba's exclusion from the OAS stemmed from resolution VI of the VIII Meeting of Consultation of Ministers of Foreign Affairs, which was adopted in Punta del Este, Uruguay, in 1962. Mexico had opposed that decision on the basis that the OAS Charter contained no provision to exclude any member from the organization. And in 1964, Mexico also voted against the OAS resolution that asked member states to break diplomatic relations with Cuba. In June 2010, therefore, Mexico might have claimed that it was the only OAS member to have maintained a relatively constant position toward socialist Cuba thanks to its recognition of Castro's government and its record of sustaining a mutually profitable relationship with it. Although Mexico's participation at the San Pedro Sula meeting was influential in the adoption of the resolution, the Mexican government did not underline its historic position, nor did it emphasize its role in the process leading to the final resolution, which repealed the 1962 decision. Mexico's relative silence on the meaning of the San Pedro Sula meeting indicated that its policy toward Cuba—and Cuba's policy toward Mexico—had changed. In fact, many things happened between the early 1960s and 2010, especially since 1990, and Cuba has lost the place it once had in Mexico's foreign policy.

In contrast with U.S.–Cuban relations, Mexico and Cuba have never been intimate enemies; on the contrary, generally speaking, the Mexican and Cuban governments maintained good communication with each other and a willingness to negotiate differences. Moreover, both governments learned how to use the bilateral relationship to satisfy their own domestic and international interests. In brief, until the end of the 20th Century, Cuba and Mexico were "convenient partners". But the increasing importance of liberal economic policies, democracy and human rights in the region toward the end of the 1990s, the end of the Cold War, Mexico's political opening and Cuba's resistance to change, modified previous understandings in Mexican-Cuban relations.

This chapter will examine how the bilateral relationship, in particular Mexican policy toward Cuba, changed over the last twenty years. It will argue that international and regional circumstances provided a favorable setting in which Mexican governments decided to adjust their policy toward Cuba according to their own interests, especially domestic ones. In other words, in a region where issues such as free trade, democracy and human rights took prominence, Presidents Ernesto Zedillo, and to an even greater extent Vicente Fox, decided to view democracy and human rights—in general, but specifically regarding Cuba—as a legitimate subject in the bilateral relationship. Fidel Castro reacted negatively, and communication between the two governments practically ended, as did their good disposition to sort out divergences. By 2004 relations had deteriorated almost to the point of rupture. Interestingly, at the beginning of the twenty-first century Mexican–Cuban relations resemble aspects of Cuba–U.S. relations: the Cuban exile community and domestic dissidents are now actors in the bilateral relationship; the Cuban government has active links with Mexico's opposition; Cuba's debt to Mexico became a bilateral conflict, as did illegal Cuban immigration; and both governments comment on each other's political processes. However, Mexico and Cuba have not broken diplomatic relations, they have continued trading with each other—however small the amount of trade—and Mexican businessmen have invested in Cuba.

In understanding the historical and contemporary bilateral relationship it is impossible to ignore the fact that Cuba and Mexico are less powerful neighbors than the regional hegemon. This partially explains why, despite significant differences, Mexico and Cuba did not become intimate enemies. Cuba and Mexico are like pieces in the regional—and international—puzzle; they have changed for different reasons, and they have to accommodate to new shapes and colors in the puzzle, but so far changes have not been deep enough to make Cuba and Mexico opponents. A convenient partnership has ended; a cycle in history has finished and it is not yet clear which form Mexican–Cuban relations will take in the future. The past, however, demonstrates how two countries with very dissimilar ideological and political positions were able to make the most of their differences, not just of their common interests. This is a useful precedent for the future.

Revolutionary Cuba and Mexico (and the United States) Become Convenient Partners

The fact that Mexico was "the only country in the region not to break diplomatic relations with Cuba in 1964"[1] became a common phrase (proudly) used by Mexican and Cuban authorities for many years. In so doing, Mexican governments implied that Mexican foreign policy was independent from that of the United States, consistent and predictable. For Cuban officials such a policy provided the regime with international recognition, a link with the region and a way of communicating with Mexican authorities. However, the history of Mexican–Cuban relations is not that simple.

As in many other Latin American countries and the United States, the Cuban revolution became not only a foreign-policy issue but also a domestic concern. In 1959, the Mexican government, self-proclaimed revolutionary, was facing social discontent, economic stalemate and political divisions, especially within the ruling party, the Institutional Revolutionary Party (PRI). The Mexican government, therefore, had to implement a policy toward Cuba that balanced the pressures from groups supporting Cuba (some of which by implication questioned the results of the "revolutionary" program allegedly implemented by the PRI), sectors of the political right, businessmen and the Catholic Church, which opposed communism, and U.S. policies toward Cuba and the region in general.

Between 1959 and 1964, the OAS focused on the Cuban revolution and its policy toward the region; these were difficult years for Mexico's foreign policy. But the Mexican government gradually shaped a policy indicating that ideological stand point was very different from that of Cuba or Communism, but that this would not force it to follow U.S. policies.[2] Castro's government, for its own reasons, reacted positively to Mexico's policy and the two countries maintained diplomatic relations based on the principle of nonintervention.[3]

At the end of the 1960s, Cuba strengthened its strategy of supporting revolution abroad, and hosted the Tricontinental Conference, which created the Organization for Solidarity of the Peoples of Africa, Asia and Latin America and the Organization of Latin American Solidarity (OLAS). This represented an opportunity for Mexico and Cuba to reinforce their mutual policy of nonintervention. The OAS again summoned a meeting to discuss Cuba's policy. On that occasion, Mexican Foreign Secretary Antonio Carrillo Flores recalled Mexico's good disposition toward Cuba, but acknowledged that he had no information regarding any act involving Mexico in accordance with the OLAS resolutions.[4] Similarly, in 1968, when social discontent in Mexico ended in confrontation between security forces and students on October 2, Cuba seems to have abstained from participating in masterminding or supporting anti-government rallies.[5] An important challenge to nonintervention, namely, Mexico's collaboration with the United States concerning intelligence activities, was also resolved, through negotiations between the two governments.[6] The most difficult case was that of Humberto Carrillo Colón, the Mexican press attaché at the embassy in Havana, whom the Cuban government accused of spying for the CIA. After Cuba disclosed the facts, presented a diplomatic protest, and published its case in its official newspaper, *Granma*, the Mexican government suspended Carrillo Colón, recalling him to Mexico and welcomed Cuban Minister of Foreign Affairs Raúl Roa, to talk the matter over; the issue was settled. In the early 1970s, President Echeverría ended other intelligence activities and Mexican–Cuban relations continued on the basis of the nonintervention "agreement."

In the 1970s, Mexican–Cuban relations improved significantly; the Mexican government implemented what has been labeled a "progressive and nationalist" foreign policy. During the October 1968 confrontation between students and the security forces, Luis Echeverría was minister of interior; in 1970, he became president. He had to formulate a domestic policy that reconciled the regime with the left; foreign policy was considered a useful instrument in this task.[7] Moreover, the 10 percent surcharge imposed by the U.S. government on all imports in 1971 drove the Mexican government to promote a policy called a "new international economic order" based on the Charter of States' Economic Rights and Duties. The Mexican government adopted Third World rhetoric and positions. Both for Echeverría's domestic opening and his progressive foreign policy, Cuba was a valuable ally, as was the international system characterized by détente between the superpowers, the increasing importance of Europe and Japan and, of course, the Third World movement. Gradually, therefore, the Mexican government put into practice a policy of rapprochement with Cuba; flights between Cuba and Mexico were reestablished; U.S.– Mexican intelligence activities ended; and Echeverría visited Cuba in 1975 (he was the first Mexican president to visit Communist Cuba).[8] Mexican policies, however, were not designed to please Cuba; as in the case of Mexico's "noninterventionist-interventionist" policy regarding intelligence and the United States, declassified U.S. documents suggest that the United States supported the idea of Echeverría becoming the Third World leader in the region to prevent Castro from taking this position.[9] Castro must have known this but Mexico's policy was beneficial for his own interests: the OAS, for example, approved a resolution whereby all member states were free to reestablish relations with Cuba. Mexico and Costa Rica promoted the resolution; in symbolic terms, it acknowledged Cuba as a legitimate member of regional politics regardless of the nature of its regime.[10] The question of Cuba's return to the organization was not raised, however, and Cuba, then or now, has not expressed any wish to do so, but the 1975 resolution was consequential in openly recognizing Cuba's importance in the region.

Cuba remained a significant interlocutor to Mexico in the late 1970s and during the 1980s, especially as the Central American conflict regionalized and Mexico implemented an active foreign policy in search of peace and stabilization: President José López Portillo actively supported the Sandinistas in Nicaragua, and the Frente Farabundo Martí para la Liberación Nacional and the Frente Democrático Revolucionario in El Salvador; his successor, Miguel de la Madrid, promoted the Contadora Group—made up of Mexico, Venezuela, Colombia and Panama—which sought for a negotiated solution to the conflict. For the Mexican government, the United States and Cuba were key to the process if peace and stability were to be achieved in Central America. The Contadora Group was not able to broker an agreement between all Central American countries but its efforts contributed to identifying the main problems and some measures that could solve them.

In addition, the North–South Meeting that took place in Cancún, Mexico, in the summer of 1981 exemplifies the willingness and capacity of Mexico and Cuba to work out differences. The purpose of the meeting was to discuss economic relations between the world's North and South to make them more just.[11] President Ronald Reagan, however, anticipated that he would not attend the summit if Fidel Castro did. The Mexican government knew that, if Reagan did not participate, other important leaders, such as UK Prime Minister Margaret Thatcher, would not either. Reagan's presence was indispensable for the viability of the meeting. Mexican Secretary of Foreign Affairs Jorge Castañeda, Sr. and President López Portillo engaged negotiations with Castro, who obviously defended his presence at the meeting as a legitimate and significant representative of the South.[12] Castro and López Portillo held a final meeting in Cozumel, with the former agreeing not to attend. The communiqué issued after Castro's visit underlined the fact that the developing countries understood and supported Cuba's rights to attend the meeting, "but given the U.S. known position, Castro's presence would determine its cancellation, damaging the negotiating process between developing and developed countries, to which President Fidel Castro has so much contributed."[13] Castro, in turn, freed "countries friendly to Cuba involved in those negotiations from any moral commitment to which they should feel inclined because of Cuba's absence."[14] Cuban Foreign Minister Isidoro Malmierca declared that not even forty "cancunes [sic]" would affect the "exemplary relations" between Mexico and Cuba.[15]

This account of the complexity in Mexican–Cuban relations identifies the major trends in the bilateral relationship for over thirty years: Cuba was a domestic issue in Mexico in terms of the support and sympathy of some groups toward the Cuban revolution, or as a means to redefine the nature or the direction of the Mexican "revolutionary" government. Cuba was also significant in terms of Mexico's foreign policy, situating Mexico in the ideological conflict of the Cold War; to prevent Cuba from supporting subversion in Mexico, and to project an independent foreign policy. The international system was decisive in Mexico's policy toward Cuba: it set limits to Mexico's action (it was one thing to maintain diplomatic relations with Cuba, and quite another to actively support the Cuban revolution, which Mexico never did), and also granted it opportunities (Mexico featured an independent foreign policy while it also collaborated with the United States in intelligence activities). The United States was the third actor in the bilateral relationship but not the determinant variable in Mexico's or Cuba's policies toward each other.

The international and domestic points of reference for Mexican–Cuban relations changed more decisively toward the end of the 1980s and in the 1990s. Mexico's economy and politics liberalized; Cuba lost its political, economic and ideological allies and, in the absence of the Soviet "threat," U.S. policy toward Cuba was influenced by domestic factors perhaps more than ever. After the collapse of Communism, Cuba again became a subject for international discussion; the main options were isolation (the U.S. preference) and constructive engagement (Canada and Europe). If the understandings between Mexico and Cuba had originated in specific circumstances, once these changed, would Mexico choose one of these policy options?

Mexico, Cuba and the United States in the post–Cold War World

As the world radically changed and the Mexican government began a process of economic opening in the mid-1980s and early 1990s, Mexican–Cuban relations maintained many of their most salient features. In 1988, after a much contested election, especially by the left headed by Cuauhtémoc Cárdenas, Fidel Castro attended the inauguration of President Carlos Salinas de Gortari.[16] Amid criticisms of the election and Castro's visit, the Cuban leader declared that he supported Salinas:

> My visit was viewed negatively but I must perforce support a government like Mexico's, which has supported us for thirty years [...] My friends are the Mexican government and Carlos Salinas de Gortari, and I am honored if my presence provided him with more support.[17]

According to the Cuban leader, it was an international duty to accept the invitation; he said that he refused to interfere in Mexican affairs because Mexico always respected Cuba: "We need Mexico. Mexico always respected us. We are loyal and on the side of (*solidarios*) with Mexico [...] This is a moment of gratitude."[18] In short; the principle of nonintervention was still part of the language of bilateral relations. Castro's visit highlighted its usefulness: the presence of foreign heads of state was symbolically important for Salinas, more so that of Castro under the circumstances, and Castro gained visibility and reinforced Cuba's links with Mexico even when the Cuban economy was in crisis and Cuba was becoming increasingly isolated within the international system.[19]

Salinas's main policy project was the North American Free Trade Agreement, which consolidated Mexico's economic liberalization. The negotiation of NAFTA marked a turning point in Mexico–U.S. relations and in Mexican foreign policy in general. In perspective, however, such change (alignment with the United States) was not radical even though Mexico's economic opening and the NAFTA agreement signaled a new direction in the country's economic policies and ideological positions. In the economic field, Mexico and the United

States became very close. Such a coincidence between them regarding the bilateral and the international economic agenda generally might have distanced Mexico from Cuba, but this did not happen.

Although the Mexican government concentrated most of its energy and resources on negotiating NAFTA, Mexico remained active in different regional diplomatic efforts, which contributed to maintaining a close and productive relationship with Cuba. Mexico and Spain summoned the I Iberoamerican summit in Guadalajara, Mexico, in July 1991 to commemorate the "encounter of two worlds" (i.e. the "discovery" of the Americas in 1492). All Iberoamerican heads of state or government attended, including King Juan Carlos I of Spain. The summit was an opportunity for Cuba to participate in a regional forum, at a time when it had lost major economic and political allies in Eastern Europe and its regime was under increasing international criticism for not democratizing. Thus, Castro's participation in the summit made Cuba visible in the region. Until 1999, the Iberoamerican summits had enabled Cuba and Mexico to maintain some of the main positions that had guided their bilateral relations for many years.

Before the Guadalajara summit, the Mexican government stated that Cuba would not be on the agenda unless there were suggestions to end the island's economic and political isolation, nor was the summit's purpose to exercise pressure on Castro, or any other leader.[20] At the Madrid summit in 1992, Cuba was a subject for discussion; participants divided into two broad groups led by Argentina and Mexico. Argentina favored adopting recommendations urging the Cuban government to democratize, while Mexico opposed such demands on the basis that they would lead to intervention in Cuba.[21] President Salinas underlined the need to respect sovereignty and tolerate differences. To the question whether he had made any suggestions to Fidel Castro, Salinas answered in the negative, for he would not like others making any recommendations to him.[22] Castro, in turn, declared that the attitudes of the Iberoamerican leaders had been frustrating, except for that of President Salinas.[23] At the IV summit in Cartagena de Indias, Presidents Carlos Saúl Menem, Argentina and Rafael Caldera, Venezuela, urged the Cuban regime to democratize. Menem suggested that he could pressure the U.S. government to lift the embargo if Castro were to open Cuba's political system.[24] At the VI summit in Santiago de Chile and Viña del Mar, 1996, Mexican President Ernesto Zedillo opposed any notion of coercing Castro, and denied the rumor that the U.S. government had requested that he ask Castro to transit to democracy.[25] Despite the views of some Latin American leaders and despite the fact that most declarations at the Iberoamerican summits supported the consolidation, defense and viability of democracies, the Mexican government defended nonintervention and the right to self-determination and opposed imposing conditions on Cuba's government.

The Mexican government took the same stance on Cuba at the Río Group meetings. At the VIII summit in September 1994, Salinas reiterated Mexico's desire for the reestablishment of Cuban–U.S. relations, always on the basis of sovereignty, justice, freedom and democracy. Once again, Argentina's position opposed Mexico's by demanding a condemnation of Cuba.[26] In a letter to Salinas, dated following the meeting, Castro stresses the value of the Mexican president as guardian of Cuba's interests in the face of the United States. Castro also expressed his annoyance at the meeting and his disapproval of the Río declaration, which emphasized the celebration of democratic elections in Latin America and the Caribbean and the link between democracy and development. To Castro, the Declaration was "a shameless intervention in Cuba's domestic affairs, and a betrayal." Finally, the Cuban leader expressed his wish that Salinas might convince Clinton that the solution to the migration problem depended on the normalization of U.S.–Cuban relations; he reminded Salinas of the response to his concern about intervention in issues pertaining to Cuba's sovereignty and independence. According to Castro's account, Salinas's answer was: "you have the formula: do not accept it."[27]

At the OAS, Mexico proposed Cuba be reinstated to full membership at the General Assembly in 1995 and 1998. Cuba was one of the major concerns of Secretary General César Gaviria, who considered that its government should move toward economic and political freedom and suggested that the inter-American community had a *responsibility* to play a constructive role in that regard.[28] Once again, member states were divided between those who supported the idea that Cuba should return to the OAS without needing to satisfy any previous condition, and those who demanded it manifest political change before being allowed to rejoin. Mexico was in the first group, Argentina and the United States in the second.[29] The shooting down of the two "Hermanos al rescate" planes in 1996 ended the discussion about Cuba's possible return to the OAS. But in 1998, Gaviria identified Cuba as the most important political problem in the hemisphere.[30] On that occasion, the Mexican government proposed the creation of mechanisms to discuss Cuba's eventual return to the OAS, similar to the UN Groups of Friends. The United States, however, stated that it was too soon to deliberate on Cuba's return to the organization, and thus the Cuban issue was no longer considered at the General Assembly.[31]

The one exception to Mexico's cautious attitude toward Cuba during Salinas's government was the Group of Three (G3) meeting in Cozumel, Mexico, in October 1991. The meeting led to speculation in many sectors; officially, the Presidents of Mexico, Colombia and Venezuela had invited Castro to explain the outcomes of the IV congress of the Communist Party that had taken place a few days earlier.[32] Cuban domestic problems, however, were the exclusive responsibility of the Cubans, according to Salinas,[33] even if, on behalf of the Colombian minister of foreign affairs, the G3 would urge democratic changes on the island.[34] Unofficially, the press suggested that the G3 presidents were trying to convince Castro to initiate a political opening in return for international support, especially much-needed oil. The meeting did not produce visible results, and it is difficult to assess whether it interfered in Cuban domestic affairs. It was clearly unusual for three Latin American governments to invite Castro to explain the decisions taken—or not—at the IV party congress but ultimately Castro attended willingly. Perhaps the most interesting consequence of the meeting in respect of Mexico's policy was Salinas's declarations a few months later in *Newsweek* magazine. Salinas recognized that Castro faced huge problems and, although Mexico respected Cuba's sovereignty, Cuba's domestic situation would be watched "with great interest because we worry about what will happen with instability there."[35] Salinas added that he had last spoken with Castro at the Cozumel meeting: "He explained his [sic] international economic situation and how they are trying to reverse it. He was confident he could get through it, but we [the G3 leaders] were not."[36]

In the political and diplomatic fields, in short, the Mexican government preserved two key pillars of the bilateral relationship: the defense of nonintervention and the right to self-determination in Cuba.[37] Mexico offered Cuba a regional presence, and Cuba still regarded Mexico as a valuable interlocutor, as Salinas's mediation between Clinton and Castro in 1994 demonstrates. In 1994, Cuban rafters were arriving at U.S. coasts in such significant numbers that President Clinton considered the need for a migration agreement with Cuba. Clinton asked Salinas to persuade Castro to enter negotiations with the United States. With the assistance of writer Gabriel García Márquez, Salinas convinced Castro to enter negotiations, and the migration accord was signed in September 1994.[38] In their accounts of this episode, Clinton and Castro underline the fact that they recognized Salinas as the sole mediator between them.[39] The Cuban leader asked Salinas to invite Clinton and enjoin to agree to discuss the economic consequences of the U.S. embargo with the Cubans. Castro required only Clinton's assurance to the Mexican president that he would be willing to debate the issue.[40]

Consistent with its position against the imposition of economic sanctions on Cuba since the early 1960s, the Mexican government opposed the 1992 Torricelli Act (Cuban Democracy Act) and the 1996 Helms-Burton Act (the Cuban Liberty and Democratic Solidarity (*LIBERTAD*) Act), which tightened the U.S. embargo on Cuba. Despite such continuity, it must be said that Mexico's policy has been directed toward the United States rather than toward Cuba. Mexico has defended its autonomy regarding trading partners and it has objected to the extraterritorial application of U.S. law. The Mexican government argued that the Torricelli Act violated essential principles of international law, especially that of nonintervention.[41] Its reaction to the Helms-Burton Act zeroed in on its clauses on trafficking with expropriated property and the denial of visas to businessmen and their families trading with or investing in Cuba (Titles III and IV). Mexico and Canada contemplated the possibility of convening a complaint panel according to NAFTA regulations, but did not do so in the end. The Mexican government, however, issued an "antidote law" (*Ley de protección al comercio y la inversión de normas extranjeras que contravengan el derecho internacional*), whereby any company established in Mexico would be sanctioned for compliance with foreign laws. Given the international opposition to the law, including the European threat to take the issue to the World Trade Organization, President Clinton postponed the application of Titles III and IV of Helms-Burton. Mexico's position concerning the Torricelli and Helms-Burton laws illustrates the importance of the United States in Mexican–Cuban relations. U.S. policy allows Mexican governments to defend foreign-policy principles and their capacity to decide autonomously, and it allows Cuba to exploit Mexican—and international—disagreement with U.S. measures in terms of its confrontation with the United States. International rejection of the Torricelli Act or Helms-Burton Act demonstrates in Cuba's view that the island is the victim of the policies of the great power and is right in defending itself.

Mexico's policy toward Cuba, however, was not completely unchanged. During the Salinas government, the Cuban exile community became visible in Mexican–Cuban relations for the first time since the Cuban Revolution. Contrary to what happened in the case of the United States and Cuba, Cuban exiles had not influenced, or shaped, Mexican policy toward Cuba—at least not publicly. In 1992, President Salinas met with Jorge Mas Canosa, leader of the Cuban American National Foundation and Carlos Alberto Montaner, leader of the Cuban Liberal Union in Mexico City. Montaner justified the secrecy of the meetings as necessary "in order to avoid difficulties for the Mexican government."[42] The Mexican government, in turn, did not disclose much about Salinas's conversations with Mas Canosa and Montaner, which had been "private" rather than "secret," but it clarified that the Cuban government had been informed of the meetings "following diplomatic courtesy."[43] The press suggested that the Mexican President wanted to convince the exile community that NAFTA would not ultimately benefit Cuba.[44] According to The *Wall Street Journal*, Salinas and the exile leaders reached an "understanding" whereby the exile community in the United States would not hamper the conclusion of NAFTA while Mexico would maintain trade with Cuba at current levels; forego renegotiating Cuba's debt; deny Cuba access to the San José Agreement (sales of discounted petroleum); and would not grant guaranteed credits to Mexican businessmen investing in Cuba.[45]

The Mexican government denied any possible link between NAFTA and relations with Cuba and clarified that President Salinas had only wanted to hold talks with representatives of different political positions regarding Cuba.[46] A spokesman for CANF also denied the existence of any agreement between Salinas and the exiled leaders but gave assurances that the campaign against NAFTA was ready to be launched (although it did not happen).[47]

Mexican–Cuban relations survived the end of the Cold War; the regional agenda that prioritized issues such as free trade, democracy and human rights; and even a rapprochement between Mexico and the United States. Mexico continued to defend traditional positions regarding nonintervention and the right to self-determination in Cuba, while the Cuban government avoided criticizing Mexico's policy—including economic policies—and both governments recognized each other as valid interlocutors. The most important change in bilateral relations was Salinas's approach to the Cuban exile community. But even so, there are reasons to believe that Salinas's meetings with Mas Canosa and Montaner were related to the conclusion—and success—of NAFTA and not to any issue regarding Mexican–Cuban relations. Even after these meetings, Castro accepted Salinas's mediation to negotiate a migration agreement with the United States.

By the end of the twentieth century, Mexican–Cuban relations during the Salinas years and the beginning of Ernesto Zedillo's government were not explained by ideological sympathy or "tradition"; rather, it was a period when Mexico and Cuba were still useful to each other. Salinas's purpose was to consolidate Mexico's economic, rather than political, opening. In this sense, policy toward Cuba was very useful: political processes were a domestic issue and should not be influenced or directed from abroad, either in Cuba, Mexico or anywhere else.[48] Cuba, in turn, benefited from Mexico's positions by gaining a presence and a similar position in regional diplomatic forums.

Democracy and Human Rights in the Bilateral Relationship

The end of the twentieth century was also the beginning of the end of an era in Mexican–Cuban relations. The Cold War had finished; Mexico and Cuba had to find their places in the international puzzle. In so doing, the two countries redefined how they related to each other, which meant a gradual deterioration of the bilateral relationship. Such a deterioration was not inevitable; the choices made by the governments of Mexico and Cuba were consistent with their own interests but these no longer resulted in policies that could be accommodated bilaterally and be advantageous to both parties. Democracy and human rights became critical topics in bilateral relations; the Cuban dissidents became a new actor just as Cuba's active links with the Mexican opposition were a new strategy for Cuba.[49] In May 2004, Mexico and Cuba would be closer than ever to breaking diplomatic relations.

One forum where Mexican governments had reiterated their long-standing position of nonintervention and support for Cuba's right to self-determination would become the site where changes in bilateral relations became most visible. At the IX Iberoamerican summit in 1999 in Havana, President Ernesto Zedillo declared that democracy was necessary to preserve and strengthen national sovereignty, and that nations would be sovereign only by recognizing the essential freedom to think, express their views, act, participate and dissent.[50] And, while in Havana, Secretary of Foreign Affairs Rosario Green met Elizardo Sánchez Santa Cruz, president of the Cuban Commission for Human Rights and National Reconciliation. This was the first time that a Mexican official publicly met a Cuban dissident. Green assured that her meeting with Sánchez Santa Cruz did not represent interference in Cuban affairs, and would not overshadow the bilateral relationship; it was just a new way of conducting diplomacy by "talking to the people".[51] According to Elizardo Sánchez, his meeting with Green had demonstrated Mexico's commitment and solidarity with all Cubans while the Cuban ministry of foreign affairs expressed its concern about the attitude that the Cuban people would assume since the Cuban—and the Mexican—people had always understood very clearly Benito Juárez's idea that respect for the rights of others leads to peace.[52]

Members of the Mexican opposition also met with Cuban dissidents in November 2000 during the inter-parliamentarian meeting. Senator Luis H. Álvarez and deputy José Antonio Herrán Cabrera, both from the National Action Party (PAN), met dissidents Oswaldo Payá, Elizardo Sánchez Santa Cruz, Osvaldo Alfonso and Héctor Palacios, among others, to examine the situation of human rights in Cuba. Cuban officials argued that it was an unfriendly gesture toward their country.[53]

Despite the fact that in 1999 Castro's government allowed all foreign officials willing to meet Cuban dissidents to do so in Havana, and that it had previously established links with different political positions in Mexico, Cuban dissidents became a new and visible actor in the bilateral relationship. Various reasons explain the relevance of Cuba's dissidents: first, the increasing role of the opposition in Mexico from the right or the left, which was an essential element in Mexico's political opening; and second, the importance of issues such as democracy and human rights for Mexico's political actors. Both events had a great influence in Mexican–Cuban relations.

At the X Ibero-American summit in Panama City, in 2000, differences between the Cuban and Mexican governments were more evident than before. As a result of an ETA attack in Spain, the heads of state approved a declaration condemning terrorist activities, but they did not include Castro's allegation that there had been a plan to murder him during the meeting. The Cuban leader complained about this; Zedillo's response was that the declaration did not exclude any kind of terrorist activity. Castro, however, indicated that the Declaration on Terrorism had been supported by the president of a "different" Mexico, "guided by principles, interests, and commitments imposed by the free trade agreement concluded with its northern neighbor."[54] Clearly, Castro wanted to denounce the fact that Mexico was closer to the United States; its policies were no longer autonomous or independent.[55] For many years, Mexico's "autonomous and independent" policies—some of them truly so, others only so in appearance—were very useful to Cuba, which underlined the fact that Mexico did not comply with U.S. policies. Castro's reaction to the Declaration on Terrorism implied that he no longer considered this to be the case; Mexico and the United States were on the same side. Mexico's "alignment" with the United States, in Castro's view, was not favorable to Cuba.

After more than seventy years of ruling Mexico, the PRI lost the presidential election to the PAN in 2000. The new government headed by Vicente Fox implemented a "new" foreign policy that would contrast with that of the PRI to underline change in Mexico and the international system: a legitimately democratic country in a post-Cold War world should implement a foreign policy to prioritize free trade, the promotion of democracy and the respect for human rights internationally.[56] In so doing, Mexico would not only project a new international image but it would also contribute to consolidating domestic democratic change. Additionally, Mexico would openly seek a "strategic relationship" with the United States.[57] Mexico's "new" foreign policy radically changed relations with Cuba—and ended an era in bilateral relations.[58]

The first important reason behind the deterioration was Mexico's vote at the United Nations Human Rights Commission in Geneva. Except for 1999, Mexico had traditionally abstained in voting resolutions calling on the Cuban government to improve the situation of civil and political human rights.[59] In 2001, Mexico's vote became the subject for much speculation: Mexican ambassador to Cuba, Ricardo Pascoe, suggested Mexico should abstain while the Mexican Congress requested that President Fox vote in accordance with constitutional principles of foreign policy and against any resolution that violated Cuba's sovereignty; some intellectuals asked the President to vote in favor of the resolution. Cuban Foreign Minister, Felipe Pérez Roque, averred that Secretary Castañeda would do anything to condemn Cuba since he was "susceptible to accepting pressures from the United States."[60] In the end, the Mexican government abstained on the basis that the UNHRC had not treated the question in a balanced manner but, from 2002 until the transformation of the Commission into the Human Rights Council in 2006, it voted in favor of the resolution. Voting in such a way was inadmissible—possibly constituting a betrayal—to Castro's government.

The Cuban dissident movement remained an actor in bilateral relations: in February 2002 President Fox visited Havana and met with Oswaldo Payá, Martha Beatriz Roque Cabello, Raúl Rivero, Héctor Palacio Ruiz, Osvaldo Alfonso and Manuel Cuesta Morúa. Fox had been welcomed and accompanied by Castro on his first day in Havana, and apparently he informed the Cuban leader of his meetings with dissidents. Fox justified his meetings with Cuban dissidents by the fact that his foreign policy was generally concerned about the observance of human rights, and Cuba could not be the exception.[61]

Relations between Mexico and Cuba became increasingly complicated during and after the UN conference on Financing for Development that took place in the City of Monterrey, Mexico, in March 2002. At the end of his speech, Castro announced that he had to leave the conference because of a "special situation created by his participation in it."[62] Shortly after the conference, a *Granma* editorial asserted that the Mexican government had asked Castro to leave the conference before the arrival of President George W. Bush so that they would not meet. After Mexico voted in favor of the resolution presented at the UN Human Rights Commission a few days later, Castro disclosed the import of a telephone conversation with President Fox held before the Monterrey conference, in which Fox effectively asked Castro to leave before Bush arrived—as well as requesting moderation in his comments on the United States.[63]

In his speech on May 1, 2004, once again after Mexico voted in favor of the resolution presented at the UN Human Rights Commission, Castro remarked that the Mexican Congress had asked the President to abstain from voting on "the resolution requested by President Bush." Castro indicated that all the influence and prestige that Mexican foreign policy had gained for being irreproachable, which had emerged from a true revolution, had turned into ashes. The border between the United States and Mexico—according to Castro—was no longer at the Río Bravo, but well within Mexico. Worst of all, Mexico's news concerning its vote in Geneva had been announced in Washington.[64] Two days later, Secretary of Foreign Affairs Luis Ernesto Derbez, and Secretary of Interior Santiago Creel recalled the ambassador to Cuba, Roberta Lajous, and declared Orlando Silva, counselor for political affairs at the Cuban embassy in Mexico, *persona non grata*. The Mexican government also requested that Cuban ambassador, Jorge Bolaños, leave Mexico. The Mexican government justified its decision on the basis that members of Cuba's Communist Party (PCC) had violated the principle of nonintervention by discussing certain domestic issues in Mexico without consideration of the institutional framework and diplomatic procedures.[65] The secretaries might have referred to a number of meetings between members of the PCC, embassy officials and leaders of the opposition party, the Party of the Democratic Revolution (PRD), in which they discussed a statement by Carlos Ahumada in Cuba; Mexican businessman Ahumada had fled to Cuba after Mexican television showed videos of him bribing officials of the Mexico City government, who were PRD members.[66]

Mexico and Cuba did not break diplomatic relations in 2004 but the recall of ambassadors signaled that the bilateral relationship had changed significantly: new issues, such as democracy and human rights, replaced the more traditional language of nonintervention. Mexico intervened in Cuban internal affairs by supporting the idea that the Cuban government should improve the human-rights situation on the island, and consider a political opening; Cuba, in turn, intervened in Mexico's domestic affairs by pursuing active links with the opposition. Neither government seemed willing to negotiate their conflicting positions. For the Mexican government, it was legitimate to discuss human rights and democracy in Cuba; for the Cuban government this was unacceptable. Cuba's resistance to change made it difficult for it to accommodate to a more democratic Mexico and a non Cold-War world.

The Second PAN Government: A "Normal" Relationship?

Foreign policy has not been a priority for Felipe Calderón's government, but one of its most important objectives when taking power was to improve relations with Latin American countries, especially Cuba. This raises an interesting question: why should a *panista* government supporter of democracy, human rights and free trade, one seeking to forge close relations with the United States, wish to improve relations with Cuba? A possible answer refers precisely to the conduct of relations by the previous *panista* government. During Fox's government, Cuba remained a domestic issue: different public positions regarding Cuba were expressed openly and freely—something that had only happened to the same degree in the early 1960s. Some political sectors and parts of public opinion still supported Cuba—for what it was, or for what it had symbolically been in the past. Policy toward Cuba, therefore, was a subject for discussion in Congress and the media, and once again, it was difficult to distinguish policy toward Cuba from Mexican positions toward the United States. More importantly, for different reasons, including the U.S. security agenda after September 11, foreign policy during Fox's government was perceived to have failed: relations deteriorated with Cuba, Venezuela, Argentina and other Latin American countries, and Castañeda's "strategic relationship" with the United States did not materialize. Calderón's government thought that Mexican foreign policy might recover some respect and influence by improving relations with Latin American governments.

Calderón's government succeeded in restoring communication with the Cuban government. The UN Council on Human Rights replaced the commission; members agreed not to pass resolutions regarding specific countries but to implement a universal periodic review whereby governments report on the actions taken to protect human rights in their countries under a UN policy of equal treatment for all countries in assessing the situation of human rights. Mexican ambassador Luis Alfonso de Alba was the Council's first president and one of his main purposes was to promote this process. Cuban officials considered that this change to the evaluation of the state of human rights in all countries demonstrated Mexico's willingness to improve relations with Cuba, although Mexican officials declared that new procedures at the Council were not necessarily directed toward Cuba.[67] In any case, the fact that Mexico no longer has to vote at international forums assessing the human-rights situation in Cuba removed a reason for conflict between the two countries.

Second, both governments appointed new ambassadors. Gabriel Jiménez Remus, close to President Calderón and well known in Cuba, replaced José Ignacio Piña, while Manuel Aguilar Flores replaced Jorge Bolaños.[68] Secretary of Foreign Affairs Patricia Espinosa visited Havana in March 2008 and December 2009; Cuban Minister Felipe Pérez Roque visited México City in October 2008. During his visit, Pérez Roque declared that relations between Mexico

and Cuba had normalized and were continuing to progress.[69] The most important result of the visit was the conclusion of a Memorandum of Understanding
on immigration. Given U.S. policy of wet-foot/dry-foot, many Cubans had
been arriving on Mexican territory to make their way to the United States by
land. The Cuban government refused to accept deportation of undocumented
Cubans who had entered Mexico by land because of "national security concerns." The memorandum thus accepted that the Mexican government can
deport any Cuban national illegally entering into Mexico by land or sea.

A third indication of improved Mexican–Cuban relations was the renegotia-
tion of Cuba's debt. Cuba's National Bank and the Mexican *Banco Nacional de
Comercio Exterior* (Bancomext) had reached an agreement in April 2002 to
restructure Cuba's debt, calculated in US $380 million. According to the agree-
ment, Cuba's guarantees were the resources of two telecommunication enterprises: Etecsa and Telefónica Antillana. In the context of increasing bilateral
difficulties, however, Cuba failed to recognize the agreement twenty-four days
after it was signed, and withdrew the resources of these companies as payment
guarantees.[70] Bancomext sued Cuba at a tribunal in Turín, Italy, and requested
the seizure of the money the companies held in European banks. Cuba, in turn,
countersued Mexico at the International Chamber of Commerce in Paris. Both
tribunals resolved in favor of Mexico in 2004 but Cuba refused to pay and sued
Bancomext in 2006 in a provincial tribunal in Havana demanding compensation
of US $600 million.[71] Calderón's government recognized that solving the debt
problem was a pre-condition to improving relations; in February 2008 Mexico
and Cuba agreed to restructure US $413 million. Cuba had fifteen years to
repay at 6 percent interest and five years' grace for the principal, and no commercial guarantees. Mexico would open a credit line for US $25 million to
promote exports to the island.[72]

Finally, Cuba joined the Río Group and participated for the first time at the
extraordinary meeting in Salvador de Bahía, Brazil, in December 2008.
Although traditionally Brazil had been the major advocate of Cuba's inclusion
in the Río Group, Mexico did not visibly oppose this step and it actually held
the pro témpore secretariat (*secretaría pro témpore*) of the group when Cuba first
attended the meeting as a full member.

Two issues tested the improvement of bilateral relations: the influenza A
(H1N1) epidemic in Mexico in 2009 and the hunger strikes initiated by two
Cuban dissidents, Orlando Zapata and Guillermo Fariñas in the first semester of
2010. At the beginning of 2009, the Mexican government confirmed that President Calderón would visit Havana, possibly in May. U.S. President Barack
Obama visited Mexico in April and there was still no news about Calderón's
trip to Cuba. Speculation suggested that, after Obama's successful visit, Mexico
would not want to risk good relations with the United States by strengthening
relations with Cuba.[73] But it was the influenza virus that in the end prevented
Calderón visiting Cuba, at least in 2009. Cuba was one of the few countries that

suspended air travel with Mexico as the epidemic broke out. The Mexican government expressed its surprise and indicated that this decision discriminated against Mexicans and infringed World Health Organization recommendations.[74] Even though at the time Fidel was no longer President, his reaction to Calderón's declarations on Mexican television resulted in new difficulties in bilateral relations. In a televised interview, Calderón said that he meant to go to Cuba but, since flights between the countries had been suspended, he could not go.[75] In his "Reflexiones", Fidel argued that the Mexican government had not informed the world of the epidemic, as it was waiting for Obama's visit, and that Calderón was "threatening" not to go to Cuba.[76] After an exchange of "Reflexiones" and bulletins issued by the Mexican government, flights between Mexico and Cuba were reestablished and Ambassador Jiménez Remus met Raúl Castro in Havana.

The death of dissident Orlando Zapata was another test of the "normalization" of relations. The communiqué issued by the ministry of foreign affairs indicates a more "balanced" policy toward Cuba: it lamented Zapata's death, expressed the Mexican government's concern for the health of Guillermo Fariñas, and called on the Cuban government to safeguard the health and dignity of its prisoners. On the other hand, Mexico openly recognized that it could not judge the situation of human rights in other countries since Mexico faced many challenges in that arena. The bulletin also underlined the importance of sovereignty, and indicated that a constructive and close relationship with Cuba was a priority and that "[our] links with that country are based on a State view and not ideological postures."[77]

The Future: Relations Between *a* Caribbean Island and Mexico?

The Mexican government did not choose between isolation and constructive engagement in the last twenty years, for many different reasons. Mexico's domestic politics, capacities, relations with the United States and the history of Mexican–Cuban relations itself made it very difficult for Mexican governments to adopt a policy of isolation of Cuba, or of constructive engagement. Not that any of these were successful in achieving their purposes, but Mexico could not find a viable alternative either. As the twentieth century came to an end, the last PRI government decided to comment on Cuba's political process while the first PAN government criticized it more directly. In any case, even without trying to isolate Cuba, Mexican governments have not been able to influence or promote changes on the island. In fact, it has not always been clear whether this was a convenient aim of Mexico's policy toward the island. But, before relations deteriorated, Mexico was considered by many in the country and abroad as a possible mediator between Cuba and the United States, or even in Cuba's eventual opening. This remains an open question. Yet, after Fox's government, Mexico's participation in Cuba's political process or relations with the United

States is unlikely, although perhaps not impossible. The Cuban government's decision to free a number of political prisoners in July 2010 indicates that Spain could be a more influential actor.

As long as there is high uncertainty concerning political succession or eventual democratization in Cuba, it is difficult to determine the features of Mexican–Cuban relations in the future. In the absence of eventful circumstances in either country or a more aggressive U.S. policy toward Cuba, relations between Mexico and Cuba will be like relations between *any* Caribbean island and Mexico. It is still too early to identify whether there will be anything "special" about them. This does not mean that Mexico and Cuba will be unimportant to each other: at least two problems underline the need for communication and disposition to negotiate between the two countries. The first refers to illegal Cuban immigration into Mexico and its transit to the United States. This is a bilateral and a domestic problem. Mexico faces a huge challenge regarding Mexican immigration to the United States, and Central American immigration to Mexico and to the United States through Mexico. Moreover, this is not only a problem with respect to Mexico–U.S. relations but also concerns human trafficking, violation of human rights, etc. In consequence, fluid communication with Cuba is essential if, at a minimum, Cuban immigration is to be controlled. Second, although Cuba's debt to Mexico is not extremely high, Mexico might want to insist on the subject if only for domestic and formal reasons, demanding reasons why Mexico should permit Cuba not to pay.

Other issues might emerge on the way. Surely, the United States will continue to be a third actor in the bilateral relationship, but its influence may vary if Cuba and the United States find a way to initiate a less hostile and more productive relationship.

NOTES

Preface

1 I am grateful to Rafael Hernández for having suggested the subtitle, which also recalls Wayne Smith's *The Closest of Enemies*.

1 The United States and Cuba Have Never Had Normal Relations

1 Ramiro Guerra, *La expansión territorial de los Estados Unidos* (Havana: Editorial de Ciencias Sociales, 1975); Lars Schoultz, *That Infernal Little Cuban Republic: The United States and the Cuban Revolution* (Chapel Hill: University of North Carolina Press, 2009); Louis A. Pérez, Jr., *Cuba and the United States: Ties of Singular Intimacy* (Athens: University of Georgia Press, 1990).

2 After losing all its mainland colonies in Spanish America, Spain called Cuba the "ever-faithful isle."

3 Raymond L. Garthoff, "The Cuban Missile Crisis: An Overview," in *The Cuban Missile Crisis Revisited*, James A. Nathan, ed. (New York: St. Martin's Press, 1992), 41.

4 Ibid., 231.

5 Ibid., 134.

6 Aleksandr Fursenko and Timothy Naftali, *"One Hell of a Gamble": Khrushchev, Castro and Kennedy, 1958–1964* (New York: W.W. Norton & Company, 1997).

7 Ernest R. May and Philip D. Zelikow, eds., *The Kennedy Tapes: Inside The White House during the Cuban Missile Crisis* (Cambridge, MA: Harvard University Press, 1997), 657. Earlier, General Shoup had referred to Cuba as "that little pipsqueak of a place," 181.

8 Quoted in Hugh Thomas, *Cuba: The Pursuit of Freedom* (New York: Harper & Row Publishers, 1971), 101.

9 Lars Schoultz, *Beneath the United States: A History of U.S. Policy Toward Latin America* (Cambridge, MA: Harvard University Press, 1998), xv.

10 Oscar Zanetti, "El comercio exterior de la República neocolonial," in *Anuario de estudios cubanos* 1, Juan Pérez de la Riva *et al.* (Havana: Editorial de Ciencias Sociales, 1975), 45–126.

11 Schoultz, *That Infernal Little Cuban Republic*, 200.
12 Leland L. Johnson, "U.S. Business Interest in Cuba and the Rise of Castro," *World Politics* 17 (April 1965), 442.
13 Berlin was a frequent topic of discussion by the ExComm. May and Zelikow, eds., *The Kennedy Tapes*, 90, 98–99, 115, 186, 284–286, 309 and 340.
14 William McKinley's "Third Annual Message," December 5, 1899:

> This nation has assumed before the world a grave responsibility for the future good government of Cuba. The new Cuba yet to arise from the ashes of the past must be bound to us by *ties of singular intimacy* and strength if its enduring welfare is to be assured. Whether those ties shall be organic or conventional, the destinies of Cuba are in some rightful form and manner irrevocably linked with our own. We must see to it that free Cuba be a reality, not a name, a perfect entity, not a hasty experiment bearing within itself the elements of failure.
> (in John T. Woolley and Gerhard Peters, *The American Presidency Project* (online), Santa Barbara, CA: University of California (hosted), Gerhard Peters (database) www.presidency.ucsb.edu/ws/?pid=29540; italics added)

15 Phillip Brenner, "Thirteen Months: Cuba's Perspective on the Missile Crisis," in Nathan, ed., *The Cuban Missile Crisis Revisited*, 187–217.
16 Garthoff, "The Cuban Missile Crisis," 43.
17 Quoted in Jon Lee Anderson, *Che Guevara, A Revolutionary Life* (New York: Grove Press, 1997), 509.
18 Brenner, "Thirteen Months," 196.
19 Critical oral history has been applied to the Missile Crisis, the Bay of Pigs invasion, the collapse of U.S.–Soviet détente in the Carter–Brezhnev period and the U.S. war in Vietnam. Four conferences have been held on the Missile Crisis: Hawk's Cay (1987), Moscow (1989), Havana (1992) and Havana (2002). See www.watson-institute.org/project_detail.cfm?id=33.
20 Norman Boucher, "Our Men in Havana," *Brown Alumni Magazine* (January–February 2003). See www.brownalumnimagazine.com/january/february-2003/our-men-in-havana.html.
21 In an email dated July 11, 2008, Jorge I. Domínguez suggested that Castro's fury may have been partly due to his seeing the connection between the no-invasion pledge and the on-site inspections for the first time upon reading the Kennedy–Khrushchev letters (Jorge I. Domínguez to Marifeli Pérez-Stable, July 11, 2008).
22 In a 1982 retrospective, the following members of the Kennedy administration denied that the United States had ever made a formal, unconditional commitment not to invade Cuba: Dean Rusk, Robert McNamara, Roswell Gilpatrick, Theodore Sorensen and McGeorge Bundy. Jorge I. Domínguez, *To Make the World Safe for Revolution* (Cambridge, MA: Harvard University Press, 1989), 45–46.
23 Ibid., 49.
24 James G. Blight, Bruce J. Allyn and David A. Welch, *Cuba on the Brink: Castro, the Missile Crisis and the Soviet Collapse* (New York: Pantheon, 1993), 252.
25 Michael Dobbs, *One Minute to Midnight: Kennedy, Khrushchev, and Castro on the Brink of Nuclear War* (New York: Alfred A. Knopf, 2008), 140–145 and 297–303.
26 Julia Preston and Samuel Dillon, *Opening Mexico: The Making of a Democracy* (New York: Farrar, Straus and Giroux, 2004).
27 In December 1992, George H.W. Bush, Brian Mulroney and Carlos Salinas signed NAFTA in San Antonio, Texas. A year later, the U.S. Congress ratified the treaty and President Clinton's signature made it official. NAFTA went into effect on January 1, 1994.
28 Ricardo Becerra, Pedro Salazar and José Woldenberg, *La mecánica del cambio político en México*, 3rd ed. (Mexico City: Cal y Arena, 2005).

29 Louis A. Pérez, Jr., *Cuba under the Platt Amendment, 1902–1934* (Pittsburgh, PA: University of Pittsburgh Press, 1986).

30 Jorge I. Domínguez, *Cuba: Order and Revolution* (Cambridge, MA: Harvard University Press, 1978); Frank Argote-Freyre, *Fulgencio Batista: From Revolutionary to Strongman* (New Brunswick, NJ: Rutgers University Press, 2006).

31 Domínguez, *Cuba*, 54–109.

32 Thomas G. Paterson, *Contesting Castro: The United States and the Triumph of the Cuban Revolution* (New York: Oxford University Press, 1994).

33 Domínguez, *Cuba*, 58–66.

34 Piero Gleijeses, *Shattered Hope: The Guatemalan Revolution and the United States, 1944–1954* (Princeton, NJ: Princeton University Press, 1991).

35 *Revolución*, September 1, 1960, 1–2.

36 James G. Blight and Peter Kornbluh, eds., *Politics of Illusion: The Bay of Pigs Invasion Reexamined* (Boulder, CO: Lynne Rienner Publishers, 1998).

37 Fursenko and Naftali, *"One Hell of a Gamble"*, 319–338, on Kennedy's reticence to abandon the idea of overthrowing Castro.

38 William H. Attwood, recorded statement, November 8, 1965, (9–10), John F. Kennedy Library Oral History Program. See www.jfklibrary.org/NR/rdonlyres/77EC2D43–1AD9–4E60–8937-D027A9DC2A21/43833/Attwood-WilliamH_oralhistory.pdf.

39 In a letter to the editor, Jean Daniel thus summarized Kennedy's message to Castro. Jean Daniel, letter to the editor, *International Herald Tribune* (September 4, 1994).

40 Jean Daniel, "When Castro Heard the News," *New Republic*, December 7, 1963, 7–9.

41 Ibid.

42 See Kennedy's speech at American University on June 10, 1963, and his address to the American people on July 26, 1963, on the Nuclear Test Ban Treaty that, in his words, opened "the path of peace" possible "for the first time in many years." John F. Kennedy (commencement address, American University, Washington, DC, June 10, 1963); John F. Kennedy, "Radio and Television Address to the American People on the Nuclear Test Ban Treaty" (speech, White House, Washington, DC, July 26, 1963). See www.jfklibrary.org/Historical+Resources/JFK+in+History/Nuclear+Test+Ban+Treaty.htm.

43 Arthur M. Schlesinger, Jr., *A Thousand Days: John F. Kennedy in the White House* (Boston, MA: Houghton Mifflin, 1965), 506–531.

44 Attwood, John F. Kennedy Library, 7.

45 Jean Daniel, "Unofficial Envoy: An Historic Report from Two Capitals," *New Republic*, December 14, 1963, 15–20.

46 "Nikita Khrushchev to Fidel Castro, January 31, 1963," in Lawrence Chang and Peter Kornbluh, eds., *The Cuban Missile Crisis, 1962: A National Security Archive Documents Reader* (New York: New Press, 1992), 319.

47 Carmelo Mesa-Lago, *The Economy of Socialist Cuba: A Two-Decade Appraisal* (Albuquerque: University of New Mexico Press, 1981), 77–107; Domínguez, *To Make the World Safe for Revolution*, 79–112.

48 Marifeli Pérez-Stable, *The Cuban Revolution: Origins, Course and Legacy*, 2nd ed. (New York: Oxford University Press, 1999), 121–152.

49 Marifeli Pérez-Stable, "Caught in a Contradiction: Cuban Socialism between Mobilization and Normalization," *Comparative Politics* (October 1999), 63–82.

50 Domínguez, *To Make the World Safe for Revolution*, 78–112.

51 James G. Blight and Peter Kornbluh, "Dialogue with Castro: A Hidden History," *New York Review of Books* (October 6, 1994). See www.nybooks.com/articles/2128.

52 Department of State, Secret, "Normalizing Relations with Cuba," March 27, 1975. See www.gwu.edu/~nsarchiv/NSAEBB/NSAEBB269/index.htm.

53 Quoted in Blight and Kornbluh, "Dialogue with Castro."

54 Piero Gleijeses, *Conflicting Missions: Havana, Washington and Africa, 1959–1976* (Chapel Hill: University of North Carolina Press, 2002).

55 Quoted in Blight and Kornbluh, "Dialogue with Castro."

56 Ibid.

57 Ibid.

58 In February 1963, the Kennedy administration banned travel to Cuba by U.S. citizens and permanent residents. In July, the Treasury Department prohibited all financial transactions between the United States and Cuba.

59 Domínguez, *To Make the World Safe for Revolution*, 157–162.

60 Wayne S. Smith, *The Closest of Enemies* (New York: W.W. Norton & Company, 1987), 128–142 on Ethiopia and the Shaba incident.

61 Jimmy Carter, "Address at Commencement Exercises at the University of Notre Dame," May 22, 1977, in Woolley and Peters, *The American Presidency*.

62 Marylin Berger, "Cyrus Vance, A Confidant of Presidents, Is Dead at 84," *New York Times*, January 13, 2002.

63 William LeoGrande, *Our Own Backyard: The United States in Central America, 1977–1992* (Chapel Hill: University of North Carolina Press, 1998).

64 Jeanne J. Kirkpatrick, *Dictatorship and Double Standards: Rationalism and Reason in Politics* (New York: American Enterprise Institute and Simon & Schuster, Inc., 1982).

65 James Chace, "The Turbulent Tenure of Alexander Haig," *New York Times*, April 22, 1984.

66 "Reagan Says Haig Met Key Cuban," *New York Times* (January 28, 1982); Barbara Crossette, "U.S. Willing to Try Talks with Cuba on Easing Tensions," *New York Times*, March 26, 1982.

67 "U.S., Cuba Resume Normal Migration—Transcript," *U.S. Department of State Bulletin* (February 1985). See http://findarticles.com/p/articles/mi_m1079/is_v85/ai_3621169/?tag=content;col1.

68 Joseph B. Treaster, "Radio Marti Goes on Air and Cuba Retaliates by Ending Pact," *New York Times*, May 21, 1985.

69 Guillermo Martínez, "To Avoid a New Mariel, Revive Legal Cuban Migration," *Miami Herald*, May 28, 1987.

70 Kenneth N. Skoug, "Cuba's Growing Crisis," *Department of State Bulletin* 87 (September 1987). See http://findarticles.com/p/articles/mi_m1079/is_v87/ai_5278939/?tag=content;col1.

71 Alfonso Chardy, "U.S.–Cuban Relations Thawing Immigration Deal is American Goal," *Miami Herald*, October 11, 1987; R.A. Zaldivar and Martin Merzer, "Cuban Immigration to Resume U.S.–Castro Agreement Could Bring at Least 23,000 a Year," *Miami Herald*, November 21, 1987.

72 Jorge I. Domínguez, *La política exterior de Cuba (1962–2009)* (Madrid: Editorial Colibrí, 2009), 491–566.

73 Domínguez, *To Make the World Safe for Revolution*, 226–230.

74 G.R. Berridge, "Diplomacy and the Angola/Namibia Accords," *International Affairs* 65 (Summer 1989), 463–479.

75 Jorge I. Domínguez, "U.S.–Cuban Relations from the Cold War to the Colder War," *Journal of Interamerican Studies and World Affairs* 39 (Autumn 1997), 50.

76 Pascal Fletcher, Reuters News Agency, "Cuba Signals an End to Military Intervention Abroad," *Miami Herald*, December 7, 1989.

77 Gabriel García Márquez, "Operation Carlota," *New Left Review* 101–102 (January–April 1977). See www.newleftreview.org/?view=945.

78 Figures for rebel groups and militias can be found in Raúl Castro, "Discurso pronunciado en la graduación del III curso de la escuela básica superior, 'General

Máximo Gómez'", *El Orientador Revolucionario* 17 (1967): 11. The same source mentions the existence of 3,591 rebels. The figure of 8,000 appears in a document declassified by the ministry of the interior as part of a package for a conference on the Bay of Pigs invasion in March 2001. When Jorge I. Domínguez asked about the difference in the two figures, the former Interior Minister Ramiro Valdés replied that the correct figure was given in 1967.

79 Quote is from a letter in my possession, dated January 24, 1961, written by Müller from the underground in Cuba to newly inaugurated U.S. President John F. Kennedy. For his anti-Castro activities, he spent fifteen years in prison. From Alberto Müller to John F. Kennedy, January 24, 1961.

80 Figures for the lives lost in the struggles between the government and the opposition in the 1960s vary widely and are, for now, hard to verify. At the time, the government held summary trials and quickly executed those who received death sentences; estimates range from 7,000 to 18,000. In the mid-1960s, Castro admitted to about 20,000 "counterrevolutionary prisoners"; estimates range from 50,000 to 100,000. Using Castro's figure, Cuba's per capita political imprisonment (1 in 35) ranks first in Latin America; Uruguay in the 1970s and 1980s comes in second (1 in 50). I computed the Cuban per capita figure; Uruguay's is from Amnesty International, "Mental Health Aspects of Political Imprisonment in Uruguay: An Amnesty International Special Briefing" (New York: Amnesty International, 1983), 1. The 20,000 figure appears in Lee Lockwood, *Castro's Cuba, Cuba's Fidel* (New York: Vintage Books, 1969), 230.

81 Human-rights violations in Cuba during the 1960s—by the Cuban government, the U.S. government and the Cuban opposition—should be gauged by international agreements such as the International Bill of Human Rights, which includes the Universal Declaration on Human Rights and the International Covenant on Civil and Political Rights, the American Convention on Human Rights, the Inter-American Convention to Prevent and Punish Torture and the four Geneva conventions (1949) and their two protocols (1977), as well as UN and OAS agreements on humanitarian international law, protection of civilians during wars and proper treatment of war prisoners. Task Force on Memory Truth and Justice, *Cuban National Reconciliation* (Miami: Latin American and Caribbean Center, Florida International University, 2003). See http://marifeliperez-stable.com/cuban-national-reconciliation/.

82 Blight and Kornbluh, *Politics of Illusion*, 15–16. This volume is an edited transcript of the proceedings held in 1995 on the Bay of Pigs invasion. Participants included former U.S. and Soviet government officials, Cuban opposition members and scholars.

83 "78 Are Believed Killed as Cuban Jetliner Crashes in Sea after Blast," *New York Times*, October 7, 1976; the actual death toll was seventy-three; Robert D. McFadden, "Cuban Attaché at U.N. Is Slain From Ambush on Queens Road," *New York Times*, September 12, 1980. For a detailed Cuban government list of terrorist acts against targets in Cuba and abroad, see: www.cubavsterrorismo.com/interface.sp/design/cronologia/index.tpl.html. For a partial list of violent acts perpetrated by Omega 7, the main exile terrorist organization in the 1970s and 1980s, see: "Bombings and Slayings Claimed for Omega 7," *Miami Herald*, January 16, 1983.

84 The United Nations has sponsored twelve multilateral conventions that classify as terrorism actions such as kidnapping of or attacks against, planes or ships, assaults against officials and diplomats, taking hostages and financing terrorism.

85 "Legacy of Terror," *New York Times*, July 16, 1978; "Pro-Castro Cubans in Puerto Rico Are Terrorists' Targets," *New York Times*, October 21, 1979; Robert D. McFadden, "Cuban Refugee Leader Slain in Union City," *New York Times*, November 26, 1979; "Bomb Hits Miami Cigar Factory," *New York Times,* January

14, 1980; Richard Wallace, "Bombs Rock Little Havana Firms," *Miami Herald*, January 12, 1983.

86 Robert M. Levine, *Secret Missions to Cuba: Fidel Castro, Bernardo Benes, and Cuban Miami* (New York: Palgrave, 2001).

87 Smith, *The Closest of Enemies*, 160–163.

88 Peter Kornbluh, ed., *Bay of Pigs Declassified: The Secret CIA Report on the Invasion of Cuba* (New York: New Press, 1998), 330.

89 "138 Cuban Prisoners Reject Castro Dialogue," *Washington Post*, December 15, 1978.

90 "Exiles Confer with Castro," *Washington Post*, November 20, 1978; "Castro Would Free 3,000," *New York Times*, November 23, 1978; Ward Sinclair, "The Two Sides of a Negotiator for Castro's Prisoners," *Washington Post*, December 3, 1978.

91 Brian Hufker and Gray Cavender, "From Freedom Flotilla to America's Burden: The Social Construction of the Mariel Immigrants," *Sociological Quarterly* 31 (Summer 1990), 321–335; Benigno E. Aguirre, "Cuban Mass Migration and the Social Construction of Deviants," *Bulletin of Latin American Research* 13 (May 1994), 155–183.

92 The referendum garnered 60 percent support. The referendum did not affect bilingual education in public schools or any program funded by the state or federal government, but it prohibited the use of local funds for promoting other cultures or languages other than English or the "American" culture. George Volsky, "Approval of Anti-bilingual Measure Causes Confusion and Worry in Miami," *New York Times*, November 9, 1980. In 1993, the English–only measure was repealed.

93 Alejandro Portes and Alex Stepick, *City on the Edge: The Transformation of Miami* (Berkeley: University of California Press, 1993). CANF focused largely on matters related to U.S.–Cuba policy, FACE mostly on the accomplishments of the exile community.

94 María de los Angeles Torres, *In the Land of Mirrors: Cuban Exile Politics in the United States* (Ann Arbor: University of Michigan Press, 1999).

95 Guillermo Martínez, "Cuban Exiles Pour Money into Congressional Races," *Miami Herald*, September 27, 1982; Helga Silva, "Group is a Cuban-born Who's Who," *Miami Herald*, May 21, 1983; Stuart Taylor Jr., "Rising Voice of Cuban-Americans," *New York Times*, March 7, 1984; Jon Nordheimer, "Cuban-American Leader Builds a Foundation of Power beyond Miami," *New York Times*, July 12, 1986.

96 David Hoffman, "Bristling Attack on Communism," *Washington Post*, May 21, 1983.

97 Patrick J. Kiger, *Squeeze Play: The United States, Cuba and the Helms-Burton Act* (Washington: Center for Public Integrity, 1997), 2.

98 George Lardner, Jr., "How Lobbyists Briefed a Rebel Leader," *Washington Post*, October 8, 1990.

99 Carlos Harrison, "U.S.–Cuba Agreement Bolstered Immigration Rights Written into the Law," *Miami Herald*, December 25, 1987. In 1988, CANF reached an agreement with the Department of State that granted 1,500 third-country Cubans immediate entry and allowed for another 1,500 a year thereafter. As a result, more than 10,000 people resettled in the United States. "Out of Limbo," *Miami Herald*, June 21, 1988.

100 Patrick J. Haney and Walt Vanderbush, *The Cuban Embargo: The Domestic Politics of an American Foreign Policy* (Pittsburgh, PA: University of Pittsburgh Press, 2005), 44–45.

101 Christopher Marquis, "Bomb Fails to Halt U.S.–Cuba Forum," *Miami Herald* May 27, 1988; Sandra Dibble, "Bombing Jolts S. Dade Neighborhood Travel Agency with Cuba Ties," *Miami Herald*, March 28, 1989; Arnold Markowitz, "Miami's

Acts of Terrorism Led U.S. in '88," *Miami Herald*, September 13, 1989; Sandra Dibble, "Little Havana Museum Bombed," *Miami Herald*, June 15, 1990.

102 Gerald E. Poyo, *"With All, and for the Good of All": The Emergence of Popular Nationalism in the Cuban Communities of the United States, 1848–1898* (Durham, NC: Duke University Press, 1989).

103 John L. Offner, *Unwanted War: The Diplomacy of the United States and Spain over Cuba, 1895–1898* (Chapel Hill: University of North Carolina Press, 1992). The administrations of Grover Cleveland (1893–1897) and William McKinley (1897–1901) resisted pressures from Congress, the media, public opinion, some business sectors and the émigrés on extending to the Cuban Liberation Army the status of belligerency. Such a recognition would have allowed the rebels to purchase and receive arms from the United States legally. Just as important, Cleveland and McKinley both hoped for a negotiated settlement whereby Spain granted reforms and the rebels laid out their arms. Recognizing the Liberation Army as belligerents would have precluded that outcome which, of course, never happened either.

104 John Lawrence Tone, *War and Genocide in Cuba, 1895–1898* (Chapel Hill: University of North Carolina Press, 2006).

105 Paterson, *Contesting Castro*, 72, 83, 98 and 115. Prío and eight of his associates were indicted for violating U.S. neutrality laws by sending money and weapons to Cuba from the United States. After making bail, Prío and the Immigration and Naturalization Service reached an agreement: the former president would suspend his activities and the INS would not deport him. During the 1950s, the FBI worked closely with the Cuban embassy in Washington to keep watch on Cuban exiles.

106 Offner, *Unwanted War*.

107 Fernando Ortiz, "La crisis política cubana sus causas y remedios," in Julio LeRiverend, ed., *Órbita de Fernando Ortiz* (Havana: Ediciones Unión, 1973), 112.

108 Manuel Márquez Sterling, *Doctrina de la República* (Havana: Secretaría de Educación, 1937), 27.

2 "Next Christmas in Havana"

1 Cuba*INFO*, March 20, 1990, 1.
2 Ibid., April 20, 1991, 1.
3 Ibid., October 5, 1990, 1.
4 Ibid., August 2, 1991, 2; August 12, 1991, 2.
5 Ibid., October 4, 1991, 1.
6 Ibid., July 19, 1990, 2.
7 Ibid., July 19, 1990, May 9, 1991.
8 Ibid., April 6, 1990, 3 and June 22, 1990, 2.
9 Ibid., April 6, 1990, 2.
10 Ibid., February 8, 1990, 2.
11 Ibid., February 14, 1991, 1. The Council for Inter-American Security charged $3 for calls predicting the date on which Castro's government would collapse. Three prizes were offered: (1) a three-day, all-expenses-paid Havana vacation; (2) a trip to Washington to attend a conference on Cuba's democratization; and (3) a box of Cuban cigars.
12 Ibid., February 26, 1990, 5.
13 Ibid., March 20, 1990, 7; June 22, 1990, 8; January 24, 1991, 4.
14 Ibid., February 26, 1990, 5.
15 Ibid., March 20, 1990, 1.
16 Edward González and David Ronfeldt, *Cuba Adrift in a Postcommunist World* (Santa Monica, CA: Rand National Defense Institute, 1992), vii and ix.

17 Donald E. Schulz, *The United States and Cuba: From a Strategy of Conflict to Construc-tive Engagement* (Carlisle Barracks, PA: Strategic Studies Institute, U.S. Army War College, 1993), 1.
18 Section 1703.7 of the Cuban Democracy Act reads: "to be prepared to reduce the sanctions in carefully calibrated ways in response to positive developments in Cuba." www.state.gov/www/regions/wha/cuba/democ_act_1992.html. Clinton's first secretary of state, Warren Christopher, often mentioned the recourse to cali-brated steps in response to changes in Cuba.
19 Stephen M. Walt, "Two Cheers for Clinton's Foreign Policy," *Foreign Affairs* (March/April 2000), 63–79, makes a critical case in Clinton's favor; Richard N. Haas, "The Squandered Presidency," *Foreign Affairs* (May/June 2000), argues the opposite. See also Norman J. Ornstein and Mark Schmitt, "Dateline Campaign '92: Post-Cold War Politics," *Foreign Policy* (Summer 1990), 169–175, for an analysis of the intersection of foreign and domestic policies.
20 "Brazil Flexes New Muscle in Another Trade Fight," *New York Times*, March 27, 2001; Jane Bussey, "Brazil, U.S. Split FTAA Talks in Miami," *Miami Herald*, Sep-tember 30, 2003.
21 Cuba*INFO*, February 8, 1993, 1.
22 Ibid., April 30, 1993, 2.
23 Ibid., February 8, 1993, 3.
24 Ibid., May 21, 1993, 2.
25 At least seven bills were introduced in Congress during the Clinton years, almost all sponsored or co-sponsored by Democrats; Representative Ron Paul (R-TX) intro-duced HR 1181 to lift the embargo and Senator Pat Roberts (R-KS) co-sponsored S 2617 to normalize trade with Cuba. The two mentioned bills and HR 1943, HR 2229, HR 883, HR 3173, HR 229 can be found through http://thomas.loc.gov/.
26 I computed the average using www.dhs.gov/xlibrary/assets/statistics/yearbook/2004/Yearbook2004.pdf
27 Cuba*INFO*, September 4, 1994, 6. The numbers given reflect only the Cubans rescued by the U.S. Coast Guard.
28 Ibid., January 15, 1993, 2.
29 Ibid., September 24, 1993, 3 and October 15, 1993, 3–4.
30 Ibid., August 5, 1994, 9–10.
31 Ibid, September 1, 1994, 5–6.
32 Ibid, 6.
33 Siro del Castillo, "Part II Interdicted: The Rafters Go to Guantánamo," University of Miami Digital Library Program, 2004. See http://balseros.miami.edu/PartII-Guantanamo.htm.
34 Cuba*INFO*, September 22, 1994, 1–4.
35 The Refugee Act of 1980 brought the United States into line on refugees as per the UN Convention and Protocol Relating to the Status of Refugees. See www.unhcr.org/protect/PROTECTION/3b66c2aa10.pdf. See als: Edward M. Kennedy, "Refugee Act of 1980," *International Migration Review* 15 (Spring–Summer 1981), 141–156.
36 Max J. Castro, "The New Cuban Immigration in Context," *The North-South Agenda* 58 (October 2002).
37 Cuba*INFO*, May 18, 1995, 1–7 and 12–13. Quotes from Helms, Burton and Goss on 5, Chiles on 6–7, *Miami Herald* poll results on 13, Sheehan on 3. Graham, Mas Canosa and Alarcón were quoted in Steven Greenhouse, "U.S. Will Return Refu-gees to Cuba in Policy Switch," *New York Times*, May 3, 1995.
38 Cuba*INFO*, October 12, 1995, 1–6. As staff consultant with the Western Hemi-sphere Subcommittee of the House of Representatives Foreign Affairs Committee (1991–1993), Richard A. Nuccio formulated the carrot-and-stick approach of Track I and Track II of the Cuban Democracy Act. Later Nuccio served as special

advisor to the president and the secretary of state for Cuba and designed the Clinton administration's measures of 1995.

39 Cynthia Corzo, "Anuncio alivia a exiliados que desean viajar a Cuba," *El Nuevo Herald*, October 7, 1995.
40 José Luiz Sánchez, Jr., "Exiliados desafían la lluvia con patriótica marcha," *El Nuevo Herald*, October 15, 1995.
41 Cuba*INFO*, October 12, 1995. Alarcón quote on 4, Gramm's, Menéndez's and Graham's on 6.
42 Helen Dewar, "Senate Rejects Cloture on Anti-Cuba Bill," *Washington Post*, October 13, 1995.
43 Cuba*INFO*, October 12, 1995, 7.
44 Ibid., November 2, 1995, 1–2 and December 20, 1995, 1–2.
45 Carmelo Mesa-Lago, *Are Economic Reforms Propelling Cuba to the Market?* (Miami: North-South Center, University of Miami, 1994).
46 Foreign Broadcast Information Service, *Latin America—Cuba: Fourth Congress of the Cuban Communist Party*, October 15, 1991, 1–24, 9–15, for the shortfalls in the first nine months of 1991.
47 Andrew G. Walder, ed., *The Waning of the Communist State: Economic Origins of Political Decline in China and Hungary* (Berkeley: University of California Press, 1995); William S. Turley and Mark Selden, eds., *Reinventing Vietnamese Socialism: Doi Moi in Comparative Perspective* (Boulder, CO: Westview Press, 1993); Susan L. Shirk, *The Political Logic of Economic Reform in China* (Berkeley: University of California Press, 1993).
48 Marifeli Pérez-Stable, "Caught in a Contradiction: Cuban Socialism between Mobilization and Normalization," *Comparative Politics* (October 1999). For the concept of "mobilizational authoritarianism," I am indebted to William S. Turley, "Party, State, and People: Political Structure and Economic Prospects," in Turley and Selden, eds. *Reinventing Vietnamese Socialism*.
49 See articles 14 (state owner of fundamental, not all, means of production), 17 (allows for joint ventures) and 18 (foreign trade no longer exclusively state-controlled). See www.gacetaoficial.cu/html/constitucion_de_la_republica.html
50 Juan Antonio Blanco, "Una obligación ética," *Encuentro* 25 (Summer 2002), 283–293. In an email dated July 23, 2009, Blanco—a former Cuban diplomat—noted that a Clinton official told him that, if the reforms had continued, the president would have moved towards the normalization of relations in his second term. From Juan Antonio Blanco to Marifeli Pérez-Stable, July 23, 2009.
51 John Price, "Cuban Parliament Passes New Law to Drum up Foreign Investment," *Associated Press*, September 6, 1995.
52 Foreign Broadcast Information Service, *Latin America 1992*, March 11, 1992, 5.
53 *Granma*, October 31, 1992, 4.
54 *CubaFax Update*, December 31, 1992.
55 Pérez-Stable, *The Cuban Revolution*, 183–186.
56 Foreign Broadcast Information Service, 25.
57 *El Nuevo Herald*, September 9, 1993.
58 Pérez-Stable, *The Cuban Revolution*, 181–183.
59 Pablo Alfonso, "Tres décadas cubanas en pie por los derechos del hombre," *El Nuevo Herald*, January 22, 2006. Adolfo Rivero, Edmigio López and Enrique Hernández were the other founding members.
60 In 1988, the Cuban government invited a UN delegation for an on-site, human-rights observation. The CCPDH brought more than 1,000 people to give testimony before the UN envoys.
61 Ariel Hidalgo, *Disidencia ¿Segunda Revolución Cubana?* (Miami: Ediciones Universal, 1994).

62 Kiger, *Squeeze Play*, 35.

63 Paul Hendrickson, "Of Burning Ambition and Orlando Bosch; For Miami's Cubans, the Return of Castro's Archenemy Rekindles the Old Hopes," *Washington Post*, May 12, 1988; Ann Louise Bardach, *Cuba Confidential: Love and Vengeance in Miami and Havana* (New York: Random House, 2002), 171–222.

64 *CubaINFO*, February 26, 1990, 6.

65 Alfonso Chardy and Ana Santiago, "3 Exiles Captured during Cuba Raid," *Miami Herald*, January 9, 1992; Chardy and Santiago, "Cuba Orders Firing Squad for 3 Miami Exile Raiders," *Miami Herald*, January 12, 1992; Pablo Alfonso and Mimi Whitefield, "Leader of Raid Executed, Cuban Government Says," *Miami Herald*, January 21, 1992.

66 Alfonso Chardy, "Miami Group Launches Coastal Raid on Cuba," *Miami Herald*, October 14, 1992; Christopher Marquis, "Cuba Gives Evidence on Hotel Attack," *Miami Herald*, October 27, 1992.

67 Sandra Dibble, "Bosch Freed on Parole Conditions of Release Are Limited"; Andrés Viglucci, "Exiles See Bosch as a Man Who Would Not Capitulate," *Miami Herald*, July 18, 1990.

68 Duncan Campbell, "The Bush Dynasty and the Cuban Criminals," *Guardian*, December 2, 2002.

69 For examples of Miami corruption investigations involving Cuban Americans, see: "Police Corruption Charges Still Being Probed, Officers Say," *Miami Herald*, July 11, 1982; Lisa Hoffman and George Stein, "Former Cops, Ex-Newsman Busted in Coke Ring," May 3, 1984; Jeff Leen and Reinaldo Ramos, "Scandal Probe Widens in Hialeah," March 4, 1986; Justin Gillis and Stephen J. Hedges, "Subpoena Hints Federal Probe's Focus Is Carollo," October 8, 1986; Jeff Leen, "Martínez Strikes a Defensive Stance, Hialeah Mayor Claims Political Vendetta," March 1, 1987; and David Hancock, "Exile Spokesman Faces Fraud Charges among Dozens S. Floridians Targeted in Medicare Probe," October 13, 1993. For examples of corruption by other ethnic groups, see: Peter K. Eisinger, "Political Transition in Boston, 1884–1933: Some Lessons for Contemporary Cities," *Political Science Quarterly* 93 (Summer 1978), 217–239; Steven P. Erie, "Politics, the Public Sector and Irish Social Mobility: San Francisco, 1870–1900," *Western Political Quarterly* 31 (June 1978), 274–289; and Humbert S. Nelli, "John Powers and the Italians: Politics in a Chicago Ward, 1896–1921, *Journal of American History* 57 (June 1970), 67–84.

70 Carlos A. Forment, "Political Practice and the Rise of an Ethnic Enclave: The Cuban-American Case, 1959–1979," *Theory and Society* 18 (January 1989), 47–81.

71 Americas Watch and the Fund for Free Expression, *Dangerous Dialogue: Attacks on Freedom of Expression in Miami's Cuban Exile Community* (August 1992) at http://memoria.fiu.edu/memoria/watch_reports/report_02.pdf.

72 Lisandro Pérez was the institute's founding director; Modesto Maidique was FIU president at the time.

73 Alfonso Chardy, "Foundation Decries Threats against Herald," *Miami Herald*, January 31, 1992.

74 Human Rights Watch/Americas and Free Expression Project, *Dangerous Dialogue Revisited: Threats to Freedom of Expression Continue in Miami's Cuban Exile Community* (November 1994). www.hrw.org/sites/default/files/reports/US94N.PDF

75 "Keys Get Balloons Meant to Stir Revolution in Cuba," *Miami Herald*, February 15, 1990; Karen Branch, "Exiles Send Hope and More to Cuba," *Miami Herald*, March 20, 1990; "The Propaganda Balloon Action against Poland," *BBC Summary of World Broadcasts*, March 11, 1982.

76 *CubaINFO*, April 20, 1990, 5; June 4, 1990, 5; August 24, 1992, 11. Though not within Cuba's territorial waters, the Cuban Freedom Flotilla was well within the up to 200-mile maritime jurisdiction under the UN Law of the Sea Convention.

77 Pedro Sevsec, "Mas Canosa Analiza Disidencia en Cuba," *El Nuevo Herald*, July 22, 1990.
78 Anne-Marie O'Connor, "Miami Cuban Exile Leaders Argue over Best Method to Oust Castro," *Palm Beach Post*, November 5, 1990.
79 David Lawrence Jr., "Who Will Determine Cuba's Destiny?" *Miami Herald*, July 29, 1990.
80 Alfonso Chardy, "Group Selective in Exile Unity Effort," *Miami Herald*, June 17, 1991.
81 Domínguez, *To Make the World Safe for Revolution*, 222.
82 Ibid., 236.
83 Jane Franklin, *The Cuban Revolution and the United States: A Chronological History* (Melbourne: Ocean Press, 1992), 239.
84 Alcibíades Hidalgo, "Saddam's Tough to Persuade. Cuba Tried," *Washington Post*, March 9, 2003.
85 Armando Valladares, *Against all Hope: The Prison Memoirs of Armando Valladares*, Andrew Hurley, trans. (New York: Knopf, 1986).
86 Four organizations sent delegations to Cuba: Amnesty International, the Washington DC-based Institute for Policy Studies, the Association of the Bar of the City of New York and the UNHRC Cuba working group. The latter held in-depth interviews with some ninety Cubans out of nearly 1500 who had requested to meet with the group. Notwithstanding an official pledge to the UNCHR not to harass these citizens, state security subsequently hounded them. See Aryeh Neier, "In Cuban Prisons," *New York Review of Books*, June 30, 1988; "Human Rights in Cuba: An Update," *U.S. Department of State Bulletin* (April 1989); and Alice H. Henken, Mary Jane Camejo, Richard J. Hiller, Michael H. Posner, Stephen J. Ritchin and Kenneth Roth, "Human Rights in Cuba: Report of a Delegation of the Association of the Bar of the City of New York," *Record of the Association of the Bar of the City of New York* 43 (November 1988).
87 Cuba*INFO*, March 20, 1990, 6.
88 Ibid., February 28, 1991, 2.
89 Ibid., July 5, 1991, 3.
90 Ibid., November 15, 1991, 1.
91 Ibid., December 13, 1991, 1.
92 Ibid., February 18, 1992, 4 and March 9, 1992, 1–2; *Washington Times*, February 26, 1992. The 1992 resolution upgraded Rivas Posada's post to special rapporteur, a charge usually reserved for the most flagrant violators of human rights. The three Cuban exiles honored by the Russians were Carlos Franqui, David Moya and Ricardo Bofill.
93 Cuba*INFO*, December 4, 1992, 1–3 and December 18, 1992, 2.
94 Juan O. Tamayo, "UN Panel Puts Cuba on Rights Abusers' List," *Miami Herald*, April 24, 1999.
95 Ibid.
96 Cuba*INFO*, August 2, 1991, 3–4 and November 15, 1991, 3.
97 Ibid., August 24, 1992, 4. González words also applied to Alberto Fujimori, who had just engineered the *autogolpe* in Peru.
98 Ibid., July 1, 1994, 6–7.
99 Declaración de Viña del Mar: Primera parte. Sexta Cumbre Iberoamericana de Jefes de Estado y de Gobierno (Santiago and Viña del Mar, Chile, November 7–11, 1996). See www.segib.org/documentos/11/esp/1.%20Primera%20parte%20La%20Gobernabilidad%20para%20una%20democracia%20eficiente%20y%20participativa.pdf.
100 Cuba*INFO*, August 24, 1992, 5–6.
101 Ibid., July 6, 1993, 6.

102 Ibid., November 2, 1995, 6–7.
103 Ibid., November 21, 1996, 6–8.
104 Ibid., November 13, 1997, 6. Gustavo Arcos, Osvaldo Payá, Rafael León and Elizardo Sánchez signed the letter.
105 Ibid., October 26, 1998, 5.
106 Ibid., August 24, 1992, 4–6.
107 Ibid., July 1, 1994, 6–7.
108 Ibid., October 26, 1998, 5.
109 Between 1960 and 1975, trade between Spain and Cuba totaled just under $1.4 billion at 1967 exchange rates (pesetas–dollars). Computed from Enrique Palazuelos Mansó, "La balanza de pagos entre Cuba y España," *Afers Internacionals* 8 (Spring 1986), 19–48, tables on 21 and 23.
110 John D. Harbron, "What is Spain's Role in Post-Castro Cuba?" *Miami Herald*, October 10, 1994.
111 George W. Schuyler, "Perspectives on Canada and Latin America: Changing Context... Changing Policy?" *Journal of Inter-American Studies and World Affairs* (Spring 1991), 19–58.
112 Donna Rich Kaplowitz, *Anatomy of a Failed Embargo: U.S. Sanctions against Cuba* (Boulder, CO: Lynne Rienner Publishers, 1998), 151–152 and 218.
113 Ibid., 153–155, quote on 155.
114 John M. Kirk and Peter McKenna, *Canada–Cuba Relations: The Other Good Neighbor Policy* (Gainesville: University Presses of Florida, 1997), 122–145.
115 Ouellet quote appears on page 149.
116 "Spain and Canada's Dialogue with Cuba," FRIDE Activity Brief, Madrid, February 19, 2009. 3.
117 Andrés Oppenheimer, "Spat over Refugees Strains Spain's Relations with Cuba," *Miami Herald*, July 19, 1990.
118 "EEC/Cuba: Spain and Community Suspend Aid," *European Report* 1606 (July 25, 1990), 1.
119 Reuters News Service, "Castro: Solution Is Near on Refugee Dispute with Spain," *Miami Herald*, July 30, 1990.
120 CubaINFO, September 7, 1990, 2.
121 Carlos Solchaga, "Cuba: perspectivas económicas," *Encuentro* 3 (Winter 1996–1997), 43–53.
122 Michael Becker, "Cuba Has Investment Interest; Nation Thinks U.S. Firms May Help End Embargo," *Fort Lauderdale Sun Sentinel*, April 9, 1995.
123 "Freer Cuba Travel Raises Trade Hopes; Businesses Seek Open Markets," *Chicago Tribune*, October 8, 1995.
124 CubaINFO, October 12, 1995, 6.
125 Ibid., April 27, 1995, 2.
126 Ibid., January 18, 1996, 1–2.
127 Ibid., February 8, 1996, 3 and March 4, 1996, 5–6. In his first trip, Richardson also raised matters pertaining to the exit fees charged by Havana to U.S.-bound immigrants and brought up the issue of the U.S. fugitives residing on the island. On the first, Havana agreed to reduce the fee from $600 to $300 for 1,000 needy cases per year. The second matter is still pending as Cuba demands reciprocity.
128 Gail Epstein Nieves, "Basulto Warned before First Trip," *Miami Herald*, March 8, 2001, news article based on testimony rendered at the trial of five Cuban spies arrested in 1999.
129 John Dorschner, "Clear and Present Danger," *Miami Herald*, February 16, 1997. This paragraph and the next two are based on Dorschner's article.
130 Nieves, "Basulto Warned before First Trip."
131 Grupo de Trabajo y Apoyo a Concilio Cubano International Support Commission,

"Unprecedented Cry for Assembly in Cuba!!! Hundreds Confront Castro Demanding Freedom of Speech, the Castro Regime Rejects them." See www.fiu.edu/~fcf/concilio.html.

132 Marifeli Pérez-Stable, "El caso CEA," *Encuentro* 10 (Fall 1998), 85–88. Review of Maurizio Giuliano, *El caso CEA: Intelectuales e inquisidores en Cuba* (Miami: Ediciones Universal, 1998). Haroldo Dilla's two CEA anthologies on democracy in Cuba were especially irritating to the PCC: *La democracia en Cuba y el diferendo con los Estados Unidos* (1995) and *La participación en Cuba y los retos del futuro* (1996).

133 Marifeli Pérez-Stable, "Misión cumplida: de cómo el gobierno cubano liquidó la amenaza del diálogo," *Encuentro* 1 (Summer 1996), 25–31.

134 Reginald K. Brack, Jr., Joelle Attinger and Cathy Booth, "Interview: Fidel's Defense," *Time*, March 11, 1996.

135 Cuba*INFO*, February 29, 1996 and *El Nuevo Herald*, February 21 and 22, 1999.

136 *El Nuevo Herald*, February 21 and 22, 1999; Walter Oppenheimer, "La Eurocámara condena a Cuba y la ley Helms-Burton," *El País*, March 15, 1996; and Resolution Adopted by the Council of the International Civil Aviation Organization at the Twentieth Meeting of Its 148th Session on 27 June, 1996. See www.icao.int/icao/en/nr/1996/pio199606_e.pdf.

3 "Half Drunk and Throwing Bottles at Each Other"

1 David González, "A Higher Profile for the Dissidents in Cuba," *New York Times*, November 17, 1999.

2 Pascal Fletcher, "Cuba Is Not Changing, Castro says," *Reuters*, January 11, 1998.

3 "El trabajo del Partido en la coyuntura actual," *Media Monitoring*, August 22, 1996. The document appeared as a series of articles in *Granma*.

4 Jorge I. Domínguez, "Government and Politics," in Rex A. Hudson, ed., *Cuba: A Country Study*, Library of Congress (Washington, DC: U.S. Government Printing Office, 2002), 254–255. While the PCC had loosened membership conditions in 1991, the increase was still impressive in light of the times.

5 Pérez-Stable, *The Cuban Revolution*, 184.

6 Mimi Whitefield and Mary Beth Sheridan, "Cuba Poll: The Findings," *Miami Herald*, December 18, 1994. Fourteen Central American pollsters interviewed 1,002 Cubans in all but the Eastern provinces; they used a 46-question instrument. The government forbade them to ask questions about Fidel Castro or other leaders.

7 "¡El futuro de nuestra Patria será un eterno Baraguá!" *Granma*, March 25, 1990, 2–3.

8 Luis Báez, Entrevista a Raúl Castro: "Hoy la prioridad política e ideológica es buscar comida", *El Mundo*, September 23, 1994. See www.elmundo.es/papel/hemeroteca/1994/09/23/mundo/7434.html.

9 PCC documents can be found at www.pcc.cu/congresos_asamblea/cong5.php; for *La Patria es de Todos*, see www.cartadecuba.org/la_patria.htm.

10 See Ley 88 de Protección de la Independencia Nacional y de la Economía de Cuba, at www.cubanet.org/ref/dis/021699.htm.

11 "Crackdown Underlines Commitment to One-Party Rule," *Latin American Regional Report: Central America and the Caribbean*, August 19, 1997, 2; "Even Friendly Countries Shocked by Crackdown," *Latin American Regional Report: Central America and the Caribbean* (March 1999) 2.

12 Carlos A. Romero, "Venezuela y Cuba. 'Una seguridad diferente'," *Nuevo Mundo Mundos Nuevos*, March 30, 2009, http://nuevomundo.revues.org/index55550.html.

13 The links for the seven reports on Cuba appear at the Inter-American Commission on Human Rights, Organization of American States, at www.cidh.org/publications.htm.

14 A year later, *Granma* announced that Christmas would subsequently be a holiday in

Cuba. John Rice, Associated Press, "Cuba Declares Christmas a Holiday," *New York Times*, December 1, 1998.

15 *Mensajero de la paz y la esperanza. Textos de la visita de Su Santidad Juan Pablo II a Cuba* (Miami: Ediciones Universal, 1998).

16 Pablo Alfonso, "Piden una acción más comprometida a la Jerarquía; el clero cubano de las provincias orientales," *El Nuevo Herald*, September 22, 1999.

17 Mauricio Vicent, "Castro acusa a EEUU y los disidentes de sabotear la Cumbre de La Habana," *El País*, November 3, 1999.

18 Pascal Fletcher, "Vatican Envoy Says Church in Cuba Making Progress," *Reuters*, December 3, 1999.

19 Cuba*INFO*, February 26, 1998, 8–9.

20 José Miguel Larraya, "Aznar recibe en la Moncloa a un destacado opositor al régimen cubano," *El País*, October 27, 1999, and "Aznar asegura que Castro es el principal obstáculo para que se den cambios en Cuba," *El País*, November 15, 1999.

21 José Miguel Larraya and Mauricio Vicent, "Las medidas del Gobierno cubano impiden una cálida acogida al Rey en las calles," *El País*, November 16, 1999. Pérez Roque served as Cuban foreign minister from 1999 to 2009.

22 Discurso del Rey Juan Carlos I en la cena oficial, Palacio de las Convenciones, Cumbres Iberoamericanas de Jefes de Estado y de Gobierno, November 15, 1999. See http://cumbresiberoamerica.cip.cu/compendios_informativos/cumbres_iberoamericanas/cumbres/ix-cumbre-iberoamericana/discurso-del-rey-juan-carlos-i-en-la-cena-oficial.

23 José Miguel Larraya, "Don Juan Carlos se despide de La Habana con el deseo de que 'Cuba se abra a Cuba'," *El País,* November 18, 1999.

24 Geri Smith, "Even Fidel's Friends Are Saying "Enough,'" *Business Week Online*, November 18, 1999.

25 Cuba*INFO*, August 29, 1996, 6. Roberto Robaina González was Cuba's foreign minister between 1993 and 1999.

26 Cuban Liberty and Democratic Solidarity (LIBERTAD) Act of 1995, Rept. 104–202, 104th Cong., 1t sess. (July 24, 1995): 2:13. "The Cuban government engages in the illegal international narcotics trade and harbors fugitives from justice in the United States."

27 Cuba*INFO*, October 10, 1996, 8 and May 2, 1996, 5.

28 Ibid., November 21, 1996, 6–7.

29 Ibid., February 6, 1997, 5–6 and May 1, 1997, 5–6.

30 The EU and ACP were bound by the Lomé Convention, which granted former European colonies preferential access to European markets, valued at $17 billion in the late 1990s. See *Economic Eye on Cuba*, at www.cubatrade.org/eyeont.html#10.

31 Cuba*INFO*, April 30, 1988, 5–6.

32 Ibid., January 11, 1999, 6.

33 "Spain and Canada's Dialogue with Cuba."

34 Cristina Warren, "Canada's Policy of Constructive Engagement with Cuba," FOCAL Background Briefing, Ottawa, May 2003.

35 Francesc Bayo, "Las relaciones políticas entre España y Cuba," Documentos CIDOBC. 16 (2006). See www.cidob.org/es/publicaciones/documentos_cidob/.

36 Cuba*INFO*, June 13, 1996, 3.

37 Larry Rohter, "Latin American Nations Rebuke the U.S. for the Embargo on Cuba," *New York Times*, June 6, 1996.

38 Cuba*INFO*, June 13, 1996, 3–4. Resolution passed on a 23–1 vote with ten abstentions; the United States was the lone opponent.

39 Annual Report of the Inter-American Juridical Committee to the General Assembly (August 29, 1996), at www.oas.org/cji/eng/INFOANUAL.CJI.1996.ING.pdf.

40 Hal Klepak, *Cuba's Military 1990–2005: Revolutionary Soldiers during Counter-*

Revolutionary Times (New York: Palgrave Macmillan, 2005), 129–135; Mark Falcoff, *Cuba the Morning After: Confronting Castro's Legacy* (Washington, DC: AEI Press, 2003), 225–228.

41 "Trade, and America's Family Feud," *Economist*, March 1, 1997.

42 Robert L. Muse, "A Public International Law Critique of the Extraterritorial Jurisdiction of the Helms-Burton Act (Cuban Liberty and Democratic Solidarity Act (LIBERTAD) Act of 1996)," *George Washington Journal of International Law and Economics* 30, no. 2/3 (1996–1997), 207–270.

43 Cuba*INFO*, August 1, 1996, 1–5. Quotations by White House on WTO, Clinton on working with allies, Burton on Title III waiver and by Díaz-Balart and CANF president appear on 2 and 4.

44 Mark P. Sullivan and Maureen Taft-Morales, "Cuba: Issues and Legislation in the 106th Congress." Congressional Research Service, Library of Congress. January 11, 2001, 10.

45 John H. Jackson and Andreas F. Lowenfeld, "Helms-Burton, the U.S., and the WTO," *American Society for International Law* (March 1997), at www.asil.org/insight7.cfm.

46 "American Survey," *Economist*, March 1, 1997.

47 Sullivan and Taft-Morales, "Cuba," 10–12; Cuba*INFO*, May 21, 1998, 1–2.

48 Joel Glass, "Clinton Faces Trouble over His Pledge to EU on Helms-Burton Act," *Lloyd's List*, 3.

49 Cuba*INFO*, September 14, 1999; "Truce between Washington and Brussels May Collapse," *Latin American Regional Report: Central America and the Caribbean* (August1999), 6.

50 Sullivan and Taft-Morales, "Cuba," 10–11.

51 Woolley and Peters, *The American Presidency Project*.

52 Robert L. Muse, "The Current Embargo on Cuba: What Is Required to End It and How Might That Happen?" Paper presented at *Imperatives for a New Cuba Policy*, conference at the University of California Center, Washington, DC, October 16, 2007.

53 Jack Payton, "End Embargo, Pope Urges," *St. Petersburg Times*, January 26, 1998.

54 Cuba*INFO*, March 20, 1998, 2. Quotes in the previous paragraph can be found on 1.

55 Christopher Marquis, "Lawmakers from Miami at Odds with CANF," *Miami Herald*, January 29, 1998. Two weeks later CANF and the lawmakers mended fences: The foundation dropped the proposal and pledged to use existing channels for humanitarian aid; the lawmakers agreed to work together rather than at cross-purposes. See Christopher Marquis, "Lawmakers, Exile Lobby Reach Accord on Cuba Aid," *Miami Herald*, February 14, 1998.

56 Cuba*INFO*, April 30, 1998, 1; July 9, 1998, 1; and October 1, 1998, 1.

57 Ibid., May 21, 1998, 2–3.

58 Ibid., October 26, 1998, 1–2.

59 Patrick J. Haney and Walt Vanderbush, *The Cuban Embargo: The Domestic Politics of an American Foreign Policy* (Pittsburgh, PA: University of Pittsburgh Press, 2005), 110–118.

60 Tim Weiner, "U.S. Ready to Ease Some Restrictions in Policy on Cuba," *New York Times*, January 5, 1999.

61 Mireya Navarro, "Miami Generally Welcomes Easing of Ban," *New York Times*, January 6, 1999.

62 Cuba*INFO*, January 11, 1999, 1–3; James C. McKinley, Jr., "Cuba Attacks as 'Deceptive' Clinton's Easing of the Embargo," *New York Times*, January 10, 1999.

63 Cuba*INFO*, January 11, 1999, 2, for the estimated annual sales and Díaz-Balart's quote.

64 Ibid., October 27, 1999, 1–2.
65 Associated Press, "U.S. Governor in First Visit to Castro's Cuba," *New York Times*, October 24, 1999; *Economist*, October 30, 1999, 32.
66 Cuba*INFO*, May 25, 1999, 1–3.
67 Karen DeYoung, "U.S. Businesses Encouraged to Trade with Cuba," *Washington Post*, July 28, 1999.
68 Cuba*INFO*, November 23, 1999, 3.
69 Nicole Winfield, "El suavizamiento del embargo: 'del lobo un pelo'," *El Nuevo Herald*, September 24, 1999.
70 Cuba*INFO*, October 27, 1999, 2.
71 The Cuban Democracy Act exempted medical sales from the embargo while requiring the American president to certify, through on-site inspections, that the medical products were being used for the intended purposes. TSRA allowed medical sales but on the terms specified by the CDA. Unsurprisingly, U.S. medical sales to Cuba have been insignificant.
72 Steven A. Holmes and Lizette Alvarez, "Congress Addressed Importing Medicine and Exporting to Cuba," *New York Times*, October 6, 2000.
73 "Easing of Embargo Rejected by Havana," *Latin American Regional Report: Caribbean & Central America*, October 31, 2000, 6.
74 Haney and Vanderbush, *The Cuban Embargo*.
75 Larry Rohter, "Wave of Bombings Stop in Cuba but Tensions Persist," *New York Times*, October 13, 1997.
76 Ann Louise Bardach and Larry Rohter, "A Bomber's Tale: Taking Aim at Castro Key Cuba Foe Claims Exiles' Backing," *New York Times*, July 12, 1998 and "A Bomber's Tale: Decades of Intrigue Life in the Shadows, Trying to Bring down Castro," *New York Times*, July 13, 1998.
77 Cuba*INFO*, September 11, 1997, 1–2; "Cuban Exiles Say *Times* Articles Are Baseless," *New York Times*, July 14, 1998. Recently declassified documents suggest a Posada–Mas Canosa connection in the mid-1960s; an FBI 1966 report released in 2005 indicates a "trustworthy source" saying Mas Canosa paid Posada $5,000 to carry out anti-Castro operations in Mexico. See the National Security Archive, "Posada Carriles Built Bombs for, and Informed on, Jorge Mas Canosa, CIA Records Reveal," at www.gwu.edu/~nsarchiv/NSAEBB/NSAEBB288/index.htm.
78 Task Force on Memory Truth and Justice, 61–62.
79 Susana Bellido and Cynthia Corzo, "Flotilla Peacefully Passes Cuba," *Miami Herald*, May 18, 1997.
80 See, for example, the work of the Directorio Democrático Cubano at www.directorio.org/.
81 Article 32 of the Cuban Constitution states: " Dual citizenship is not recognized. Therefore, when a foreign citizenship is acquired, the Cuban one will be lost." Yet, it also adds: "Formalization of the loss of citizenship and the authorities empowered to decide on this is prescribed by law." Cuban Constitution, art. 32. www.constitutionnet.org/files/Cuba%20Constitution.pdf. In *Citizenship Laws of the World* (2001), the U.S. Office of Personnel Management says on page 60:

> Many countries automatically revoke citizenship upon a person's acquisition of a foreign citizenship, but this is known not to always be the case in Cuba. Former citizens of Cuba should not assume that acquisition of a new nationality has released them from obligations and responsibilities associated with Cuban citizenship. Voluntary loss of citizenship is permitted by Cuban law; however, it is necessary to first acquire the permission of the Council of State. See www.opm. gov/EXTRA/INVESTIGATE/is-01.PDF. As far as I know, there is no public record of the Council of State having formalized Mas Canosa's loss of citizenship or that of any other naturalized U.S. citizen born in Cuba.

82 Marifeli Pérez-Stable, "Estrada Palma's Civic March: From Oriente to Havana, April 20–May 11, 1902," *Cuban Studies* 30 (2000), 113–21.

83 The full debate can be found at http://video.google.com/videoplay?docid=4983270 361571655161#. I translated the excerpts quoted.

84 Damián J. Fernández, *Cuba and the Politics of Passion* (Austin: University of Texas Press, 2000) looks at the role of passion in Cuban politics.

85 Cynthia Corzo, "La muerte interrumpe tenaz lucha," *El Nuevo Herald*, November 24, 1997.

86 Corzo, "Deceso deja profundo vacío en exilio cubano," in ibid.

87 Bellido and Corzo, "Flotilla Peacefully Passes Cuba."

88 Beginning in 1991, Florida International University conducted intermittent opinion polls in South Florida's Cuban-American community. The question on the sale of food and medicine was first asked in 1993. See the comparison at Institute for Public Opinion Research and Cuban Research Institute, Florida International University, *2000 FIU/Cuba Poll,* www.fiu.edu/~ipor/cuba2000/index.html.

89 Rick Bragg, "For Cuban-Americans, a Void Lingers 2 Years After a Leader's Death," *New York Times*, September 12, 1999.

90 "Castro in Quotes," *The Guardian*, February 19, 2008, at www.guardian.co.uk.

91 Discurso pronunciado por Fidel Castro Ruz, Presidente de la República de Cuba, en el acto por el aniversario 60 de su ingreso a la universidad, efectuado en el Aula Magna de la Universidad de La Habana, el 17 de noviembre de 2005," at www.cuba.cu/gobierno/discursos/2005/esp/f171105e.html.

92 Carlos M. de la Cruz and Carlos A. Saladrigas, "'Exiles Deserve understanding'," *Miami Herald*, April 18, 2000.

93 Charles Lane, "And a Child Shall Lead Them," *New Republic*, January 24, 2000.

94 Jim DeFede, "Leave the Driving to CANF," *Miami New Times*, February 17–23, 2000.

95 Kirk Nielsen, "The Sánchez Solution," *Miami New Times*, April 13, 2000.

96 Rick Bragg, "Stand over Elian Highlights a Virtual Secession of Miami," *New York Times*, April 1, 2000; Peter T. Kilborn, "Miami Area's Mayors Ride a Volatile Political Wave," *New York Times*, April 17, 2000.

97 "Civic Leaders Sought to Bring a Compromise," *Miami Herald*, April 23, 2000; Carlos Saladrigas, "Cubans Need a Vision," *Miami Herald*, May 12, 2000.

4 "We Need to De-Americanize the Problem of Cuba"

1 Richard L. Berke, "Bush 'Is My Commander,' Gore Declares in Call for Unity," *New York Times*, September 30, 2001.

2 Bush had a larger reelection margin in the Electoral College (6.5 percent to Wilson's 4.3 percent); Wilson had a larger share of the popular vote (3.1 percent to Bush's 2.5 percent).

3 Jim Burns, "Bush to Waive Title Three of Helms-Burton Law against Cuba," *CNS News* and *Cubanet*, July 16, 2001. See http://cnsnews.com and www.cubanet.org, for quotes by Díaz-Balart, Ros-Lehtinen and Menéndez.

4 George Gedda, Associated Press, "Bush Suspends Law on Cuba Lawsuits," *Yahoo News* and *Cubanet*, July 17, 2001. See http://news.yahoo.com.

5 George W. Bush, "Statement: Toward a Democratic Cuba," July 13, 2001. Woolley and Peters, *The American Presidency Project*, (database) www.presidency.ucsb.edu/ws/?pid=63565.

6 Nick Miroff, "Guantánamos's New Guests Get Little Attention in Havana," *World Press Review*, January 22, 2002, at www.worldpress.org/Americas/371.cfm.

7 "La Habana dispuesta a negociar pese al embargo," *El Nuevo Herald*, February 19, 2002. The figures cited do not include Cuban Americans.

8 Joe Sharkey, "Trips to Cuba for Commercial Reasons Are Increasingly Becoming a Reality for Americans," *New York Times*, January 10, 2001.

9 Pablo Alfonso, "Bush y el Congreso discrepan sobre Cuba," *El Nuevo Herald*, February 19, 2002.

10 In 2001–2005, Mel Martínez led the Department of Housing and Urban Development. Otto Reich first served as Assistant Secretary of State for the Western Hemisphere under a recess appointment and then as U.S. Special Envoy for the Western Hemisphere. Both left after Bush's first term, Reich for private life and Martínez for the Senate.

11 Christopher Marquis, "It's Republican vs. Republican on Cuba," *New York Times*, July 28, 2002.

12 TradeStats ExpressTM generates U.S. trade statistics at http://tse.export.gov. Using http://tse.export.gov/NTDMap.aspx?UniqueURL=qit4rk45wbpjjaqzhxrni b45–2009–11–2–15–52–3. I generated a table for U.S. exports to Cuba between 1992 and 2008.

13 "Castro Welcomes One-off US Trade," *BBC Americas*, November 17, 2001, at http://news.bbc.co.uk/2/hi/americas/1662346.stm.

14 U.S.–Cuba Trade and Economic Council, "Economic Eye on Cuba," May 2009, www.cubatrade.org/CubaExportStats.pdf. Since 1993, medical exports had been authorized under the Cuban Democracy Act. Strict licensing procedures kept these exports at minimal levels: $3.6 million under Clinton and a negligible $197,000 under Bush.

15 United States International Trade Commission, *U.S. Agricultural Sales to Cuba: Certain Economic Effects of U.S. Restrictions* (July 2007), 3–5 and 3–6, at www.usitc. gov/publications/pub3932.pdf.

16 Remy Jurenas, "Exempting Food and Agriculture Products from U.S. Economic Sanctions: Status and Implementation," Congressional Research Service, U.S. Library of Congress, January 20, 2006.

17 Jonathan R. Coleman, "U.S. Agricultural Sales to Cuba: Certain Economic Effects of U.S. Restrictions," Office of Industries, U.S. International Trade Commission, June 2009, 12.

18 U.S.–Cuba Trade and Economic Council, "Economic Eye on Cuba."

19 *Present Dangers: Crisis and Opportunity in American Foreign and Defense Policy*, ed. Robert Kagan and William Kristol (New York: Encounter Books, 2000); James Mann, *The Rise of the Vulcans: The History of Bush's War Cabinet* (New York: Vintage Adult, 2004).

20 Scott W. Carmichael, *True Believer: Inside the Investigation and Capture of Ana Montes, Cuba's Master Spy* (Annapolis, MD: Naval Institute Press, 2007). Montes avoided the death penalty by agreeing to tell American intelligence officers all she knew.

21 Facts and Figures 2003. *Federal Bureau of Investigation*, at www.fbi.gov/libref/facts-figure/counterintell.htm.

22 Rick Bragg, "I.N.S. Official Is Convicted on Charges of Espionage," *New York Times*, May 31, 2000; Noah Bierman, Frances Robles and Casey Woods, "Suspects Led Low-profile Lives," *Miami Herald*, January 10, 2006; Del Quentin Wilber and Mary Beth Sheridan, "State Department Retiree Accused of Spying," *Washington Post*, June 6, 2009. Former INS official Mariano Faget served five years in prison; former FIU professor Carlos Álvarez received a five-year sentence and his wife, Elsa Prieto, a three-year sentence. Walter Kendall Myers and his wife Gwendolyn Steingraber Myers accepted a plea bargain; both agreed to cooperate fully with U.S. authorities. Myers is serving life in prison and Steingraber Myers was sentenced to seven years.

23 Remarks by Former U.S. President Jimmy Carter at the University of Havana, Cuba, May 14, 2002, at www.cartercenter.org/news/documents/doc528.html.

24 "Remarks by the President on Cuba Policy Review," Washington, DC, May 20, 2002, at www.cubanet.org/CNews/y02/may02/21e5.htm.

25 Jorge I. Domínguez, *A Constitution for Cuba's Political Transition: The Utility of Retaining (and Amending) the 1992 Constitution* (Miami, FL: Institute of Cuban and Cuban-American Studies, University of Miami, 2003).

26 "Cuba: Bioweapons Threat or Political Punching Bag?," Terrorism Project, Center for Defense Information, Washington, DC, at www.cdi.org/terrorism/cuba-pr. cfm#_ftnref1.

27 Rosa Townsend, "Powell se retracta de las acusaciones de bioterrorismo contra La Habana," *El País,* May 15, 2002.

28 David González, "Carter and Powell Cast Doubt on Bioarms in Cuba," *New York Times,* May 14, 2002.

29 Steven R. Weisman, "In Stricter Study, U.S. Scales Back on Cuba Arms," *New York Times,* September 18, 2003.

30 Mark P. Sullivan, "Cuba: U.S. Restrictions on Travel and Remittances," January 25, 2010, Congressional Research Service, 4–5.

31 Nancy San Martín, "Rules Changed on Cuba Trips," *Miami Herald,* March 25, 2003.

32 Duncan Currie, "Why Cuba's Historic Civil Society Gathering Was So Import-ant," *The Weekly Standard,* May 26, 2005.

33 David González, "Cuba Arrests a Score of Dissidents Linked to a U.S. Diplomat," *New York Times,* March 20, 2003; Tim Weiner, "Cuba Arrests 8 in Hijacking of Havana Ferry," *New York Times,* April 5, 2003; Anita Snow, "Cuba Executes Three Men for Ferry Hijacking," *Independent,* April 12, 2003, at www.independent.co.uk/ news/world/americas/cuba-executes-three-men-for-ferry-hijacking-594227.html.

34 Daniel P. Erikson, *The Cuba Wars: Fidel Castro, the United States, and the Next Revolution* (New York: Bloomsbury Press, 2008), 78–81.

35 Ibid., 82.

36 Commission for Assistance to a Free Cuba, "Report to the President," May 2004. See www.state.gov/documents/organization/32334.pdf. Secretary Powell ended up as the sole chairman when Mel Martínez decided to run for the Senate. The docu-ment became known as the Powell Report.

37 Commission for Assistance to a Free Cuba, "Report to the President," July 2006, at http://2006–2009.cafc.gov/index.htm.

38 Pablo Alfonso, "Payá viaja de Washington a Roma para reunirse con el Papa," *El Nuevo Herald,* January 7, 2003.

39 U.S. Department of State, "Support for a Democratic Transition in Cuba," January 28, 1997, at http://web.gc.cuny.edu/dept/bildn/cuba/publications/usacubarela-tions/supportforademocratictransition.pdf.

40 Cuban Assets Control Regulations, 31 CFR Part 515, *Federal Register* 69, 115 (June 16, 2004).

41 "Castro Wilts under the Sun," Reuters, *New York Times,* June 24, 2001; Mary Jordan, "Castro Falls, but Says He's 'in One Piece'," *Washington Post,* October 22, 2004.

42 The documents pertaining to amending Articles 3, 11 and 137 can be found at Ter-rorismo, *Granma.* www.granma.cubaweb.cu/terrorismo.

43 Respuesta confeccionada por la Comisión de Asuntos Constitucionales y Jurídicos de la Asamblea Nacional que le fue entregada a Osvaldo Payá acerca de su proyecto el 18 denoviembre del 2002 y enviada posteriormente por correo el 26 de noviem-bre del mismo año. http://cuba-l.unm.edu/?nid=19534&cat=cd.

44 Christopher Bodeen, "China's Changes Astonish Fidel Castro," *Associated Press,* February 28, 2003.

45 Speech delivered by Dr. Fidel Castro Ruz, President of the Republic of Cuba, at

the Commemoration of the 60th Anniversary of his admission to University of Havana, in the Aula Magna of the University of Havana, on November 17, 2005, at www.cuba.cu/gobierno/discursos/2005/ing/f171105i.html.

46 *Revolución*, June 9, 1960, 1.

47 Nancy San Martín, "Cuba Announces New Restrictions on Diplomats," *Miami Herald*, March 19, 2003.

48 "Congelan la petición cubana sobre Cotonú," EFE, *El Nuevo Herald*, May 1, 2003.

49 Gabriela Cañas, "La Unión Europea adopta sanciones diplomáticas contra Cuba," *El País*, June 6, 2003.

50 Marika Lynch, "D.C. Foes of Cuba Embargo Quit Group," *Miami Herald*, April 24, 2003.

51 "Tormenta intelectual por la represión en Cuba," Agence France Presse, *El Nuevo Herald*, May 5, 2003.

52 Andrés Oppenheimer, "Listen Carefully to Latin America's Response to Cuba's Repression: Silence," *Miami Herald*, April 10, 2003.

53 Wilfredo Cancio, "Fusilan a tres cubanos tras juicio sumario," *El Nuevo Herald*, April 12, 2003.

54 Marika Lynch, "Cuba Is Re-elected to U.N. Rights Panel; U.S. Angered," *Miami Herald*, April 30, 2003.

55 In his Roundtable presentation, Castro mentioned that on March 31–April 1, Cason had gone to José Martí International Airport to persuade hijacker Adermis Wilson to give up the Soviet-made AN-24 aircraft and the forty-six passengers on board. Should he continue to the United States, Cason told Wilson, he would face serious charges for air piracy. Castro—who had been at the airport for a few hours already—and Cason talked to the hijacker together. The incident represented a moment of truce between the Comandante and the chief U.S. Interests Section. Neither man succeeded in dissuading Wilson, who landed in Key West where he was tried, convicted and sentenced to twenty years in prison in July 2003. See Jennifer Babson, "Castro Attempted to Halt Hijack, Witnesses Testify," and "Cuban Convicted of Hijacking Plane," *Miami Herald*, July 10 and July 11, 2003.

56 Comparecencia especial del Presidente de la República de Cuba, Fidel Castro Ruz, en la Mesa Redonda sobre los más recientes acontecimientos en nuestro país y el incremento de las acciones agresivas del gobierno de Estados Unidos contra nuestro pueblo, el 25 de abril de 2003, at www.cuba.cu/gobierno/discursos/2003/esp/f250403e.html.

57 Mauricio Vicent, "La crisis del canapé," *El País*, July 6, 2003.

58 Andrés Oppenheimer and Nancy San Martín, "U.S. Vote May End up Aiding Cuba at U.N.," *Miami Herald*, April 17, 2003.

59 "Cuba Executions Meant to Avert 'Migration Crisis, War' with U.S.," *Miami Herald*, April 19, 2003.

60 Lynch, "Cuba Is Re-elected to U.N. Rights Panel." UNCHR nominations are put forward by the UN's Economic and Social Council but regional governments decide on the slate.

61 "Los Grammy Latinos podrían venir a Miami," *El Nuevo Herald*, February 13, 2001.

62 American Civil Liberties Union, "Overview of the Cuban Ordinance Case," at www.aclufl.org/take_action/students/case_of_the_month/2000/overview0400. cfm. In July 1996, Miami-Dade County passed the ordinance in the emotionally charged atmosphere after the Cuban Air Force had downed two civilian planes over international waters. The measure banned county vendors from doing business with any organization that dealt with Cuba, prohibited contractors from visiting Cuba and gave elected commissioners the authority to grant waivers. Until 2000, it was common practice for many American cities to issue ordinances on foreign matters, for example, divestiture of South African investments during the apartheid era.

63 Edward Walsh, "Justices Limit States on Sanctions; Court Rejects Mass. Law on Firms Doing Business with Burma," *Washington Post*, June 20, 2000.

64 Andrés Viglucci, Jordan Levin and Charles Rabin, "Protests Jeopardize Safety at Event, Show Chief Says," *Miami Herald*, August 21, 2001. In 1999, when the Cuban orchestra Los Van Van performed in Miami, Cuban exiles had pelted eggs, soda cans and other items at concertgoers.

65 Jon Pareles, "Latin Grammys Go on Minus Cubans," *New York Times*, September 4, 2003.

66 Mirta Ojito, "Latin Grammy Show Puts Miami to the Test," *New York Times*, September 3, 2003. After 9/11, the Bush administration required Cubans to submit visa applications six-to-eight weeks in advance of travel dates. According to the State Department, the applications arrived late and their visas could not be processed in time.

67 Carol Rosenberg, "Lobbying for Latin Grammys Challenged," *Miami Herald*, March 6, 2001.

68 Ibid.

69 Liz Balmaseda, "Each Side in Rift Claims Legacy," *Miami Herald*, July 26, 2001; Rui Ferreira, "Dieciséis directivos salen de la FNCA," *El Nuevo Herald*, August 8, 2001; Dana Candy, "Cuban Exile Group Fractured as Hardliners Quit Board," *New York Times*, August 8, 2001.

70 Oscar Corral, "2 Groups Differ on Cuba, Not on Use of Power," *Miami Herald*, March 29, 2004.

71 Corral, "Poll: Hard Line on Cuba Endures," *Miami Herald*, March 11, 2004. The Advocates' first action was to hire the Miami-based Campaign Data Inc. to survey 600 Cuban-American registered voters in South Florida. The poll showed steadfast embargo support and outright rejection of the Varela Project. An independent expert hired by the *Herald* to review the Cuba Democracy Advocate poll said: "The very one-sided way in which the questions are asked really leads the respondent to an answer. I can say that this particular survey is useless in determining attitudes toward Cuban policy."

72 Pablo Bachelet, "Cuban Exile Group Cleared of Violations," *Miami Herald*, June 21, 2007. The Federal Election Commission had investigated the PAC for alleged illegal links between the PAC and Cuba Democracy Advocates. www.uscubapac. com/agendaofpac.html. I did not find a webpage for Cuba Democracy Advocates.

73 See: Cuba Study Group, www.cubastudygroup.org.

74 Andrés Oppenheimer, "Poll Says Exiles Shifting from Hardline Positions," *Miami Herald*, May 16, 2002.

75 Tim Henderson, "Aerial View of Rally Shows Flaws in Estimates," *Miami Herald*, April 4, 2003. Air Flight Services used a $400,000 camera made to take high-resolution photos and then proceeded to count the marchers, one by one. The *Herald* also published the photos in sequence with the number of marchers in each take.

76 Jorge Mas Santos, "Entre cubanos está la solución," *El Nuevo Herald*, February 2, 2001.

77 Oscar Corral, "CANF Outraged by Return of Dozen Cubans," *Miami Herald*, July 27, 2003.

78 Rui Ferreira, "Al aire las diferencias entre la Fundación y Díaz-Balart," *El Nuevo Herald*, July 25, 2003.

79 Domingo Moreira, "Project Varela Leads Cuba to Freedom," *Miami Herald*, June 5, 2002.

80 Institute for Public Opinion Research and Cuban Research Institute, Florida International University, *2000 FIU Cuba Poll,* www.fiu.edu/~ipor/cuba2000/index. html and *2007 FIU Cuba Poll,* www.fiu.edu/~ipor/cuba8/. I compiled the percentages

cited by adding either the strongly favor/mostly favor categories or mostly oppose/ strongly oppose categories. In the question on the timing of political change in Cuba, I combined the categories of within 1 year/in 2–5 years and those of in 6–10 years/ over 10 years/never.

81 José J. Basulto, "Ayudemos al pueblo cubano," *El Nuevo Herald*, November 11, 2001.

82 Kathryn McConnell, "Private Groups Rally to Send Disaster-Relief Aid to Cuba," at www.america.gov/st/foraid-english/2008/November/20081121134256AKllenn oCcM0.5089075.html&distid=ucs; Jaweed Kalim, "U.S. Curbs Post-Storm Aid to Cuba," *Miami Herald*, September 27, 2008.

83 See Brian Latell, *After Fidel: The Inside Story of Castro's Regime and Cuba's Next Leader* (New York: Palgrave Macmillan, 2005) for an analysis of how the two brothers have ruled Cuba since 1959.

84 Lázaro Barredo Medina, "Ningún enemigo podrá derrotarnos," *Granma*, August 18, 2006, www.granma.cubaweb.com.

85 Vivian Sequera, Associated Press, "Raúl Castro to U.S.: Normalize Ties," www. fiu.edu/~fcf/rcqastr10501.html; Associated Press, "U.S. Still Considers Attack on Island, Cuban Leader Says," *Miami Herald*, April 16, 2001.

86 "Briefing on U.S. Policy toward Cuba by Thomas Shannon, Assistant Secretary of State for Western Hemisphere Affairs," August 23, 2006, http://2002–2009-fpc. state.gov/71065.htm.

87 Raúl Castro, "Trabajar con sentido crítico y creador, sin anquilosamiento ni esquematismos," *Granma,* July 27, 2007.

88 Javier Mestre, "En torno a la encomiable tozudez del socialismo cubano," *Rebelión*, August 27, 2007, www.rebelion.org; Mauricio Vicent, "Cuba inicia el debate del cambio," *El País*, September 11, 2007; "Repiten consulta popular de los 90," *Reforma*, September 21, 2007, www.reforma.com; Rafael Alcídes, "Ideas sueltas en La Habana," *Encuentro en la red*, October 8, 2007, www.cubaencuentro.com; Pedro Campos, "Más socialización pidió el pueblo en el debate del discurso de Raúl," *Kaos en la red*, October 16, 2007, www.kaosenlared.net.

89 Raúl Castro, "Nuestra batalla de hoy es la misma iniciada el 26 de julio de 1953," *Granma*, July 27, 2008.

90 "El gobierno comienza a vender insumos en pesos convertibles a los campesinos," *Encuentro en la red*, March 18, 2008; "Decreto-Ley No. 259 sobre la entrega de tierras ociosas en usufructo," *Granma*, July 18, 2008; "Se inicia proceso de entrega de tierras estatales ociosas en usufructo para incrementar la producción de alimentos," *Granma*, September 15, 2008.

91 The International Republican Institute issued Cuban Public Opinion Survey in 2007, 2008 and 2009, www.iri.org. In 2007 NTS Consulting Limited conducted a telephone survey on two sets of questions, governance and the economic situation. Project directors Sergio Díaz-Briquets and Jorge Pérez-López submitted their findings, "Public Opinion in Cuba at a Time of Transition: An Independent Assessment," to the Pan American Development Foundation. Freedom House has released two special reports based on qualitative interviews: "Change in Cuba: How Citizens View Their Country's Future," September 15, 2008 and "Another 'Special Period' in Cuba? How Citizens View Their Country's Future," March 20, 2009, www.freedomhouse.org.

92 Jesús Ríos and Johanna Godoy, "Personal Freedom, Self-concept and Well-being among Residents of Havana and Santiago de Cuba," Paper presented at the First Latin American Congress of Public Opinion, Colonia del Sacramento, Uruguay, April 12–14, 2007.

93 Domínguez, *To Make a World Safe for Revolution.*

94 Jeff Franks, "Cuba Oil Claims Raise Eyebrow in Energy World," *Reuters*, October 24, 2008. Cuba announced that the offshore fields could contain 20 billion barrels, which oil experts considered "hard to believe but not out of the realm of possibility."

95 "Ingresa Cuba al Grupo Río," *Granma*, November 14, 2008.
96 Paul Knox, "Graham Protests against Cuban Trials," *Globe and Mail*, April 8, 2003, www.theglobeandmail.com.
97 Table 15.3: Visitantes por países, *Anuario Estadístico de Cuba 2008*, www.one.cu/aec2008/esp/15_tabla_cuadro.htm.
98 Table 376–0051: Canadian Direct Investment Abroad and Foreign Direct Investment in Canada, Statistics Canada, www.statcan.gc.ca. Post-1998 data are "suppressed to meet the confidentiality requirements of the *Statistics Act*."
99 Table 8.4: Intercambio comercial de mercancías por países seleccionados y áreas geográficas, *Anuario Estadístico de Cuba 2008*.
100 Nancy San Martin, "Canada Protests Embargo-Case Verdict," *Miami Herald*, April 5, 2002; Paul Harris, "The Long Ordeal of James Sabzali," April 16, 2005, www.escritoire.ca/images/Sabzali.pdf.
101 Jeff Sallot, "U.S. Sees Strategic Advantage in Ottawa's Cuban Ties," *Globe and Mail*, December 19, 2006.
102 Table 8.4: Intercambio comercial de mercancías por países seleccionados y áreas geográficas.
103 "Cuba–China Relations," *Cuba Facts* 21 (May 2006), http://ctp.iccas.miami.edu/FACTS_Web/Cuba%2520Facts%2520Issue%252021%2520May%25202006.htm; Marc Lacey, "In Stores, Hints of Change under New Castro," *New York Times*, May 2, 2008.
104 Bosco Esteruelas, "La UE congela su relación con Cuba por la represión de disidentes," *El País*, May 1, 2003; "La UE revisa su política frente a Cuba tras los últimos episodios de represión en la isla," *El País*, June 5, 2003; Mauricio Vicent, "Castro renuncia a la ayuda humanitaria de la UE y al diálogo político con los Quince," *El País*, July 28, 2003, "La Habana estima 'correcto' el intento de Madrid de favorecer el diálogo con la UE," *El País*, October 20, 2004 and "La UE reanuda la cooperación con Cuba después de cinco años de congelamiento de las relaciones," *El País*, October 23, 2008; Patricia Grogg, "Cuba–UE: Nuevos peldaños en la colaboración," *IPS*, March 20, 2009, http://cubaalamano.net/sitio/client/report.php?id=980.
105 "Cuban Policy in the Middle East: A Cuba–Iran Axis?" *Focus* 55 (June 7, 2004), http://ctp.iccas.miami.edu/FOCUS_Web/Issue55.htm; "The Growing Iran-Cuba Strategic Alliance," *Focus* 76 (May 16, 2006), http://ctp.iccas.miami.edu/FOCUS_Web/Issue76.htm; "Recibe Raúl a Presidente de Irán," *Granma*, September 16, 2006; "Recibió Raúl a Enviado Especial del Presidente iraní," *Granma*, January 8, 2009; "Sostiene Raúl encuentros bilaterales como parte de la Reunión Ministerial del MNOAL," *Granma*, April 30, 2009.
106 Susan B. Glasser, "Russian to Dismantle Spy Facility in Cuba," *Washington Post*, October 18, 2001.
107 Peter Finn, "Russian Bombers Could Be Deployed to Cuba, *Washington Post*, July 22, 2008.
108 Oleg Mityayev, "Russian Revitalizes Relations with Cuba," *Ria Novosti*, February 4, 2009, http://en.rian.ru/analysis/20090204/119973885.html; "Raul's Pragmatic Approach," *Latin American Regional Report: Caribbean & Central America* (November 2008), 11–12 and "Cuba: Russian Tractors Re-seed Cuba," *Latin American Regional Report: Caribbean & Central America* (February 2009), 10–11.
109 Léster Delgado Sánchez, "Los pactos sobre derechos humanos: un paso en el camino," *Temas* (July–September 2009), 65–74.
110 "La historia dirá quién tiene la razón," *Granma*, December 14, 2007.
111 "Address of His Holiness Benedict XVI to the Bishops of Cuba on Their 'Ad Limina' Visit," *Vatican News*, www.vatican.va, May 2, 2008.
112 "Cubans Mushrooming in Venezuela's Sensitive Sectors," *El Universal*, February 4,

2010, http://english.eluniversal.com/2010/02/04/en_pol_esp_cubans-mushrooming-i_04A3390933.shtml.

113 Carlos A. Romero, "Venezuela y Cuba: 'Una seguridad diferente'," *Nuevo Mundo Mundos Nuevos*, March 30, 2009, http://nuevomundo.revues.org/index55550.html.

5 "The Policy We've Had in Place for 50 Years Hasn't Worked"

1 Remarks by the President at the Acceptance of the Nobel Peace Prize, December 10, 2009, Oslo, Norway, www.whitehouse.gov/the-press-office/remarks-president-acceptance-nobel-peace-prize.

2 "Discurso pronunciado por el General de Ejército Raúl Castro Ruz, Presidente de los Consejos de Estado y de Ministros, en la clausura del IV Período de Sesiones de la Asamblea Nacional del Poder Popular, el 20 de diciembre de 2009, Año del 50 Aniversario del Triunfo de la Revolución," *Granma*, December 21, 2009. Translation is mine.

3 Remarks of Senator Barack Obama: Renewing U.S. Leadership in the Americas, May 23, 2008, Miami, FL, www.barackobama.com/2008/05/23/remarks_of_senator_barack_obam_68.php.

4 In the elections between 1994 and 2000, Ros-Lehtinen ran unopposed. Before 2008, her victory margins ranged from 24 to 40 percentage points. Lincoln Díaz-Balart ran unopposed in the elections between 1992 and 1996 and 2000 and 2002. His victory margins ranged from 18 to 56 percentage points. His brother Mario won his first election by 30 points, ran unchallenged in 2004 and won by 16 points in 2006. See "Election Statistics," Office of the Clerk of the U.S. House of Representatives, http://clerk.house.gov/member_info/electionInfo/index.html.

5 Darío Moreno and María Ilcheva, "Cuban Americans in the 2008 Election," *Cuban Affairs* 3 (December 2008), wwwcubanaffairsjournal.org.

6 Lesley Clark, "Democrats Torn between Party, GOP Allegiances," *Miami Herald*, March 9, 2008.

7 Frances Robles, "House Passes Bill Easing Cuba Travel Restrictions," *Miami Herald*, February 25, 2009; Lesley Clark and Frances Robles, "Showdown on Cuba Policy Not over Yet," *Miami Herald*, March 11, 2009.

8 Realities in Cuba, Floor Statement by Sen. Robert Menéndez delivered on March 2, 2009, http://miamiherald.typepad.com/files/realities20in20cuba2003.02.2009.pdf; Lesley Clark, "Cuba Bill Opens Obama–Menéndez Rift," *Miami Herald*, March 3, 2009; Juliet Eilperin, "Nominations on Hold for Top 2 Science Posts," *Washington Post*, March 3, 2009; Changing Cuba Policy—In the United States National Interest, Staff Trip Report to the Committee on Foreign Relations, United States Senate, One Hundred Eleventh Congress, February 23, 2009 (Washington, DC: U.S. Government Printing Office, 2009).

9 "More Democrats Oppose Lifting Cuba Travel Ban," *Miami Herald*, November 7, 2009.

10 "Pro-Cuba Embargo Money Flows to US Lawmakers," AP, *Miami Herald*, November 16, 2009.

11 Wilfredo Cancio Isla, "Florida's U.S. Senate Candidates Unified on Cuba," *Miami Herald*, December 22, 2009. At the time, the candidates were Charlie Crist and Marco Rubio, Republicans, and Kendrick Meeks and Maurice Ferré, Democrats. At first, Rubio trailed Crist badly. By April 2010, the tables had been turned: Crist bolted the Republican Party and launched his campaign as an independent. Meeks was the likely Democratic nominee.

12 Jim Wyss, "Capitol Hill Bills Could Change Business between the U.S. and Cuba," *Miami Herald*, September 28, 2009. The three plausible bills were: Freedom to Travel Act, sponsored by Senators Byron Dorgan (D-ND) and Michael Enzi (R WY);

Western Hemisphere Energy Security Act, sponsored by Representative Jeff Flake (R-AZ); and Agricultural Facilitation Act, sponsored by Representative Jerry Moran (R-KS). On April 21, 2010, a British Petroleum oil rig exploded in the Gulf of Mexico near the Louisiana coast. Prospective off-shore drilling in Cuban waters—indeed all such drilling—may long be in abeyance.

13 David Rogers, "2007 Defeat of Rangel Amendment," March 9, 2009, http://uscubanormalization.blogspot.com/2009_03_01_archive.html.

14 Bendixen & Associates, "The Miami-Dade County Electorate: An Exit Poll Study of 2008 General Election Voters" (Miami, FL: November 13, 2008).

15 Institute for Public Opinion Research, Brookings Institution and Cuba Study Group, 2008 Cuba/US Transition Poll, www.fiu.edu/~ipor/cuba-t/Cuba-T.pdf. In February 2009, the Cuba Democracy Advocates released a poll showing 72 percent of Cuban Americans supporting the embargo and 58 percent favoring the 2004 restrictions on family travel. As was the case in an earlier poll conducted for the same organization, the new poll raised methodological concerns. Alfonso Chardy and Luisa Yánez, "Embargo Popular, New Poll Indicates," *Miami Herald*, February 4, 2009.

16 Bendixen & Associates, "National Survey of Cuban Americans" (Miami, FL: April 20, 2009) www.bendixenandassociates.com/studies/National_Survey_of_Cuban_Americans_on_Policy_towards_Cuba_FINAL.pdf.

17 Gerardo Reyes, "U.S. in Favor of Havana Concert," *Miami Herald*, August 8, 2009.

18 The Cuba Study Group commissioned Bendixen & Associates to conduct the polls before and after the Juanes concert. See www.bendixenandassociates.com/studies/PreConcertJuanesCuba.pdf and www.bendixenandassociates.com/studies/PostConcertJuanesCuba.pdf.

19 Jordan Levin, "Poll: Cuban Americans Change Tune about Juanes Concert in Havana," *Miami Herald*, October 1, 2009.

20 According to an email from Executive Director Ricardo Herrero, the New Cuban+American Majority PAC (NCAM) is a non-partisan, federal Political Action Committee which was established to support federal candidates who champion legislation toward Cuba focused on helping the Cuban people and advancing the national interests of the United States. NCAM raises funds from individuals and other committees to contribute to, and educate, candidates running for the United States Congress who support the right of all U.S. persons to travel freely to Cuba and who seek to increase the free flow of resources, information and interaction between the United States and the Cuban people (Ricardo Herrero to Marifeli Pérez-Stable, 30 January 2010). NCAM's webpage—www.ncampac.org—was scheduled to go live in the fall of 2010.

21 Fact Sheet: Reaching out to the Cuban People (April 13, 2009), The White House, www.whitehouse.gov/the_press_office/Fact-Sheet-Reaching-out-to-the-Cuban-people.

22 "Cuba da cuenta de la medida de EE UU con un breve anuncio en la televisión," EFE, *El País*, April 14, 2009.

23 Orlando Oramas León, "Las enmiendas sobre Cuba aprobadas en EE.UU.," *Granma*, March 23, 2009; "Prensa oficial asegura que el embargo se mantiene," *El Nuevo Herald*, March 24, 2009.

24 Remarks of Senator Barack Obama.

25 Remarks by the president at the Summit of the Americas, Port of Spain, Trinidad and Tobago, April 17, 2009, www.whitehouse.gov/the_press_office/Remarks-by-the-President-at-the-Summit-of-the-Americas-Opening-Ceremony.

26 Press Conference by the President, Port of Spain, Trinidad and Tobago, April 19, 2009, www.whitehouse.gov/the_press_office/Press-Conference-By-The-President-In-Trinidad-And-Tobago-4/19/2009.

27 Lesley Clark, "Obama Aims to Renew Migration Talks with Cuba," *Miami Herald*, May 23, 2009.

28 In 1982, the State Department first included Cuba on the list for its history of abetting and aiding armed groups abroad. In 1992, however, Havana announced that it would no longer support these groups. In 2005, it ended the policy of giving safe haven to American fugitives. Obama's State Department kept Cuba on the list, saying it "publicly opposes" the U.S.-led war against Al Qaeda terrorists and maintains close ties with state sponsors of terrorism like Iran and Syria. Other than the U.S. government and hardliners, most experts do not see the Cuban government as a national security threat for the United States. See Council on Foreign Relations, "State Sponsors: Cuba," March 23, 2010, www.cfr.org/publication/9359/state_sponsors.html; Brandon Bloch, "Washington's Double Standard on Cuba: Havana as a Spurious 'State Sponsor of Terrorism'," Council on Hemispheric Affairs, September 14, 2009, www.coha.org/washington%E2%80%99s-double-standard-on-cuba-part-i-cuba-as-a-%E2%80%9Cstate-sponsor-of-terrorism%E2%80%9D/. On February 2, 2010, then-Director of National Intelligence Dennis C. Blair, presented the Annual Threat Assessment of the US Intelligence Community for the Senate Select Committee on Intelligence, www.dni.gov/testimonies/20100202_testimony.pdf. The U.S. intelligence assessment made no mention of current support for terrorist groups by Cuba. The island is mentioned twice: as part of the group of anti-American countries led by Venezuela in Latin America and as a concern that the regime may once again resort to a sudden mass migration as an escape valve for its economic troubles.

29 "EEUU deja a Cuba en la lista de países terroristas," *El Nuevo Herald*, May 1, 2009.

30 "Raúl Castro dice que Cuba está lista para hablar con EEUU sobre derechos humanos y presos políticos," *IBLNEWS*, April 17, 2009, www.iblnews.com/story.php?id=46986.

31 Fidel Castro, "Obama y el bloqueo," April 21, 2009, www.cubadebate.cu/index.php?tpl=design/especiales.tpl.html%26newsid_obj_id=14849. The "five heroes" were arrested, tried and convicted of spying on anti-Castro groups in South Florida. Havana claims that the men's charge was to stop violence against Cuba, thus, the label of "antiterrorists."

32 Raúl Castro, "No hay pretexto político ni moral que justifique la continuidad del bloqueo," April 29, 2009, ://emba.cubaminrex.cu/Default.aspx?tabid=25342.

33 Matthew Lee, "U.S.–Cuba Talks on Immigration to Resume," *Miami Herald*, May 31, 2009.

34 Releases Pertaining to Cuba, U.S. Department of State, www.state.gov/p/wha/ci/cu/rls/index.htm. Havana's public statements on the migration and postal talks can be found, respectively, at *Tribuna de La Habana*, www.tribuna.co.cu/etiquetas/2009/Julio/15/declaracion-prensa.html and Declaraciones del Ministerio de Relaciones Exteriores, http://america.cubaminrex.cu/Declaraciones/Articulos/Informaciones/2009/Dec170909.html.

35 Alfonso Chardy and Rui Ferreira, "South Florida Sees Upswing in Family Travel to Cuba," *Miami Herald*, September 10, 2009; Frances Robles, "U.S.–Cuba Travel Flourishing," *Miami Herald*, October 5, 2009.

36 Andrea Rodríguez, AP, "Almost 300,000 Cubans Abroad Visited Island in '09," *Washington Post*, January 27, 2010.

37 Wilfredo Cancio Isla, "EEUU retoma intercambio cultural con Cuba," *El Nuevo Herald*, August 23, 2009; XIII Congreso Latinoamericano de Ciencias del Mar-COLACMAR, VIII Congreso de Ciencias del Mar-MARCUBA, 4to. Taller Internacional PESCA 2009, *"Ciencias marinas: Integración para el desarrollo,"* Palacio de Convenciones de La Habana, October 26–30, 2009, www.colacmarcuba2009.com/ProgramaCientifico.pdf; Larry Rother, "Opening Arms and Ears to Cuban Music,"

New York Times, November 19, 2009; "U.S. Science Delegation Completes Hopeful Three-Day Visit to Cuba," www.aaas.org//news/releases/2009/1207cuba. shtml; Nick Miroff, "Scientists Work to Protect Cuba's Unspoiled Reefs," *National Public Radio*, December 8, 2009, www.npr.org/templates/story/story. php?storyId=121177851; Ginger Thompson, "Trying to Sway America's Cuba Policy with Song," *New York Times*, December 29, 2009. For example, twelve Cuban actors traveled to the University of Alabama in July to mount a joint production of Shakespeare's *A Midsummer Night's Dream*; the play was presented in Birmingham and Havana. Sarasota-based USA Youth Debates obtained a Department of the Treasury license to take fifteen students to meet their counterparts on the island. For the first time since the founding of the Latin Grammys, Omara Portuondo—a Cuban artist living in Cuba who was nominated for a Latin Grammy—received a visa to attend the ceremony and a Grammy in the category of Best Contemporary Tropical Album. Carlos Varela, a singer whose songs needle the government and are often banned from the Cuban airwaves, came to the United States to remix an album with Jackson Browne, met with legislators, had lunch with senior White House officials and gave concerts in several cities. On May 15, 2010, Varela performed in Miami. Sponsored by the American Association for the Advancement of Science, a U.S. science-policy delegation traveled to Cuba November 10–13 to explore research areas of mutual interest for U.S.–Cuba scientific collaboration.

38 James Anderson, Associated Press, "NM Gov. on Cuba Mission, Plans White House Report," *Miami Herald,* August 25, 2009; Will Wissert, Associated Press, "NM Gov. Cheers US, Cuban Openness to Better Ties," *Miami Herald*, August 28, 2009.

39 Paul Haven, Associated Press, "US Diplomat Met with Cuban Dissidents in Havana," *Miami Herald*, September 30, 2009.

40 Juan O. Tamayo, "Cuba Allows U.S. Access to Jailed Dual Citizens," *Miami Herald*, October 15, 2009.

41 In 2008, DAI received a $6 million grant from USAID to promote democracy in Cuba. Neither DAI nor Gross had ever worked in Cuba. An independent consultant, Gross had worked with DAI before and submitted a $500,000 Cuba proposal. He traveled to the island five times, a frequency that surely sounded all the alarms at state security. Inexperience, *naïveté* or, as a congressional staffer told the *Washington Post*: "We agree with the program, but this is rookieville." Nary Beth Sheridan, "Judy and Alan Gross's Family Is at the Heart of the Standoff between Washington and Cuba," *Washington Post*, May 21, 2010.

42 In the past, DAI had received unwanted for its links to anti-Chávez activities in Venezuela and for lobbying the Philippine government to allow foreign companies into air and sea transport industries. See Michael Collins, "Arrest of Alleged American Spy in Cuba Further Sets Back U.S.–Cuban Relations," *Americas Program Report* (Washington, DC: Center for International Policy, January 14, 2010).

43 Ley 88 de protección de la economía nacional y la independencia de Cuba, February 16, 1999, Cubanet, www.cubanet.org/ref/dis/021699.htm.

44 Marc Lacey and Ginger Thompson, "Cuba Detains a U.S. Contractor," *New York Times*, December 12, 2009; Juan O. Tamayo, "Envoys Get to See Jailed American," *Miami Herald*, December 29, 2009.

45 Andrea Rodríguez, Associated Press, "Cuba: Detained U.S. Contractor Was Spying," *Miami Herald*, January 6, 2010; Matthew Lee, Associated Press, "U.S. Denies Detained American in Cuba Is a Spy," *Miami Herald*, January 7, 2010.

46 Mary Beth Sheridan, "Pro-democracy Program in Cuba Questioned after Man Detained," *Washington Post*, December 25, 2009.

47 United States Government Accountability Office, *U.S. Democracy Assistance for Cuba*

Needs Better Management and Oversight (November 2006) www.gao.gov/new.items/ d07147.pdf and *Continued Efforts Needed to Strengthen USAID's Oversight of U.S. Democracy Assistance for Cuba* (November 2008), www.gao.gov/new.items/d09165. pdf. For questionable practices and improper expenditures, see pages 36–37 of the 2006 report. For the $83 million disbursed from 1996 to 2008 and the competitive award ratios, see pages 1 and 3 of the 2008 report. For USAID's Cuba program, see: "Latin America and the Caribbean: Cuba," USAID, www.usaid.gov/locations/ latin_america_caribbean/country/cuba/index.html.

48 Oscar Corral, "Is U.S. Aid Reaching Castro Foes?" *Miami Herald*, November 15, 2006. USAID grants are spent on a wide array of activities from university programs to companies that ship goods to Cuba. USAID prohibits cash handouts to Cuban dissidents for fear the regime brand them as mercenaries but, in fact, that is exactly what the opposition is called by Cuban authorities.

49 Sheridan, "Pro-Democracy Program in Cuba Questioned after Man Detained."

50 Michael Collins, "Democracy Promotion Programs under Fire as Fallout from Spy Arrest Continues," *Americas Report* (Washington, DC: Center for International Policy, April 19, 2010).

51 Remarks by the President in Address to the Nation on the Way Forward in Afghanistan and Pakistan, United States Military Academy at West Point, West Point, NY, December 1, 2009, www.whitehouse.gov/the-press-office/remarks-president-address-nation-way-forward-afghanistan-and-pakistan; Remarks by the President at the Acceptance of the Nobel Peace Prize.

52 Hillary Rodham Clinton, Remarks on the Human Rights Agenda for the 21st Century, Georgetown University, Washington, DC, December 14, 2009www. state.gov/secretary/rm/2009a/12/133544.

53 Theodore Piccone, "The Obama Administration Clarifies Approach to Human Rights," *Global Post*, www.globalpost.com/dispatch/worldview/091218/obama-clinton-human-rights.

54 U.S. Department of State, *Trafficking in Persons Report* (June 2009). www.state.gov/ documents/organization/123357.pdf.

55 "U.S. Ambassador Makes First Speech at International Court," *Associated Press*, November 19, 2009. In August, Secretary Clinton had called the U.S. absence from the International Criminal Court "a great regret," a sign of diminishing hostility even if the Obama administration has not moved to sign the Rome Treaty, which Bill Clinton had done only to have George W. Bush withdraw his signature. See Mary Beth Sheridan, "Clinton Regrets U.S. Not Part of Court," *Washington Post*, August 7, 2009.

56 See pages for the Democratic Republic of Congo, Sudan and East Africa at USAID, www.usaid.gov/. For the humanitarian situations in Eastern Congo and Sudan, see the Human Rights Watch reports, *"You Will Be Punished": Attacks on Civilians in Eastern Congo*, December 14, 2009, www.hrw.org/en/reports/2009/12/14/you-will-be-punished-0 and *The Way Forward*, October 6, 2009, www.hrw.org/en/ reports/2009/10/06/way-forward.

57 "Democracy and Governance in Nigeria," USAID, www.usaid.gov/our_work/ democracy_and_governance/regions/afr/nigeria.html.

58 Nigeria summary in Human Rights Watch, *World Report 2009*, www.hrw.org/en/ node/79250.

59 Ibid., *Cuba's Repressive Machinery: Forty Years after the Revolution* (June 1999), www. hrw.org/en/reports/1999/06/01/cubas-repressive-machinery.

60 Ibid., *New Castro, Same Cuba: Political Prisoners in the Post-Fidel Era* (November 2009), www.hrw.org/en/reports/2009/11/18/new-castro-same-cuba-0.

61 Hillary Rodham Clinton, Remarks on the Human Rights Agenda for the 21st Century.

62 The calendar for 2008–2011 can be found at the Human Rights Council Universal

Periodic Review, www.upr-info.org/IMG/pdf/uprlist.pdf. Forty-eight countries are reviewed per year in three sessions.

63 "Cuba in Protest over UN Rights Report," *Caribbean Net News*, February 2, 2009, www.caribbeannetnews.com/news-13939–5–5–.html.

64 Summary Prepared by the Office of the High Commissioner for Human Rights in Accordance with Paragraph 15 (A) of the Annex to Human Rights Council Resolution 5/1: Cuba, November 28, 2008, http://lib.ohchr.org/HRBodies/UPR/Documents/Session4/CU/A_HRC_WG6_4_CUB_3_E.pdf. See paragraphs 1, 7, 15, 24 and 29.

65 "We Can't Release Political Prisoners Because We Have None," *National Post*, February 10, 2009, www.nationalpost.com/m/story.html?id=1274414.

66 Gustavo Capdevilla, "Cuba Passes UN Review with Flying Colours," *IPS*, February 11, 2009, http://ipsnews.net/news.asp?idnews=45737; Sixty-fourth General Assembly, Third Committee (Social, Cultural and Humanitarian Rights), United Nations, October 20, 2009, www.un.org/News/Press/docs/2009/gashc3955.doc.htm; "Acusan a Cuba de 'férreo bloqueo' a verificación de derechos humanos," *El Nuevo Herald*, June 10, 2010. Manfred Nowack, the special rapporteur, had until October 30, 2010 to complete his report.

67 Informe de Cuba al Comité contra la Tortura, January 18, 2010, www2.ohchr.org/english/bodies/cat/docs/CAT.C.CUB.2.Rev.1_sp.pdf.

68 National Report Submitted in Accordance with Paragraph 15 (A) of the Annex to Human Rights Council Resolution 5/1: Cuba, November 4, 2008, http://lib.ohchr.org/HRBodies/UPR/Documents/Session4/CU/A_HRC_WG6_4_CUB_1_E.pdf. Quotes appear in paragraphs 3 and 33.

69 General Assembly Thirty-ninth Regular Session, *Resolution through Which Resolution VI of the Eighth Meeting of Ministers of Foreign Affairs of 1962 Ceases to Have Effect*, San Pedro Sula, Honduras, June 3, 2009, http://graphics8.nytimes.com/packages/pdf/world/OAS-statement.pdf.

70 Anthony L. Hall, "OAS Lifts Its Almost 50-year Ban on Cuba," *Caribbean Net News*, June 5, 2009, www.caribbeannetnews.com/news-16906–6–6–.html; Thelma Mejía, "OAS Opens Doors to Cuba without Conditions," *IPS*, June 3, 2009, www.ipsnews.net/news.asp?idnews=47090; Lesley Clark, "Cuba Critics Want to Punish the OAS," *Miami Herald*, June 5, 2009.

71 "El 78% de los encuestados apoya la retirada de tropas de Irak," *El País*, May 30, 2004.

72 Eugenio Hernández, "Zapatero Greeted by Two Fronts in Spain's First Official Visit to the United States since the Iraq War," *DC World News Examiner*, October 12, 2009, www.examiner.com/x-24559-DC-World-News-Examiner~y2009m10d12-Spains-socialist-Premiere-first-official-visit-to-the-US-since-Iraq-war.

73 Valentina Pop, *EU Observer*, February 1, 2010, http://euobserver.com/9/29377.

74 Miguel González and Mauricio Vicent, "'Decidle a Raúl que si él no da pasos tampoco yo podré darlos,'" *El País*, October 25, 2009.

75 "El embajador de Cuba dice que no necesitan 'intermediarios' para hablar con EE UU," *El País*, October 27, 2009.

76 "Zapatero: le toca a Cuba 'mover ficha' en el diferendo con Estados Unidos," EFE, *El Nuevo Herald*, May 25, 2009.

77 Mauricio Vicent and Miguel González, "Moratinos promete en Cuba intentar cambiar la política de la UE con la isla," *El País*, October 20, 2009.

78 Will Weissert, "Spanish FM Shuns Dissidents during Cuba Visit," *San Diego-Union Tribune*, October 19, 2009, www3.signonsandiego.com/news/2009/oct/19/cb-cuba-spain-101909/.

79 Mauricio Vicent, "37 presos políticos de Cuba cuestionan la política de Moratinos," *El País*, October 27, 2009.

80 Negotiations for the EU–Central America association agreement were concluded by the EU–Central American summit on May 19, 2010 while the EU–Mercosur summit resulted in the renewal of negotiations aimed at reaching such an agreement.

81 Paul Hare, "The Odd Couple: The EU and Cuba 1996–2008," www.brookings.edu/papers/2008/09_cuba_hare.aspx. The EU also issued what are called joint actions to block U.S. sanctions against member states for trading with Iran and Libya. See "EU Respond to US Extra-Territorial Laws with Blocking Statute," *EuropaWorld*, February 8, 2001, www.europaworld.org/issue45/eurespondtous2801.htm.

82 Vicent and González, "Moratinos promete en Cuba."

83 Vicent and González, "Moratinos promete en Cuba." Nelson Alberto Aguiar Ramírez is the freed prisoner, Omelio Lázaro Angulo received his exit permit and Pedro Hermosilla is the Spaniard accused of bribery. After Aguiar's release, there are Fifty-three prisoners of conscience (out of the original seventy-five) still in jail. Elsa Morejón—Dr. Oscar Elías Biscet's wife—received a temporary exit permit to travel to Spain for medical treatment. While in the United States to visit her son, Morejón met with President Bush on January 24, 2008. In November 2007, the president had awarded Dr. Biscet the National Medal of Freedom; his son accepted it in his place. Canadian Foundation for the Americas (FOCAL), *Chronicle on Cuba* (January 2008), 58, http://cubasource.org/pdf/Chronicle012008.pdf and President Bush Honors Medal of Freedom Recipients, White House Press Release, November 5, 2007, www.genome.gov/Pages/Newsroom/NHGRIRelatedReleases/WHRelease_PresidentialMedalRecipients_20071105-.pdf.

84 In February 2008, for example, Cuban authorities freed seven prisoners of conscience—jailed in the Black Spring of 2003—after Spain's intercession. "Cuba Releases Imprisoned Activists," *Amnesty International*, February 18, 2008, www.amnesty.org/en/news-and-updates/good-news/cuba-releases-imprisoned-activists-20080218; "Cuba: Three Journalists Released from Prison and Flown to Spain," *International PEN*, February 21, 2008, www.internationalpen.org.uk/index.cfm?objectid=FA05D450-E0C4-ED84–02D33C8061941583.

85 Helene Zuber, "Zapatero a Der Spiegel: 'Europa es líder mundial de valores democráticos'," *Der Spiegel*, November 23, 2009, http://bloquedeleste.com/zapatero-a-der-spiegel-europa-es-lider-mundial-en-valores-democraticos.

86 "Spain Says Cuba's Castro Committed to Reform," *Reuters*, October 20, 2009, www.reuters.com/article/idUSTRE59J0S020091020.

87 *World Report 2010*, Human Rights Watch, www.hrw.org/en/world-report-2010/cuba.

88 Yáñez is one of the Spanish Socialist Worker's Party's lions on human rights and relations with Latin America, a veteran militant against fascism since 1962 as well as an opponent of the "Left's totalitarian pathology—which is communism in power."

89 Miguel González, "Cuba justifica la expulsión de Yáñez porque su visita 'no era inocente'," *El País*, January 6, 2010. Yánez—a former secretary of state for Iberoamerica, had been denied a Cuban visa in 2008 to attend a meeting of Cuesta Morúa's Progressive Arc.

90 Luis Yáñez-Barnuevo, "Cuba en el corazón," *Dominio Público*, January 9, 2010, http://blogs.publico.es/dominiopublico/1763/cuba-en-el-corazon/.

91 Miguel González, "Cuba justifica la expulsión de Yáñez porque su visita 'no era inocente'," *El País*, January 6, 2010.

92 Comparecencia del señor ministro de Asuntos Exteriores y de Cooperación (Moratinos Cuyaubé), para informar sobre la política exterior y de seguridad común, con especial atención a las cuestiones relativas a Oriente Próximo y Cuba. A petición propia, (Número de expediente 214/000130,) *Diario de sesiones del Congreso de los Diputados*, December 22, 2009, 4, www.congreso.es/public_oficiales/L9/CONG/DS/CO/CO_456.PDF.

93 "Moncloa corrige a Moratinos: No se presionará a la UE para que cambie la postura con Cuba," *Libertad Digital*, January 4, 2010, www.libertaddigital.com/mundo/moncloa-corrige-a-moratinos-no-se-presionara-a-la-ue-para-que-cambie-la-postura-con-cuba-1276380502; "Zapatero matiza a Moratinos sobre la política hacia Cuba," *El País*, January 9, 2010.

94 "Zapatero afirma que es posible que visite Cuba en 2009," *EcoDiario*, December 26, 2008, http://ecodiario.eleconomista.es/espana/noticias/941450/12/08/Zapatero-afirma-que-es-posible-que-visite-Cuba-en-2009.html.

95 Joint Motion for a Resolution on Prisoners of Conscience in Cuba, European Parliament, March 10, 2010, http://cubasource.org/pdf/Resolution_EP_prisoner-scuba.pdf.

96 Lázaro Barredo Medina, "El ingreso más inmediato que puede tener nuestro país es el ahorro," *Granma*, May 22, 2009.

97 Discurso pronunciado por el General de Ejército Raúl Castro Ruz, Presidente de los Consejos de Estado y de Ministros, en el Tercer Período Ordinario de Sesiones de la VII Legislatura de la Asamblea Nacional del Poder Popular, en el Palacio de Convenciones, el 1° de agosto de 2009, Año del 50 Aniversario del Triunfo de la Revolución," *Granma*, August 1, 2009.

98 "La improductividad es el abismo que amenaza tragarse los recursos humanos," *Granma*, November 11, 2009. Castro's original speech was delivered on December 7, 1970. Translation is mine.

99 Boris Moreno, "¿Hacia dónde va la barca cubana? Una mirada al entorno económico," *Palabra Nueva* (January 2010), www.palabranueva.net/contens/1001/0001011.htm. The quotes in the previous and current sentence are from Moreno.

100 Mauricio Vicent, "Cuba debe despedir a un millón de empleados estatales," *El País*, May 1, 2010.

101 "Enfrentar los retos serenamante y con más firmeza que nunca," *Granma*, July 31, 2009.

102 Larry Rohter, "In Cuba, Army Takes on Party Jobs, and May Be Only Thing That Works," *New York Times*, June 8, 1995.

103 "¡El futuro de nuestra patria será un eterno Baraguá!", *Juventud Rebelde*, March 16, 1990.

104 Raúl Castro, *Si se perdiera la revolución perderíamos la independencia, Entrevista concedida al periodista cubano Luis Báez, 11 de septiembre de 1994* (Havana: Editora Política, 1994), 7.

105 Ian Urbina, "In Cuba, Change Means More of the Same, with Control at the Top," *New York Times*, April 6, 2009.

106 "Bastión 2009: La guerra de todo el pueblo," *Granma*, www.granma.cubaweb.cu/secciones/bastion-2009/index.html, is a compedium of all articles published in *Granma* on the military exercises.

107 Marc Franc, "Cuba Begins War Games with U.S. Invasion in Mind," *Reuters*, November 27, 2009; Ariel Hidalgo, "El más temible adversario," *El Nuevo Herald*, December 5, 2009. The interior ministry also partakes in the *Bastión* exercises.

108 "Discurso pronunciado por el General de Ejército Raúl Castro Ruz, Presidente de los Consejos de Estado y de Ministros, en el Cuarto Período Ordinario de Sesiones de la VII Legislatura de la Asamblea Nacional del Poder Popular, en el Palacio de Convenciones, el 20 de diciembre de 2009, *Granma*, December 21, 2009." The first *Bastión* was held in 2004. But for the calamitous hurricane season, it would have been held again in 2008.

109 The quote is from Foreign Affairs Minister Rodríguez Parrilla's reply to the speech given by the U.S. Representative, "Foreign Affairs Minister Rodríguez Parrilla's Reply to the Speech Given by the U.S. Representative," Ministerio de Relacines

Exteriores de la República de Cuba, http://embacu.cubaminrex.cu/Default. aspx?tabid=15209. The context was the annual UN debate on a resolution condemning the U.S. embargo. For the Cuban foreign minister's speech in favor of the resolution, see: Speech Delivered by H.E. Mr. Bruno Rodríguez Parrilla, Minister for Foreign Affairs of the Republic of Cuba, at the United Nations General Assembly, under the Item "Necessity of Ending the Economic, Commercial and Financial Embargo Imposed by The United States of America against Cuba," New York, October 28, 2009, http://america.cubaminrex.cu/AGNU/Articulos/64Periodo/ Intervenciones/091028_ING.html. For Ambassador Susan Rice's speech see "Here We Go Again, United Nations General Assembly, October 28, 2009," www.undispatch.com/susan-rice-cuba-vote-here-we-go-again.

110 "Necessity of Ending the Economic, Commercial and Financial Embargo Imposed by the United States of America against Cuba," General Assembly GA/10877, www.un.org/News/Press/docs/2009/ga10877.doc.htm.

111 "España desiste de cambiar posición común de la UE con Cuba," *El Nuevo Herald*, March 15, 2010.

112 On June 14, EU foreign ministers were to uphold the Common Position while proposing a "period of reflection" regarding relations between the European Union and Cuba. Miguel González, "España busca que la UE entreabra la puerta a cambiar la política con Cuba," *El País*, June 14, 2010.

113 Hare, "The Odd Couple."

114 Promotion of Human Rights and Democratization in the EU's External Relations, European Commission's External Relations, http://ec.europa.eu/external_relations/human_rights/index_en.htm.

115 European Instrument for Democracy & Human Rights, http://ec.europa.eu/europeaid/how/finance/eidhr_en.htm.

116 "Cooperation Agreement between the European Commission and the Socialist Republic of Vietnam," *Official Journal of the European Communities*, No. L 136/28, May 14, 1996, www.delvnm.ec.europa.eu/eu_vn_relations/trade_economic/ Framework%20and%20Cooperation%20Agreement.pdf.

117 Human Rights Watch, *No Sanctuary: Ongoing Threats to Indigenous Montagnards in Vietnam's Central Highlands*, www.unhcr.org/refworld/topic,4565c22517,4565c25f 21b,44c766aa4,0.html. The report includes the Memorandum of Understanding signed by the UN Commission on Human Rights, Vietnam and Cambodia.

118 Human Rights Watch, *World Report 2006*, www.hrw.org/legacy/english/ docs/2006/01/18/vietna12249.htm.

119 Human Rights Watch, *World Report 2010*, www.hrw.org/en/node/87404.

120 Mensaje desde Cuba a los intelectuales y artistas afronorteamericanos, Unión de Escritores de Cuba (UNEAC)," December 3, 2009, www.uneac.org.cu/index.php? module=noticias&act=detalle&tipo=noticia&id=2478.

121 Mauricio Vicent, "Partidarios del Gobierno cubano golpean a las Damas de Blanco," *El País*, December 11, 2009.

122 Mauricio Vicent's articles in *El País* give an account of the protests: "Acto de repudio contra las Damas de Blanco en Cuba," March 13, 2010; "Acoso a las Damas de Blanco en su tercera jornada de protestas en Cuba," March 17, 2010; "Las Damas de Blanco retan al Gobierno cubano por cuarto día," March 18, 2010; and "Protesta en Cuba sin precedentes," March 21, 2010.

123 Vicent, "Protesta en Cuba sin precedentes."

124 Luisa Yáñez, José Cassola, Jennifer Lebovich and Fabiola Santiago, "Tens of Thousands Join Gloria Estefan in Calle Ocho March for Ladies in White," *Miami Herald*, March 25, 2010.

125 Isabel Sánchez, AFP, "Iglesia cubana insiste en apertura tras cumplir inédita mediación," *El Nuevo Herald*, May 4, 2010.

126 Mauricio Vicent, "Las Damas de Blanco podrán desfilar por La Habana," *El País*, May 3, 2010.

127 "Gobierno autoriza marchas de las Damas de Blanco," *El Nuevo Herald*, May 3, 2010.

128 "Nuestra voz es un llamado al diálogo: Entrevista con el cardenal Jaime Ortega Alamino," *Palabra Nueva*, April 19, 2010, www.palabranueva.net/contens/noticias2010/pn_1011.pdf. In the 1980s, the United States Conference of Catholic Bishops intervened on behalf of numerous political prisoners and their families. Altogether nearly 1,000 left Cuba for the United States.

129 "Conferencia de prensa del cardenal Jaime Ortega Alamino," *Palabra Nueva* (May 2010), www.palabranueva.net/contens/pn_notic.htm#1017.

130 Juan O. Tamayo, "Cuba to Transfer Political Prisoners," *Miami Herald*, May 24, 2010.

131 In mid-April, Fariñas agreed to occasional intravenous feeding. At the time of this writing, he was in an intensive care unit being fed intravenously. Having lost nearly forty-five pounds, he was in weak physical condition but stable. See Mauricio Vicent, "La Iglesia cubana anuncia mejoras en la situación de los presos políticos," *El País*, May 24, 2010.

132 Discurso pronunciado por el General de Ejército Raúl Castro Ruz, Presidente de los Consejos de Estado y de Ministros, y Segundo Secretario del Comité Central del Partido Comunista de Cuba, en la clausura del IX Congreso de la Unión de Jóvenes Comunistas, La Habana, 4 de abril de 2010, Año 52 de la Revolución," *Granma*, April 5, 2010. Translation is mine.

133 "Se reúne Raúl con autoridades de la Iglesia Católica," *Granma*, May 20, 2010 and Anneris Ivette Leyva, "Califica el Cardenal Jaime Ortega de muy positivo el diálogo entre Raúl y autoridades eclesiásticas," *Granma*, May 21, 2010. Invited by the Cuban church and government, Monsignor Mamberti was to take part in the events commemorating seventy-five years of diplomatic relations between Cuba and the Vatican. He was also scheduled to participate in the tenth Catholic Social Week, which the church holds periodically on Catholic social doctrine.

134 In 1969, the Catholic Church publicly condemned the embargo for the first time. Since then the bishops have pursued a policy of dialogue with the Cuban authorities. "Comunicado de la Conferencia Episcopal de Cuba a nuestros sacerdotes y fieles (3 de septiembre de 1969)," in Conferencia de Obispos Católicos de Cuba (eds.), *La voz de la Iglesia en Cuba: 100 documentos episcopales* (México, D.F.: Obra Nacional de la Buena Prensa, A.C., 1995).

135 In 1993 and 1994, Havana held two meetings called *La nación y la emigración*, a title that implied a separation between the two, especially regarding political diversity. In January 2010, a third encounter was held; most participants were not from the United States, a reflection of the growing diversity of receptor countries. Nonetheless, the United States is still the largest destination of Cubans leaving the island. Recent emigrants to other countries tend not to be outright regime opponents, making it easier for the authorities to engage with them. The church's call for dialogue and reconciliation recognizes the political pluralism of the diaspora and Cuba both.

136 "Nuestra voz es un llamado al diálogo: Entrevista con el cardenal Jaime Ortega Alamino."

137 Statement by the President on the Human Rights Situation in Cuba, March 24, 2010, www.whitehouse.gov/the-press-office/statement-president-human-rights-situation-cuba.

138 "U.S. Sends Official to Cuba for Migration Talks," *Agence France Presse*, February 17, 2010. As of this writing, the last time that U.S. officials pressed the issue of freeing Gross was April 1, 2010. Gross had not been charged. One way for Havana

to dispense with the matter would be to free him on humanitarian grounds or charge, try, condemn and then expel him.

139 "U.S., Cuba Hold Rare Meeting at the UN, with Haiti Focus," *Agence France Presse*, March 31, 2010. After the earthquake, Cuba allowed U.S. planes carrying aid to pass through its airspace on their way to Haiti. Juan O. Tamayo, "U.S. Keeps Cuba Informed on Gulf Oil Spill," *Miami Herald*, May 20, 2010.

140 In November 1981, Secretary of State Alexander Haig met Cuban Vice-President Carlos Rafael Rodríguez. In March 1982, Vernon Walters—retired general and ambassador at-large in Reagan's first term—traveled to Havana where he met with Rodríguez and Fidel Castro.

141 "Castros Sabotage Ending U.S. Cuba Embargo: Clinton," *Reuters*, April 9, 2010.

142 For a useful blueprint, see Vicki Huddleston and Carlos Pascual, *Learning to Salsa: New Steps in U.S.–Cuba Relations* (Washington, DC: Brookings Institution Press, 2010).

143 On June 11, the Catholic Church announced that Ariel Sigler, forty-six, had been released, the first of the twenty-six seriously ill political prisoners; six other prisoners from the Black Spring were transferred to prisons near their homes, making twelve the number of political inmates moved closer to their families. See Isabel Sánchez, "La Iglesia alentada tras la liberación de Sigler," *El Nuevo Herald*, June 14, 2010.

144 Juan Carlos Chávez, "37 Arrests Reported in Dissident Crackdown," *Miami Herald*, June 5, 2010. The two groups were *Agenda para la Transición* (Transition Agenda) and *Unidad Liberal de la República de Cuba* (Liberal Unity of the Republic of Cuba). Initially, the number arrested was given at thirty-seven but, in fact, thirty-eight dissidents were detained or prevented from leaving their homes. See "Liberan a los 38 disidentes detenidos en La Habana," *El Nuevo Herald*, June 6, 2010. Héctor Palacios—one of the thirty-seven imprisoned during the Black Spring and freed in December 2006—noted that the meeting took place all the same with a smaller group in attendance. Palacios heads the *Unidad Liberal*.

145 Brian Alexander, "Targeting Castro, Not Cuba: Considering a Smart Sanctions Approach to Cuba," *Cuba in Transition,* Papers and Proceedings of the Thirteenth Annual Meeting of the Association for the Study of the Cuban Economy (ASCE), Coral Gables, Florida, August 7–9, 2003, 293–301. Alexander uses the concept of "smart sanctions" developed by David Cortright and George López. See their edited anthology, *Smart Sanctions: Targeting Economic Statecraft* (Lanham, MD: Rowman & Littlefield Publishers, Inc., 2002).

146 Remarks by the President at the Acceptance of the Nobel Peace Prize.

147 On June 18, American and Cuban officials were to meet in Washington, DC for the third round of talks on migration. The Obama White House restored these meetings which the Bush administration had cancelled in 2004. "Reunión con EEUU sobre asuntos migratorios," *El Nuevo Herald*, June 12, 2010. An agreement against narcotrafficking is essential to U.S. national security. Should Cuba someday become a failed state, it would likely be due to the criminal violence visiting Mexico and Central America. The sooner an agreement is signed the better the chances of sidelining that dreaded future. Albeit under different directions, the current military and security forces will also serve either a democratic Cuba or one following the paths of China and Vietnam.

Essay by Ana Covarrubias: Mexico and Cuba

1 The region was understood as the Latin American countries that were OAS members; the United States. Canada and the English speaking Caribbean were excluded.

2 In Punta del Este, Mexican Secretary of Foreign Affairs Manuel Tello declared: "It seems, then, undoubtedly that there is a radical incompatibility between the membership of the Organization of American States and a Marxist-Leninist political profession..." See *Política* 2, no. 43 (February 1, 1962), p. 37.

3 In 1962, after the Punta del Este meeting, Castro explicitly recognized Mexico's nonintervention in Cuba:

> ... interventions have not come from Mexico, aggression has not come from Mexico, there are no groups of saboteurs organizing in Mexico, no arms and explosives to kill and destroy come from Mexico, there are no maneuvers against our country coming from Mexico. (*Revolución*, January 3, 1962, 5)

In 1964, after the OAS Washington meeting where members approved a resolution to break diplomatic relations with Cuba, and Mexico refused to comply with it, Fidel Castro made a "responsible declaration which also reveals his government's disposition toward Mexico:

> with the government of Mexico we are willing to talk and discuss ... to commit ourselves to maintain a policy subject to norms, inviolable norms of respect of the sovereignty of each country and not to meddle in the internal affairs of any country ... for our part, we have confidence in the Government of Mexico, and we make this responsible declaration: with the Government of Mexico we are willing to talk, and with the Government of Mexico we are willing to discuss, and with the Government of Mexico we are willing to make commitments. (*Revolución*, July 27, 1964, 2–4)

4 "Intervención del C. Lic. Antonio Carrillo Flores, Secretario de Relaciones Exteriores, al fundar los votos de México, 23 de septiembre de 1967" and "Declaraciones del C. Secretario Antonio Carrillo Flores, al regresar a México, el 25 de septiembre de 1967", both in Mexico, SRE, *Memoria de la Secretaría de Relaciones Exteriores*, September 1, 1967–August 31, 1968, pp. 391, 395–396.

5 A CIA document dated August 24, 1968 indicates that the Cuban government was trying to infiltrate arms into Mexico for the students. In another document dated September 6, 1968, the CIA questioned whether the Mexican president believed that the student uprisings were organized by the Communists with the support of the Cuban and Soviet embassies. According to the document: "There is no hard evidence that either the Cuban or the Soviet embassies have masterminded the disturbances, although it is reasonable to assume that they have at least provided some support". "Central Intelligence Agency. Intelligence Information Cable, August 24, 1968. Mexican Military Alert for Possible Cuban Infiltration of Arms Destined for Student Use", and "Central Intelligence Agency. Intelligence Information Cable, September 6, 1968, Situation Appraisal: Status of the Mexico City Student Movement", both at "LITEMPO: The CIA's Eyes on Tlatelolco. CIA Spy Operations in Mexico", National Security Archive Electronic Briefing Book 204, Posted – October 18, 2006, www.gwu.edu/~nsarchiv/NSAEBB/NSAEBB204/index.htm. Mexico's former ambassador to Cuba argued that Castro had assured him of his interest not to get involved in events in Mexico because instability in that country would not favor Cuba. Ana Covarrubias, "Mexican–Cuban relations, 1959-1988", D. Phil. thesis in International Relations, University of Oxford, 1994. If the Soviets did have any relevant participation in the student movement in Mexico, there is more reason to believe that the Cubans had a moderate position, given the difficulties in Soviet–Cuban relations at the time.

6 For the U.S. government (the CIA basically) espionage activities in Mexico, and Mexico's monitoring of Cuba's actions see Kate Doyle, "Double Dealing: Mexico's Foreign policy toward Cuba", National Security Archive, www.gwu.edu/~nsarchiv/

NSAEBB/NSAEBB83/index.htm; Philip Agee, *Inside the Company: CIA Diary* (London: Penguin 1975), and Jeffrey Morley, *Our Man in Mexico; Winston Scott and the Hidden History of the CIA* (Kansas, University of Kansas Press, 2008).

7 Yoram Shapira, *Mexican Foreign Policy under Echeverría* (London, Sage, 1978).

8 A number of Mexican delegations visited Cuba to assess the prospects of improving trade and collaboration during Echeverría's government. Cuba and Mexico signed treaties in different areas, including culture, education and scientific cooperation. The General Intergovernmental Joint Commission was established in 1978, and Mrs Echeverría also traveled to Cuba. See Covarrubias, "Mexican–Cuban relations".

9 The 1980s was a difficult decade for Cuba: economically, dependence on the Soviet Union significantly increased, and a renewed trade deficit and worsening terms of trade demonstrated that Cuba's economy was unable to stand on its own in the world. In 1987 the government recognized an economic crisis for the first time. In addition, the USSR and Cuba diverged on domestic reforms: while Gorbachev implemented *perestroika* and *glasnost*, Castro announced the "rectification" process whereby economic decision-making would become centralized and socialist, and revolutionary values would regain prominence over market forces. See Domínguez, *To Make a World Safe for Revolution*, 92, and Jorge Domínguez, "Cuba in the 1980s", *Foreign Affairs* 65, no. 1 (Fall, 1986), 121.

10 "Freedom of action of the States parties to the Inter-American treaty of Reciprocal Assistance to normalize or conduct their relations with the Republic of Cuba at the level and in the form that each State deems advisable" (OAS/Ser.F/11.16, Document 9/75, rev. 2 (English), July 29, 1975).

11 Mexico, Presidente, 1976–1982, José López Portillo, *Sexto Informe de Gobierno*, September 1, 1982, 14.

12 According to Cuban Vice-President Carlos Rafael Rodríguez, Cuba would not renounce its right to participate in the dialogue in Mexico: "It is inconceivable that Cuba be absent from a dialogue which intends to reunite the most representative elements of the countries of the south" (*Proceso*, May 4, 1981), 14.

13 *Excélsior*, August 9, 1981, 6-A.

14 Ibid, 7-A.

15 *Excélsior*, August 8, 1981, 12-A.

16 Cárdenas FDN-PRD.

17 *Proceso*, December 12, 1988, 16.

18 *Excélsior*, December 5, 1988, 26-A.

19 Salinas promoted trade and investment with Cuba. Castro visited Mexico in December 1988 to attend Salinas's inauguration; he had a well-publicized dinner party with Mexican businessmen, apparently at the suggestion of Salinas. Castro wanted to invite them to invest in Cuba. The Cuban leader had already expressed his wish to substitute imports from socialist countries to Mexican businessmen that accompanied President Miguel de la Madrid's visit to Havana shortly before he left office. See *Proceso*, December 12, 1988, 14–15.

20 *Excélsior*, July 17, 1991, 1-A, *Uno Más Uno*, July 16, 1991, 8.

21 *Clarín* quoted by *Uno Más Uno*, July 21, 1992, 21.

22 *Uno Más Uno*, July, 21, 1992, 1, 22.

23 *Uno Más Uno*, July 25, 1992, 23.

24 "Historia General de las relaciones Exteriores de la República de Argentina. Tercera Parte. La Actuación Argentina en los Foros de Alcance Regional y su Impacto en las Relaciones con Estados Unidos", www.argentina-rree.com/15/15-060.htm. At the III summit in Salvador, Brazil, Menem had declared that Cuba's isolation was not the result of economic pressures but of the "capricious attitude of one man."

25 *Uno Más Uno*, November 12, 1996, 8.

26 Carlos Salinas de Gortari, "Una mediación desconocida: el diálogo entre los presi-

dentes de Cuba y Estados Unidos", *México: un paso difícil a la modernidad*, Barcelona, Plaza y Janés, 2000, 256.

27 Ibid., 157–258.

28 "Palabras del secretario general de la Organización de los Estados Americanos César Gaviria Trujillo. Sesión inaugural del vigésimo quinto periodo ordinario de sesiones de la Asamblea General". Montrouis, Haiti, June 5, 1995, www.oas.org/speeches/speeech.asp?sCodigo=02-0321. My emphasis.

29 Claude Heller, "La cuestión cubana en los foros multilaterales", *Foro Internacional* 43, no. 3 (173) (July-September 2003), 681–682.

30 *La Jornada*, June 2, 1998, 49.

31 *La Jornada*, June 2 1998, 46, and June 3, 1998, 55. Heller, "La cuestión cubana", 683.

32 This was President Salinas's explanation of the meeting. *La Jornada*, October 24, 1991, 3; *Cambio 16 América Latina*, March 2, 1992, 8–9.

33 *La Jornada*, October 24, 1991, 3.

34 *Uno Más Uno*, October 23, 1991, 27.

35 *Newsweek*, February 3, 1992, 33.

36 Ibid.

37 Salinas's government had also favored trade and investment in Cuba.

38 The United States agreed to grant 20,000 immigrant visas per year while Cuba's government committed itself to do anything possible to stop illegal departures from Cuba and accept Mariel Cubans in U.S. prisons. See chapter 2, this volume.

39 Clinton, Salinas and Castro concur with the details of Salinas's mediation. See Salinas de Gortari, *México*, 247–263; Bill Clinton, *My Life* (New York; Vintage, 2005), 615, Fidel Castro, "La sumisión a la política imperial", August 28, 2007, Juventud rebelde. cu, www.juventudrebelde.cu/cuba/2007-08-28/la-sumision-a-la-politica-imperial/.

40 Salinas, *México*, p. 254.

41 Declarations of Mexican Secretary of Foreign Affairs, Fernando Solana, *Proceso*, October 19, 1992, 6.

42 *Proceso*, October 5, 1992, 8.

43 *Proceso*, October 12, 1992, 22.

44 Even before the meetings, some U.S. Senators had expressed their concern that free trade with Mexico would benefit Cuba as a result of Mexico's trade with the island. *Época*, May 18, 1992, 16.

45 Quoted by *Proceso*, October 19, 1992, 6–7, and October 26, 1992, 20–25.

46 *Mexico and NAFTA Report*, January 14, 1993, RM-93-01, 8.

47 *Proceso*, October 26, 1992, 23. Another episode where the Cuban exile seems to have influenced Mexico's policy refers to a group of shipwrecked Cubans that arrived on Mexican coasts and were deported to Cuba because they did not apply for political asylum in Mexico. The exile community in Miami reacted very strongly; Mexican flags were burnt outside the Mexican consulate. The Mexican government then offered to grant visas to those Cubans, who traveled to Mexico and subsequently to the United States. According to the Mexican magazine *Proceso*, Jorge Mas Canosa thanked the Mexican government. *Proceso*, September 6, 1993, 30–32.

48 Mexico's objection to the OAS actively promoting democracy and human rights in the region during the 1990s illustrates well Salinas's wish to limit Mexico's opening to the economic field. The OAS presented a good opportunity for Mexico to reinforce the idea that democracy and human rights were "strictly" domestic issues. See Ana Covarrubias, "Los derechos humanos en la política exterior de México: ¿en defensa propia o de los valores liberales?", Ana Covarrubias (coord.), *Temas de política exterior* (México, El Colegio de México, 2008), 303–332.

49 Rafael Rojas, "México y Cuba, amigos desleales", *Foreign Affairs en español* 4, no. 3 (July-September, 2004), 77–81.

50 "Versión estenográfica de las palabras del presidente Ernesto Zedillo durante la cere-
monia de clausura de la IX Reunión cumbre Iberoamericana de jefes de Estado y de
Gobierno en el salón Plenario del Palacio de las Convenciones en esta ciudad",
Havana, Cuba, November 16, 1999.

51 Mexican ambassador to Cuba, Pedro Joaquín Coldwell, had previously met with
Cuban dissidents. *Excélsior*, November 26, 1999, *La Jornada*, November 15, 1999;
both in Infolatina, http://zeus.infolatina.com.mx

52 *Excélsior,* November 26, 2999, Infolatina, http://zeu.infolatina.com.mx.

53 *Excélsior,* November 13 2000, Infolatina, http://zeus.infolatina.com.mx.

54 Mexico, Presidencia de la República, comunicado núm. 2532, Panamá, Panama
City, November 18, 2000, and *Crónica*, November 26, 2000, Infolatina, http://zeus.
infolatina.com.mx. Castro had previously declared that Mexican children knew Walt
Disney's characters better than national heroes. The Mexican government and Castro
apologized through Minister Roberto Robaina. Carlos Tello Díaz, *El fin de una
amistad. La relación de México con la Revolución cubana* (México, Planeta, 2005),
133–144.

55 There were some suggestions in 1994-1995 that one of the conditions required by
the U.S. government, and perhaps by the Congress, to assist—"rescue"—Mexico's
economy was that the Mexican government would modify its policy toward Cuba.
Miguel Ángel Valverde Loya, "Las relaciones México-Estados Unidos en el sexenio
de Zedillo", *Foro Internacional* 41, no. 4 (166) (October-December, 2001), 674.

56 A "new" foreign policy was not peculiar to Fox: President Echeverría had also
implemented a "new" foreign policy. Frequently, Mexican officials announce a
"new" foreign policy.

57 Jorge G. Castañeda, "La nueva visión estratégica de largo plazo", palabras pronuncia-
das en la Conferencia Magistral "Politica exterior de México", Universidad
Autónoma de Tamaulipas, Ciudad Victoria, February 1, 2002, *Discursos del Secretario
de Relaciones Exteriores, Jorge Castañeda (enero-junio, 2002)* (Mexico; SRE, 2002), 25.

58 Although Mexican policy toward Cuba cannot be understood without looking at
Mexico's foreign policy more broadly, the personalities of the two Secretaries of
Foreign Affairs under Fox were a significant influence on the way relations with
Cuba were conducted. Andrés Rozental argues that the history of antagonism
between Castañeda and Castro contributed to the deterioration of the bilateral rela-
tionship. Castañeda had published two books: *La utopía desarmada* and *La vida en rojo:
Vida y muerte del Che Guevara* that were critical of the Cuban government. The latter
was prohibited in Cuba. Andrés Rozental, "La agenda de política exterior de Fox:
prioridades globales y regionales", Luis Rubio and Susan Kaufman (eds.), *México.
Democracia ineficaz* (Mexico; CIDAC-Miguel Ángel Porrúa, 2006), 138–139.

59 In 1999, Mexico voted against the resolution. Former U.S. ambassador to Mexico,
Jeffrey Davidow, suggests that Mexico's vote was the result of a conversation
between President Zedillo and Fidel Castro after an international meeting in the
Dominican Republic, in which Castro underlined U.S. interventionism and asked
Zedillo what the next target of the United States would be: Havana or Chiapas?
Additionally—according to Davidow—Mexico's vote would signal its willingness to
make peace after Castro's declarations on Mexican children knowing more about
Mickey Mouse than about national heroes. Jeffrey Davidow, *El oso y el puercoespín.
Testimonio de un embajador de Estados Unidos en México* (Mexico: Grijalbo, 2003),
162–164.

60 *Proceso*, April 15, 2001, 13, and April 22, 2001, 10–11.

61 *Reforma*, February 5, 2002, www.reforma.com.

62 *Reforma*, March 22, 2002, http://busquedas.gruporeforma.com/reforma/Documen-
tos/printimpresa.aspx?DocId=238844-1066&strr=castro%20Monterrey.

63 "El culpable de lo ocurrido en Monterrey se llama Jorge Castañeda", *Granma*, March

26, 2002, www.granma.cu. The transcript of the telephone conversation was reproduced in various Mexican newspapers. *Reforma*, April 22, 2002, www.reforma.com.

64 "Discurso de Fidel Castro", *El Universal*, May 3, 2004, www.eluniversal.com.mx/pls/.

65 *La Jornada*, May 3, 2004, http://jornada.unam.mx/o'=3nlpol.php?printver=l&fly=l.

66 *Reforma.com*, October 21, 2008, http://busquedas.gruporeforma.com/reforma/Documentos/DocumentoImpresa.aspx.

67 *La Jornada*, June 21, 2007, www.jornada.unam.mx/2007/06/21/index.php?section=politica&article=022nlpol.

68 As Senator, Jiménez Remus organized a trip to Cuba in 1988, which was the first visit to the island of a group of *panistas*. Felipe Calderón was among them.

69 *La Jornada*, October 20, 2008, www.jornada.unam.mx/2008/10/20/index.php?section=politica&article=015n1pol.

70 Homero Campa Butrón, "México–Cuba: la recaída", *Foreign Affairs Latinoamérica* 9, no. 3, 2009, 73.

71 Ibid., 74.

72 Ibid.

73 One might argue, on the other hand, that an improvement in Mexican–Cuban relations would be welcomed by the United States given Obama's positions on foreign policy. During Obama's visit, Calderón declared that the U.S. embargo was not "very useful" in fostering change in Cuba, which was a different position from that taken by previous governments, which considered it a unilateral imposition that threatened sovereignty and self-determination. Campa, "México–Cuba", 78.

74 *Ibid.*, p. 76.

75 "Entrevista del Presidente Felipe Calderón con Joaquín López Dóriga sobre la influenza AHINI, jueves 7 de mayo de 2009", www.presidencia.gob.mx/prensa/entrevistas/?contenido=44806.

76 "Lo que pasó por mi mente" (May 11, 2009), and "Otra noticia que estremeció al mundo" (May 14, 2009), www.granma.cubaweb.cu/secciones/ref-fidel/art140.htm; and www.granma.cubaweb.cu/secciones/ref-fidel/art141.html.

77 Mexico, SRE, "México hace un llamado al Gobierno de Cuba a realizar las acciones necesarias para proteger la salud y la dignidad de todos sus prisioneros", March 15, 2009. Communiqué no. 074, www.sre.gob.mx/csocial/contenido/comunicados/2010/mar/cp_074.html.

INDEX

11 September 2001 84, 88, 109, 112, 161; *see also* Guantánamo Naval Base

Afghanistan 42, 84, 123, 131, 144, 192n51; *see also* Guantánamo Naval Base; torture
Africa, Caribbean, Pacific (ACP) 64, 178n30
Alarcón Quesada, Ricardo 32, 42–3, 74, 76, 78, 87, 122, 128, 130, 172n37, 173n41
Albright, Madeleine 71, 73
Alliance for Progress 4–5; *see also* Kennedy, John F.
Alpha 66, 37
Amnesty International 43, 127, 169n80, 175n8, 194n84
Angola 12–14, 16–17, 19, 25, 77–8, 168n21
Arcos, Gustavo 40–1, 176n74
Argentina 11, 42–3, 45, 63, 153–4, 161, 200n24
Auténtico Party 8
authoritarianism 34–5, 44, 109, 173n48
Axworthy, Lloyd 64; *see also* Canada
Aznar, José María 45, 48, 62–5, 108, 131–3, 178n20; *see also* Popular Party; Spain

Baker, James 27, 42; *see also* Bush, George H.W.; Malmierca, Isidoro
Baltimore Orioles 72
Basulto, José 51–3, 80–2, 102, 176n128, n130, 186n81; *see also* Brothers to the Rescue
Batista Zaldívar, Fulgencio 8–10, 17 ,167n30
Battle of Ideas 81, 93; *see also* Castro Ruz, Fidel; González, Elián
Bay of Pigs 4–5, 9, 17, 19, 51, 54, 82, 142, 166n19, 167n36, 169n78, n82, 170n88

Belén Montes, Ana 88, 182n20; *see also* spying
Black Spring (2003) 85, 92, 95–7, 108, 113–14, 133, 137, 140–1, 194n84, 198n143, n144
Bofill, Ricardo 36, 41, 175n42
Bolivia 85, 110, 130
Boliviarian Alternative for the Americas (ALBA) 110–11, 161; *see also* Chávez, Hugo
Bonne Carcassés, Félix 59
Bosch, Orlando 37–8, 174n67
Botifoll, Luis J. 99
Brazil 45, 107, 109, 111, 123, 128, 130, 140, 162, 172n20, 201n24
Brothers to the Rescue 51–2, 55, 64, 70, 78, 102, 114, 137; *see also* Basulto, José
Burton, Dan 31, 67; *see also* Helms, Jesse
Bush, George W. 83–92, 103–4, 112, 123–4, 132, 159–60, 166n27, 181n1, n2, n3, n4; n5, 182n14, 192n55, 194n83
Bush, Jeb 86, 8

Calderón, Felipe 161–3, 203n68, n73, n75; *see also* Partido Acción Nacional
Cambio Cubano xi, 40; *see also* Gutiérrez-Menoyo, Eloy
Canada 7, 25, 41, 46–9, 55, 60, 63–5, 71, 107–9, 111, 128, 152, 155, 176n111, n114, n116, 178n33, n34, 187n98, n100, 199n1
Cancún 151
Cárdenas, Cuauhtémoc 152; *see also* Partido de la Revolución Democrática
Carter, Jimmy 13–14, 16–17, 19–20, 72, 88–90, 94, 116 ,168n61, 182n23, 183n28

Castañeda Álvarez, Jorge 151, 159
Castañeda Gutman, Jorge 161, 202n57, n58, 203n63
Castro Ruz, Fidel 1–2, 4–6, 9–13, 15–16, 22, 24, 26–42, 45–6, 48–51, 53–5, 57–60, 62–5, 67, 73–82, 84–7, 90, 92–6, 98–111, 118, 121, 132, 136, 148, 151, 153–5, 157, 159–60, 163, 165n6, 166n12, n21, n24, n25, 167n32, n37, n39, n40, n46, n51, 168n53, n55, n71, 169n80n85, 170n86, n89, n90, 171n105, n11, 174n63, 175n78, 176n119, 177n131, n2; n6, 178n17, n20, 180n65, n76, 181n90, n91, 182n13, 183n34, n41, 184n44, n45, n55, n56, 186n83, 190n31, 195n98, 198n140, n145, 199n3, n5, 200n9, n19, 201n39, 202n54, n58, n59
Castro Ruz, Raúl 75, 81–2, 90, 94, 99, 101, 103–5, 107–11, 113, 120–2, 126, 133, 13–137, 140–2, 145, 168n78, 177n8, 186n85, n87, n89, n103, 188n2, 190n3, n32, 195n97, n104, n108, 197n132; see also la institucionalidad
Catholic Church 61–2, 71, 114, 142–3, 145, 149, 197n134, 198n143; see also Damas de Blanco; García Ibáñez, Dionisio; Ortega Alamino, Jaime; political prisoners
Center for the Study of the Americas 54, 177n132
Central Committee (CC) 58, 135–6; see also Cuban Communist Party (PCC)
Central Intelligence Agency (CIA) 11–13, 17, 38, 46, 149, 170n88, 180n77, 199n5, 200n6
Cernuda, Ramón 39, 40–1
Chamber of Commerce 49, 63, 74, 162
Chávez, Hugo 57, 63, 85, 110, 111, 131
Chile 24–5, 41, 43, 45, 63, 128–9, 175n99
China 13, 24, 34, 84, 94, 105, 108, 111, 123–4, 136, 145, 173n47, 184n44, 187n103, 198n147
Christopher, Warren 29, 90, 172n18
Claver-Carone, Mauricio 100, 117; see also Cuba Democracy Advocates
Clinton, Bill 24–33, 37, 55–6, 65–72, 74–45, 85–6, 88, 113, 116–17, 151–6, 179n43, n48, 182n14, 192n55, 198n141, 201n39
Clinton, Hillary 118, 124–6, 144, 192n52, n55, 193n61
Cold War xi, 1–2, 4, 8–10, 13–14, 16, 18, 23–4, 42, 46–7, 55, 57, 61, 93, 104, 112, 126–9, 137, 144–5, 148, 151–2, 156–7, 159–60, 168n75 ,172n19
Commission for Assistance to a Free Cuba 91–2, 183n36, n37
Common Position (CP) 56, 65, 67, 70, 114, 133–5, 138–40, 196n112; see also European Union
Concilio Cubano 54, 59, 176n131

Constitution 7–9, 24, 26, 34, 38, 89–90, 94, 99, 126, 128, 180n81, 183n25
Costa Rica 21, 43, 62–3, 97, 150
Cozumel 44–5, 151, 154–5
Creel, Santiago 160
Cuba Democracy Advocates 100, 185n72, 189n15
Cuba Policy Foundation 95
Cuban Adjustment Act 29, 31, 96
Cuban American National Foundation (CANF) 20–4, 32, 37, 39–40, 49, 51, 62, 65, 67, 71–2, 75–9, 81–3, 98–103, 114–16, 156 ,170n43, 180n55, 182n94, 185n77; see also Hernández, Francisco; Mas Canosa, Jorge; Mas Santos, Jorge; Moreira, Domingo; Radio Marti
Cuban Commission for Human Rights and National Reconciliation 157; see also Sánchez, Elizardo
Cuban Committee for Democracy (CCD) 40
Cuban Communist Party (PCC) 34, 54, 57–60, 72, 91, 93, 104–5, 107, 136–7, 160, 173n46, 177n132, 179n49
Cuban convertible peso (CUC) 105
Cuban Democracy Act (CDA) 24, 26–9, 43, 47–8, 50–1, 56, 89, 120, 155, 172n18, n38, 180n71, 182n14; see also Cuban Liberty and Democratic Solidarity (LIBERTAD) Act
Cuban Liberty and Democratic Solidarity (LIBERTAD) Act 25, 33, 46, 51, 155, 178n26, 179n42; see also Helms-Burton; U.S. embargo
Cuban Liberty Council (CLC) 83, 100
Cuesta Morúa, Manuel 134, 159, 194n89

Damas de Blanco 114, 131, 140–3, 196n121, n22, 197n126, n127
De la Madrid, Miguel 150, 200n19
Democracy Movement 76, 78; see also freedom flotillas; Sánchez, Ramón Saúl
Democratic Platform 40, 45
Derbez, Luis Ernesto 160
détente 1, 12–14, 144, 150, 166n19
Development Alternatives Incorporated (DAI) 122, 191n41, n42
Díaz-Balart, Lincoln 29, 38, 67, 71, 73–4, 81, 86, 101, 115, 179n43, n63, 181n3, 184n78, 188n4
Díaz-Balart, Mario 102, 115
Donahue, Thomas 74
Drug Enforcement Administration (DEA) 66
Durán, Alfredo 38
Dole, Bob 33, 56, 83
drug trade 63, 145; see also Drug Enforcement Administration (DEA); narcotraffic

Echeverría, Luis 150, 200n7, n8, 202n56
Ecuador 63, 85, 130
El Salvador 14, 24, 45, 62, 125, 150
Espinosa, Patricia 161
Estefan, Emilio 98
Estefan, Gloria 141, 197n124
ETA 158
European Economic Commission (EEC) 47–8, 176n118
European Union (EU) xi, 41, 53–8, 60, 64, 66–9, 86, 91, 95, 97, 107–9, 113, 131, 133–5, 138–40, 144–5, 178n30, 179n48, n73, 194n80, n81, 196n112; *see also* Common Position (CP)

Fariñas Hernández, Guillermo 114, 131, 142, 162–3, 197n131
Federal Aviation Administration (FAA) 52–3
Ferrer, Darsi 140
financial crisis 45, 112, 123, 136
Florida International University (FIU) 39, 88, 102, 169n72, 181n88, 182n22, 186n80
Ford, Gerald R. 12–13, 72
Fox, Vicente 44, 148, 159, 160–1, 163, 202n56, n58; *see also* Partido Acción Nacional (PAN)
Franco, Francisco 46, 132–3
Frayde, Marta 36
free trade 47, 68, 117, 119, 148, 156, 158–9, 161, 201n44
freedom flotillas 76–7

García Ibáñez, Dionisio 141; *see also* Catholic church
García Márquez, Gabriel 155, 168n77
Gaviria, César 44–5, 154, 201n28
García, Joe 99, 101, 115
Gómez Manzano, René 59
González, Elián 63, 80–5, 93, 99–100
González, Felipe 44–5, 48, 60, 132–3
Gorbachev, Mikhail 24, 105, 200n9
Gore, Al 29, 83–4, 117, 181n1
Granma 105, 110, 136, 142, 149
Grau San Martín, Ramón 8
Great Britain 47, 63, 109, 135
Green, Rosario 157–8
Groth, Carl-Johan 43
Gross, Alan 122–3, 131, 143–4, 191n41, 198n138; *see also* Development Alternatives Incorporated (DAI)
Guadalajara 44, 153
Guantánamo Naval Base 30, 66, 87, 124, 172n33, 181n6; *see also* torture
guerrillas 7, 11, 17, 36, 60, 129
Guevara, Ernesto Ché 5, 166n17, 202n58
Gutiérrez, Carlos 92
Gutiérrez-Menoyo, Eloy 40; *see also* Cambio Cubano

Haiti 144, 198n139, 201n28
Helms, Jesse 31, 33, 49, 86; *see also* Cuban Liberty and Democratic Solidarity (LIBERTAD) Act; U.S. embargo
Helms-Burton xi, 25, 33, 47, 49–51, 55–7, 63–71, 73, 75, 78, 85–6, 89–90, 107–8, 116, 122, 126, 137, 144, 155–6, 170n97, 177n136, 179n42, n45, n48, 181n3
Hernández, Francisco 67; *see also* Cuban American National Foundation (CANF)
Herrera, María Cristina xiii, 39
humanitarian assistance 71
human rights 14, 18–19, 36, 38, 41–4, 46, 50, 53, 56, 59–64, 68, 70, 75, 78, 80, 83, 86, 89, 96–7, 100, 107, 109, 113–14, 120–31, 133–5, 138–40, 142, 144–5, 148, 156–61, 163–4, 169n81, 173n60, 174n74, 175n86, 92, 177n13, 192n52, n53, n56, n57, 193n61, n62, n64, n68, 194n87, n88, 196n114, n115, n117, n118, n119, 198n137, 201n48; *see also* Cuban Committee for Human Rights and National Reconciliation; Of Human Rights; torture; UN Commission on Human Rights (UNCHR); UN Human Rights Council (UNHRC); UN Universal Periodic Review (UPR)

Iberoamerican summit 44–5, 60–2, 65, 75, 80, 153, 157
Immigration 15–16, 20–2, 26, 31–2, 78–80, 88, 112, 137, 144–5, 148, 162, 164, 168n71, 170n99, 171n105, 172n36, 190n33; *see also* Brothers to the Rescue; U.S. Coast Guard
Institutional Revolutionary Party (PRI) 7, 149, 159, 163
Insulza, José Miguel 65, 130
Inter-American Democratic Charter 130
Inter-American Juridical Committee (IAJC) 65
International Civil Aviation Organization (ICAO) 53, 55, 177n136
International Monetary Fund (IMF) 45
Iran 88, 109, 113, 120, 124, 187n105, 190n28, 194n81
Iraq 42, 47, 84, 90–2, 95–6, 112, 131–2, 193n72

John Paul II 44, 56–7, 61–3, 70–1, 81, 96, 134, 141
Johnson, Lyndon 10
Juanes 118, 189n18, n19

Kennedy, John F. 2–6, 10, 12, 14, 25, 83, 165n17, 166n13, n21, n25, 167n37, n38, n39, 168n58, 169n79
Khrushchev, Nikita 2–3, 5–6, 11, 165n6, 166n21, n25, 167n46

King Juan Carlos 45, 63, 153, 178n22, n23
Kissinger, Henry A. 12–13, 16, 72

la institucionalidad 81, 104, 135
Lage, Carlos 54, 137
Lawrence, David 39, 175n79; *see also* Mas
   Canosa, Jorge; *Miami Herald*

Machado Ventura, José Ramón 104
maleconazo 30, 36, 78
Malmierca, Isidoro 42, 151; *see also* Baker,
   James
Mas Canosa, Jorge 21, 32–7, 39, 40, 65, 76,
   99–101, 156–7, 172n37, 175n77, 180n77,
   n81
Mas Santos, Jorge 80–2, 98–9, 101–2,
   185n79
market reforms 57, 84–5, 93, 106, 146
Martínez, Mel 91, 102, 182n10, 183n36
McCain, John 117
McNamara, Robert S. 6, 166n22
Medvedev, Dimitri 109
Menem, Carlos 43, 45
Menéndez, Robert 29, 32, 86, 102, 116,
   131, 173n41, 181n3, 188n8
Mexican–American War 7
Mexico 1, 7, 9, 19, 22, 42–4, 46–7, 63, 65,
   67, 124, 128–9, 144, 147–64, 166n25,
   n28, 180n77, 189n12, 197n134, 198n147,
   199n3, n45, 200n6, n8; n11, n19, 201n26,
   n39, n40, n44, n46, n47, n48, 202n49,
   n54, n55, n57, n58, n59, 203n70, n73, n77
Miami Herald 20, 29, 32, 39, 78; see also Mas
   Canosa, Jorge
Missile Crisis 2–6, 10–12, 25, 46, 165n3, n7,
   166n15, n16, n19, n24, 167n46
mobilization 34–5, 58, 61, 80–1
Montaner, Carlos Alberto 41, 156–7
Moratinos, Miguel Ángel 132–5, 138,
   193n77, 194n79, n82, n83, 195n 92,
   n93
Moreira, Domingo 102, 185n79
Mulroney, Brian 47–8, 166n27

narcotraffic 26, 32
Nader, Ralph 83
Nascimento, Abdias 140
National Assembly 32, 35, 64, 74, 89, 94,
   110, 122, 130, 135, 137, 141
national security 2–3, 9, 14, 35, 72, 88, 113,
   130, 134, 136, 162, 168n46, 180n77,
   190n28, 198n147, 199n5, 200n6
nationalism 7–9, 17, 58, 171n102
New Cuban+American Majority PAC 119,
   189n20
Nicaragua 14, 21, 25, 27–8, 36, 62–3, 78,
   85, 110, 125, 130, 150
Nigeria 125–6, 192n57, n58
Nixon, Richard 6, 16

Nonaligned Movement 41
North American Free Trade Agreement
   (NAFTA) 7, 28, 65, 67, 152–3, 155–7,
   166n27, 201n46

Obama, Barack 23, 113–26, 129, 131–2,
   137–9, 145, 162–3, 188n3, n8, 189n24,
   190n27, n28, n31, 192n53, n55, 198n147,
   203n73
Of Human Rights 36, 42, 75
Office of Foreign Assets Control (OFAC) 3,
   2, 70, 71, 75, 86
Operation Mongoose 4
Organization of American States (OAS)
   11–12, 46, 48, 60, 66, 129–31, 147–50,
   154, 169n81, 177n13, 193n70, 199n1, n2;
   n3, 200n10, 201n48; *see also* Inter-
   American Democratic Charter; Inter-
   American Judicial Committee (IAJC)
Ortega Alamino, Jaime 61–2, 141–3,
   197n128, n129, n133, n136; *see also*
   Catholic church

Panama 2, 3, 19, 21, 63, 75, 128, 151, 158,
   202n54
Partido Acción Nacional (PAN) 158
Partido de la Revolución Democrática 160
Payá, Oswaldo 89, 92, 94, 158–9, 176n104,
   183n38, n43
Pérez, Carlos Andrés 44, 45
Pérez de Cuéllar, Javier 43
Pérez Roque, Felipe 62–3, 74, 97, 109, 137,
   159, 161, 178n21
Perot, Ross 28, 56
Platt amendment 7, 9, 23, 50, 167n29
political prisoners 19–20, 43, 51, 54, 64, 86,
   88, 99, 100, 103, 114, 120–1, 126, 128,
   132–5, 141–3, 164, 193n60, n65,
   197n128, n130, 198n143
Popular Party 48, 65
Posada Carriles, Luis 75, 180n77
Powell, Colin L. 90–2, 183n27, n28, n36
Prío Socarrás, Carlos 8
Putin, Vladimir 110; *see also* Cuban
   American National Foundation (CANF)

Radio Martí 15, 71, 78, 168n68; *see also*
   Cuban American National Foundation
   (CANF)
Reagan, Ronald 14–15, 21–2, 30, 48, 56,
   66, 88, 116, 144, 151, 168n66, 198n140
Reich, Otto 96, 182n10; *see also* Bush,
   George W
realpolitik xii, 25
religion 31, 62, 96; *see also* Catholic church;
   John Paul II; Vatican, the
remittances 30, 32–3, 55, 56, 70, 72, 86, 89,
   92, 112, 114–15, 118, 119, 132, 137,
   183n30

Reno, Janet 82
Rice, Condoleezza 92
Richardson, Bill 51, 121, 176n127
Rivero, Raúl 159
Robaina, Roberto 63, 178n25, 202n54
Roca, Vladimiro 59, 121
Rodríguez Bruno 120–1, 138, 196n109
Roque, Martha Beatriz 59, 91, 121, 159
Ros-Lehtinen, Ileana 29, 38, 71, 74, 81, 86,
  101–2, 115, 181n3, 188n4
Russia 43, 109–12, 123–4
Ryan, George 73

Salinas de Gortari, Carlos 152, 201n26, n32,
  n37, n39, n40
San Pedro Sula 129–30, 147, 193n69
Sánchez, Elizardo 36, 39, 121, 134, 157–8,
  176n104, 181n95
Sánchez, Ramón Saúl 13, 75–6, 79–82,
  181n95; see also Democracy Movement
Saramago, José 46, 95
Shannon, Thomas 103–4, 108, 186n86
Soviet Union xi, 1, 4–5, 10–12, 14–15,
  17–18, 21, 24, 26, 28, 34, 36, 42, 84, 105,
  109, 129, 144, 200n9
Spain xi, 2–3, 7, 22, 45–8, 64, 97, 108, 114,
  120, 131–5, 138, 141, 153, 158, 164,
  165n2, 171n103, 176n109, n110, n116,
  n117, n118, n119, 178n33, 194n72
Spanish Socialist Workers' Party 97
spying 72, 88, 149, 182n22, 190n31,
  191n45; see also Belén Montes, Ana
Suárez, Adolfo 46
Summit of the Americas 28, 120, 189n25

telecommunications 69, 112, 119
terrorism 4, 15, 19, 22, 38, 75, 87–8, 91,
  101, 112, 120–1, 158, 169n84, 171n101,
  183n26, n27, n42, 190n28; see also Alpha;
  Bosch, Orlando; Posada Carriles, Luis
Third World 10, 14, 150
Title III 33, 50, 65–7, 69, 75, 86, 179n43;
  see also Helms-Burton
Title IV 51, 65, 68–9, 75; see also Helms-
  Burton
Torricelli, Robert 26–7, 29
torture 124–5, 128, 169n81; see also human
  rights; Guantánamo Naval Base
Trade Sanctions Reform and Export
  Enhancement Act (TSRA) 74–5, 85,
  87–8, 116, 180n71
Trading with the Enemy Act 70
travel ban 29, 74, 86–7, 89, 100, 116, 118,
  188n9

United Nations (UN) xi, 12, 41–3, 47, 49,
  74, 110, 125, 137, 139, 159, 169n34,
  193n66, 196n109; see also UN
  Commission on Human Rights
  (UNCHR); UN Human Rights Council
  (UNHRC)
United States Agency for International
  Development (USAID) 122–3, 125–6,
  191n41, 192n47, n48, n55, n56, n57
UN Commission on Human Rights
  (UNCHR) 36, 42–4, 46, 53, 59, 78, 97,
  127, 139–40, 175n117, 197n60
UN Human Rights Council (UNHRC) 97,
  124, 127–8, 193n86
UN Universal Periodic Review (UPR) 124,
  126–8, 161, 193n62
Uruguay 4, 43, 63, 129, 147, 169n80, n92
U.S. Coast Guard 30–1, 80, 91, 172n27
U.S. Cuba Democracy Political Action
  Committee 100
U.S. embargo xiii, 9, 39, 41–5, 48, 49, 61–2,
  70, 107, 111, 113, 118, 127, 134, 138,
  155, 196n109, 203n73; see also Trading
  with the Enemy Act
U.S. farm interests 73; see also Trade
  Sanctions Reform and Export
  Enhancements Act (TSRA)

Valladares, Armando 40, 42, 175n85
Varela Project 89–90, 92, 94–5, 99–100,
  185n71; see also Payá, Oswaldo
Vatican, the 62, 71, 95, 110, 142, 197n133
Venezuela 11, 37, 43–5, 75, 85, 109–11,
  120, 130–1, 150, 153–4, 161, 177n12,
  188n112, n113, 190n28, 191n42; see also
  Chávez, Hugo
Vietnam 11, 13, 17, 24, 34, 49, 53, 60, 84,
  136, 139–40, 145, 166n19, 196n116,
  n117, 198n147

Wenski, Thomas 72
World Bank 46
World Trade Organization (WTO) 46–7,
  65–6, 68, 86, 139, 156, 179n43, n45

Xiaoping, Deng 34, 105

Zapata Tamayo, Orlando 114, 135, 143
Zapatero, José Luis Rodríguez 97, 132–3,
  135, 138, 193n72, n76, 194n85, 195n93,
  n94
Zedillo, Ernesto 148, 153, 157, 202n50, n55,
  n59
Zelaya, Manuel 85, 130

For Product Safety Concerns and Information please contact our EU
representative GPSR@taylorandfrancis.com
Taylor & Francis Verlag GmbH, Kaufingerstraße 24, 80331 München, Germany

www.ingramcontent.com/pod-product-compliance
Lightning Source LLC
Chambersburg PA
CBHW050433280326
41932CB00013BA/2099

9 780415 804516